Black British Intellectuals and Education

Ask any moderately interested Briton to name a black intellectual and chances are the response will be an American name: Malcolm X or Barack Obama, Toni Morrison or Cornel West. Yet Britain has its own robust black intellectual traditions and its own master teachers; among them are C. L. R. James, Claudia Jones, Ambalavaner Sivanandan, Stuart Hall and Paul Gilroy. However, while in the USA black public intellectuals are a feature of national life, black British thinkers remain routinely marginalized.

Black British Intellectuals and Education counters this neglect. It explores histories of race, education and social justice in Britain through the work of black scholars, educators and campaigners, from the eighteenth century, through post-war migration and into the 'post-multicultural' present. The book argues that black British thinkers have helped fundamentally to shape educational policy, practice and philosophy, and that education has been one of the key spaces in which black British identity has emerged.

Chapters explore:

- early black British intellectual life, from the slave narratives to the early twentieth-century anti-colonial movements;
- how African-Caribbean and Asian communities organized against racial inequalities in schooling in the post-Windrush era of the 1950s and 60s;
- how black intellectuals and activists developed radical critiques of education, youth and structural racism in the 1970s, 80s and 90s;
- the influence of multiculturalism, cultural studies and black feminism on education;
- current developments in black British educational work, including 'post-racial' approaches, Critical Race Theory and black social conservatism.

Black British Intellectuals and Education will be of key relevance to undergraduates, postgraduates and academics engaged in research on race, ethnicity, education, social justice and cultural studies.

Paul Warmington is Deputy Director of the Centre for Research in Race and Education at the University of Birmingham, UK.

Black British Intellectuals and Education

Multiculturalism's hidden history

Paul Warmington

LONDON AND NEW YORK

First published 2014
by Routledge
2 Park Square, Milton Park, Abingdon, Oxon OX14 4RN

and by Routledge
711 Third Avenue, New York, NY 10017

Routledge is an imprint of the Taylor & Francis Group, an informa business

British Library Cataloguing in Publication Data
A catalogue record for this book is available from the British Library

Library of Congress Cataloging in Publication Data
Warmington, Paul.
Black British intellectuals and education : multiculturalism's hidden history /
Paul Warmington.
pages cm
Includes bibliographical references and index.
ISBN 978-0-415-80935-1 (hardback) -- ISBN 978-0-415-80937-5 (paperback)
-- ISBN 978-1-315-79704-5 (ebook) 1. Blacks--Great Britain--History. 2.
Intellectuals--Great Britain--History. 3. Great Britain--Race relations--History.
4. Blacks--Great Britain--Civilization. 5. Multiculturalism--Great Britain--
History. I. Title.
DA125.N4W37 2014
305.5'5208996042--dc23
2013037148

ISBN: 978-0-415-80935-1 (hbk)
ISBN: 978-0-415-80937-5 (pbk)
ISBN: 978-1-315-79704-5 (ebk)

Typeset in Galliard
by Saxon Graphics Ltd, Derby

Printed and bound in Great Britain by
TJ International Ltd, Padstow, Cornwall

For Jeanette, Aisha and Eli, with much love

Contents

Preface

This is a book about black life in Britain. It is not about gang violence. It is not about gun crime. It is not about transracial adoption, arranged marriages or any other of the problem-victim narratives through which black Britain tends to be depicted. In this book black people are not other and black children are not other people's children. Instead, it casts black people in Britain as social agents: as thinkers and activists. It explores race, education and social justice through the vital work of black public intellectuals: writers, teachers and campaigners.

In *Black British Intellectuals and Education* black struggles are shown to have been integral to the shaping of education in post-war Britain, and education as integral to the emergence of black British identities. Sadly, the very idea of black British intellectuals is one that academics and media commentators still often fail to comprehend; witness the scrambling around for black talking heads that ensues when comments are required on urban unrest or the election of a black (American) president. Yet, as we shall see, Britain's black intellectual traditions are powerful and longstanding. They encompass both the fragile ebony towers of black academia and the grassroots black education movements carved out in parents' groups, supplementary schools and black bookshops.

Education is sometimes cited almost incidentally as central to the making of black Britain but it occupies surprisingly little space in the large-scale accounts of black British history. Moreover, where education has been covered, there has been little attempt to link together its multiple dimensions: to suggest how pre-war anti-colonial movements might have influenced post-war black community struggles around education, or how the growth of supplementary schools might relate to black arts movements or the emergence of black cultural studies.

While I hope that the book does not read too much as an elegy for independent black thought and politics, it did emerge out of a concern for lost links. In the 1980s and 90s I was lucky to work at Third World Publications in Birmingham, one of a now much diminished network of black and anti-racist publishers, distributors and bookshops. Third World's makeshift warehouse was, for me, a second university and a first-rate library. I spent four years shelving, boxing and reading what seemed to be a boundless compendium of black writing: Cedric Robinson, Ron Ramdin, Amrit Wilson and Sivanandan. Yet some of the important work that was in circulation then is now less widely read and is, in some cases, out of print. I noticed this in the work of my students – excellent and exciting young thinkers who were well versed in bell hooks and could cite Malcolm X but for whom Una Marson, John La Rose and even C. L. R. James were hazier figures.

In addition to the gaps on bookshelves and in dissertations, there was also the frustration, outside specialist circles, of too many 'square one' conversations at academic conferences and in staff rooms, wherein 'black' educational issues were discussed, if at all, as if much of the research, debates and campaigns of past decades had not happened. A good colleague once informed me, for example, that restrictions on Muslim women's dress in some European countries were not necessarily racist. That is true – but it is true at a level of vast abstraction. Whatever positions we take around race, education and social justice, there are back stories upon which we should draw, giant shoulders upon which we can stand. As this book shows, at root what black educators, parents and students want in terms of education is much the same as any of their neighbours want. However, time and time again black communities in Britain have shown willingness to act assertively in order to make educational gains. Moreover, historical conditions have given particular shape to black educational desire. Understanding something of these hidden histories helps to explain Britain's recent educational history and to explain why debates over race equality and education remain contentious.

In short, I wrote this book not just to fill a gap but because I wanted to read it, and wanted my students and colleagues to read something like it. It is an introductory text that I hope will point in the direction of some black British giants. That said, it is neither biographical nor a roll call of black heroes, though it inevitably contains traces of both. Nor does it claim to be definitive; it is just one black British history out of many that will be told. Indeed, there are figures who, in the interests of the edit, receive only passing mention here but who merit whole biographies of their own. I remember an episode of the TV comedy *Blackadder* in which Dr Johnson, played by Robbie Coltrane, proudly touts his almost finished English dictionary, only to be thrown into apoplexy when, in the course of conversation, an acquaintance uses the word 'discombobulating' ... or 'sausages'. Pulling the strands of this book together has been a bit like that and I apologize for omitting or underestimating the place of particular actors and events. Lastly, I make no nostalgic claims for particular golden ages in black British thought and educational activism; new black intellectual spaces emerge constantly and continue to give hope and produce wisdom. Thanks to those who continue to educate and inspire.

Acknowledgements

Numerous friends and colleagues have provided tremendous help in the course of producing this book. I would like, in particular, to thank those who have either offered advice on the text, provided spaces in which to discuss and revise my ideas or made available research material. Many thanks to Gargi Bhattacharyya, Black Cultural Archives, Centre for Research in Race and Education at the University of Birmingham, Critical Race Theory Discussion Group, Max Farrar, George Padmore Institute/New Beacon Books, David Gillborn, HEA Centre for Sociology, Politics and Anthropology Race Group, Institute of Race Relations/ Jenny Bourne, Zeus Leonardo, Jane Martin, Jeanette McLoughlin, Nicola Rollock and Strange Fruit. I would also like to thank colleagues at Routledge for commissioning the book and supporting its production: in particular, Anna Clarkson, Clare Ashworth, Katharine Atherton and Rachel Norridge.

And thanks most of all to my family and friends for their support and endless patience. Thanks to my father Mack, my mother Bernice and my sisters. Love to Jeanette, Aisha and Eli. I know it's been a long wait.

Parts of Chapters 1 and 8 were previously published in:

Warmington, P. (2009) 'Taking race out of scare quotes: race conscious social analysis in an ostensibly post-racial world', *Race Ethnicity and Education*, 12(3): 281–96.

Warmington, P. (2012) '"A tradition in ceaseless motion": Critical Race Theory and black British intellectual spaces', *Race Ethnicity and Education*, 15(11): 5–21.

Warmington, P. (2013) 'Agents of critical hope: black British narratives', in V. Bozalek, B. Leibowitz, R. Carolissen and M. Boler (eds) *Discerning Critical Hope in Educational Practices*, London: Routledge (in press).

I would like to express my gratitude to Taylor and Francis, and to David Gillborn and Vivienne Bozalek.

List of abbreviations

AYM	Asian Youth Movement
BME	black and minority ethnic
BPM	Black Parents Movement
CARD	Campaign Against Racial Discrimination
CCCS	Centre for Contemporary Cultural Studies
CECWA	Caribbean Education and Community Workers Association
CRC	Community Relations Commission
CRE	Commission for Racial Equality
CRT	Critical Race Theory
DES	Department of Education and Science
DfE	Department for Education
DfES	Department for Education and Skills
ESN	educationally subnormal
GLC	Greater London Council
ILEA	Inner London Education Authority
IRR	Institute of Race Relations
IWA	Indian Workers Association
LEA	Local Education Authority
LCP	League of Coloured Peoples
NAME	National Association for Multiracial Education
NLWIA	North London West Indian Association
OWAAD	Organisation of Women of Asian and African Descent
WISC	West Indian Standing Conference
WASU	West African Students Union

1 Black British intellectuals

Race, education and social justice

> The purpose of black scholarship is more than the restoration of identity and self-esteem: it is to use history and culture as tools through which people interpret their collective experience, but for the purpose of transforming their actual conditions and the totality of the society all around them.
>
> Manning Marable (2000: 2)

Introduction

Ask any moderately interested Briton to name a black intellectual and chances are the response will be an American name: Malcolm X or Barack Obama, perhaps Toni Morrison or Cornel West. Yet Britain has its own black intellectual traditions and its own master teachers, among them C. L. R. James, Claudia Jones, Ambalavaner Sivanandan, Stuart Hall and Paul Gilroy. Black Britain's intellectual flow has encompassed dialogues with Marxism, feminism, post-colonialism and postmodernism. However, while in the USA black public intellectuals are an embedded, if often embattled, feature of national life, black British thinkers remain routinely marginalized. Too often it is assumed that black communities are problems to be theorized by white intellectuals. And Britain as a whole pays the cost of that neglect.

What this book does is explore race and education through the language and ideas of black British thinkers, from the early black writers of the eighteenth century, through post-war migration and into the 'post-multicultural' present. It includes those who have campaigned and innovated in the field of education itself and those who have used their expertise as educators as a platform to address wider social developments. It examines:

- the early development of black British intellectual life, from the slave narratives to the anti-colonial movements of the early twentieth century;
- how black communities began to organize against racial inequalities in schooling in the post-Windrush era of the 1950s and 60s;
- how, from out of these grassroots struggles, black intellectuals and activists of the 1970s, 80s and 90s developed radical critiques of education, youth and structural racism;

- the influence of multiculturalism, black cultural studies and black feminism on education;
- current developments in black British educational work, including 'post-racial' approaches, Critical Race Theory and black social conservatism.

Black Intellectuals and Education offers a story of black intellectual life and how black Britain came of age in schools and other educational sites. However, its focus is not limited to schooling or to academic life. Black Britain has produced many intellectual and educational spaces outside formal settings: supplementary schools, independent community education projects, reading circles, grassroots journals, bookshops and publishing houses. *Black British Intellectuals and Education* encompasses both black academia – the ebony tower – and the organic intellectuals of the grassroots black education movements. This introductory chapter outlines the book's content and structure, giving a sense of the events, figures and concepts integral to its depiction of the relationships between black British intellectual life, education and social justice. These include the place of education in black British history, the development of black British political identities and the problematic existence of black intellectuals.

Black British history and education

Education has been central to black British history. From the eighteenth century onwards, Britain's black intelligentsia has grown up around sites of educational desire. For freed slaves and Lascar sailors, Britain was a place in which literacy became possible. In the early twentieth century there were those who arrived on colonial scholarships or hoping to find audiences as writers. In the 1960s and 70s, during what Dhondy *et al.* (1985: 43) referred to as the 'black explosion in British schools', children who are now parents and grandparents were bundled along the street to paint-peeled classrooms in new cities. Journalist Gary Younge (2012: 9) has referred to the latter period as the time during which 'our absence, not our presence [became] unimaginable'. Education, in its widest sense, is one of the spaces in which that black British presence has been felt – one of the spaces in which what it means to be black *and* British has been negotiated.

It is a story that deserves to be told because while education has been formative to black British experiences, particularly in the post-war period, existing large-scale histories, such as Peter Fryer's (1984) *Staying Power* and Ron Ramdin's (1987) *The Making of the Black Working Class in Britain*, give it surprisingly limited attention. Other very useful historical work, such as Sally Tomlinson's (2008) *Race and Education*, illuminates post-war contests over race and education but focuses primarily on policy ideology. One consequence of this has been the relegation of some of the seminal figures in black British intellectual life, such as the pioneering Harold Moody, activist John La Rose and his New Beacon circle, cultural theorist Hazel Carby and the literary historian David Dabydeen. Exploring their work – and that of newer, sometimes unpredictable black voices – helps to make sense of how and why competing understandings of education in and for cultural diversity have developed in the UK, and how these have articulated with wider issues and crises in British life.

Public intellectuals

Insofar as they have addressed race, education and social justice, the black British intellectuals included in this book have been *public* intellectuals. They have concerned themselves not only with learning theories and classroom technologies, but with relationships between education and wider social structures, with wider culture. So what might we regard as distinctive about the work of black British public intellectuals? In delineating African-American intellectual traditions, the late Manning Marable (2000: 1) referred to 'three great points of departure'. Marable (2000) characterized the work of black public intellectuals as: *descriptive* (concerned with depicting the realities of black life through black perspectives); *corrective* (aiming to critique racist values and representations); and *prescriptive* (mapping out practical possibilities for social change).

These aims can be seen, too, across centuries of black British endeavour but in the British context we can add a fourth dimension, one that might be termed *co-constructive*. For any black British public intellectual bearing witness, plotting action or offering critique has also had to answer the question: *who are they, the 'black British'*? This task has weighed on black British thinkers in a way that it has not weighed upon black Americans. This is not to trivialize the struggles waged among African-Americans to imagine and define themselves since emancipation. However, the historical challenge of defining what it means to be black British, to be black *and* British, seems of a different, more literal order. Later this chapter considers the conflicting loyalties and burdens of representation carried by black public intellectuals.

Starting points

Of course, black public intellectuals do not only contemplate race and racism, nor are they exclusively concerned with education. However, this book's starting point is that to understand the emergence of black British identities, it is necessary to understand histories of race and education – and to understand histories of race and education, it is necessary to comprehend the changing shape of black political thought in Britain. The succeeding chapters develop four overarching themes:

• Firstly, understandings of education and social justice have been fundamentally shaped by the work of black and anti-racist educators. Black activists and intellectuals have often broken new ground long before policy-makers.
• Secondly, the understandings of education that black intellectuals have developed are rooted in longer histories of black intellectual production, which need to be understood if we are to avoid trivializing debates around race and education.

- Thirdly, black British intellectual production has never been tidy or homogenous; education is one of the significant fields in which black British intellectual positions have been defined *and differentiated*.
- Fourthly, in the post-war period, as the children of Commonwealth migrants entered the schools in increasing numbers and their communities began to organize around educational injustices, education became one of the key sites in which the mass consciousness of being black *and* British developed.

Mapping black British intellectuals

This book, of course, depicts just one of many possible black British histories but, allowing for that, what kinds of figures and events populate it? Black intellectuals have long figured in British life, first emerging through the abolitionist cause and featuring in the radical populist movements of the nineteenth century. By the early twentieth century a spread of organized black political activity was evident. It included Harold Moody's League of Coloured Peoples, Ladipo Solanke's West African Students Union and the first incarnation of the Indian Workers Association. In the same period pan-African and radical anti-colonialist groupings cohered around figures such as George Padmore and Amy Ashwood Garvey, producing a formidable intelligentsia. There were direct links between these pre-war activists and some of those who organized around education, publishing and social justice in the 1950s and 60s. The pre-war hive prefigured later black British movements in its concern with anti-racism, African–Asian solidarity, community education and the welfare of young people and families.

In the post-war era the early stands taken by the black educational movements of the 1960s and early 70s against busing, school exclusions and the placement of black children in schools for the 'educationally subnormal' (ESN schools) fed into radical structural analyses of British schooling that, in the work of educators such as Bernard Coard, Farrukh Dhondy, Stella Dadzie and Gus John, drew upon experiences of teaching in British schools, Marxist analyses of education in capitalism and the radicalism emerging across the black Atlantic. In the 1980s Hazel Carby, Paul Gilroy and the new generation of black British cultural theorists inspired by Stuart Hall imagined black British youth forming active opposition to both the authoritarian dimensions of schooling and the distractions offered by facile forms of multiculturalism. These analyses contrasted with the work of Maureen Stone and later Tony Sewell, whose educational research was embedded in neo-liberal norms and a questioning of multicultural education.

From the late 1980s Stuart Hall's rethinking of articulations between race, class and gender influenced the educational writing of, for instance, Heidi Safia Mirza, whose work countered the phallo-centrism apparent in earlier accounts of the racialized processes of schooling. Tariq Modood, meanwhile, has challenged dominant modes of political blackness and their reliance on both subcultural and Marxist analytical frameworks. In recent years Critical Race Theory has re-emphasized the politics of race in education, its adherents arguing that, despite the contemporary rhetoric of social justice and cultural diversity, the function of schooling has not been to counter racial inequalities but to maintain them at manageable levels (Gillborn, 2008).

But crucially, black public intellectuals are not and never have been confined to the academy; indeed, it might be argued that black British intellectual life and academia have intersected only fitfully. The history of black education also incorporates the work of bookshops, arts groups and publishers, such as Bogle L'Ouverture and New Beacon; labour and community organizations, such as the Indian Workers Association and the Asian Youth Movements; black women's groups, including Southall Black Sisters and the Organization of Women of Asian and African Descent (OWAAD); and both black and multiracial anti-racist groups, such as the Black Parents Movement (BPM) and National Association for Multiracial Education (NAME). Today there are black public intellectuals who span the worlds of campaigning, policy-making and media commentary: from Doreen Lawrence to Trevor Phillips to Aditya Chakrabortty.

What does '*black British*' mean?

Running through this book is the story of the rise and retreat of the inclusive 'black Britishness' that shaped black intellectual work in the late twentieth century. One of its arguments is that, perhaps more than in any other sphere, it was in the schools of the 1960s, 70s and 80s that black British identities, with all their lived contradictions, took hold. So what do we mean by the term '*black British*'? When Harold Cruse or Henry Louis Gates write of black American intellectuals and activists their category remains more or less stable, their concern being exclusively with African-American traditions. In the UK, however, the term 'black' has a more complex history. It can, depending on context, denote either people of African/African-Caribbean descent or, via discourses of 'political blackness', the wider assembly of African, African-Caribbean, Asian, Arabic and mixed race peoples constructed in the post-war period of immigration – something akin to the collective referred to in the USA as people of colour.

This second, inclusive definition invokes a uniquely British form of political blackness that has been integral to the formation of black British intellectual identities. During the 1960s, 70s and 80s political blackness became a strategic political tool: an identification, through which intellectuals of colour addressed racism and social justice. Black identification became a position from which they entered into dialogue with the state, the schools and their white neighbours (Sivanandan, 1982; Alibhai-Brown, 1999; Alexander, 2002; Carrington, 2010). To adopt a term later fashioned by American Critical Race Theorists, British political blackness enabled black intellectuals to *name the contours* of racism in society.

The political blackness carved out in post-war Britain was partly a creative appropriation of American civil rights lessons; partly the organic product of struggles over work, education, immigration and racism in Britain. True, it was also a response to the mainstream political discourses of the 1950s and 60s, wherein migrants from former colonies, the New Commonwealth, were routinely grouped together under descriptors such as 'coloured' and 'immigrant'. Even terms such as 'Asian', 'West Indian' and 'African-Caribbean' were constructed in Britain, linking Indians to Sri Lankans and Jamaicans to Barbadians in ways that had not been forged in the home countries (see James and Harris, 1993). Yet, what is sometimes under-emphasized is that British blackness also had powerful antecedents in the anti-colonial alliances of the early twentieth century. As Chapter 2 of this book emphasizes, the possibilities of a powerful and inclusive British blackness were sketched out even before the post-war 'colour bar' struggles.

In this book, therefore, the use of the word 'black' does not signify mere colour, presumed cultural essence or an interest in delineating 'our side' as opposed to 'their side'; instead blackness is understood as a strategic political tool. In addition, while this book maintains a focus on intellectual endeavour by people of colour, that does not imply a charmed, self-sufficient 'black' space. After all, black intellectuals and activists in the UK have nurtured myriad multiracial alliances over decades and radical race-conscious scholarship by white thinkers such as Peter Fryer, Marika Sherwood, Jenny Bourne and Chris Searle has also contributed to black Britain's intellectual life. What 'black' denotes in this book is something about particular intellectual concerns and approaches. These might be defined as a determination to account for the social construction of race as a fully social relationship; a refusal to evade race, racialization and racism by treating them as unfortunate marginal, aberrant experiences; and recognition of the social agency of black communities. It also implies resistance to the ways in which 'racism works to suppress the historical dimensions of black life, offering a mode of existence locked permanently into a recurrent present where social existence is confined to the roles of either being a problem or a victim' (Gilroy, 1993b: 37). The story of race and education in Britain ranges far wider than the perennials of school failure and underachievement.

Decentring blackness

Since the 1980s black thinkers such as Stuart Hall, Tariq Modood and Claire Alexander have all interrogated the homogenizing tendencies of British political blackness (though not necessarily for the same reasons). They have rightly raised questions about the dominance within political blackness of certain forms of African-Caribbean maleness; the marginalization of women; the relegation of South Asian voices; the invisibility of queer sexualities; generational and class differences; the complexities of articulations between religion and race. Although Stuart Hall's (1988) proclaimed 'new ethnicities' have not entirely replaced political blackness, they have modified its claims and necessitated critical self-reflection, hastening the emergence of less stable, decentred blackness. At the same time, it is still the case that many contemporary black British intellectual currents are derived from the idiom of political blackness, even where they take issue with it. Additionally, in social policy awkward terms such as 'black and minority ethnic' (BME) are used to rephrase the idea of blackness as inclusive, as something that does not refer only to people of African descent.

So in this book the term 'black' is used in a contentious, even provocative sense: with its umbrella political meaning restored, albeit in chastened form. In part, this is because it is concerned with *histories* of black intellectual production in the UK, covering periods when much black intellectual work adhered to the uniquely British use of the term 'black'. Above all, there is a final reason why, in its coverage of educational struggles, this book unashamedly returns to a definition of blackness that has become unfashionable in recent years. For, in obsessing over the constraints of political blackness, we risk underestimating just how unique the British inclusive definition of blackness is, or was. There is still a story to be told about what the creation of that idiom achieved among people of colour in Britain.

As James Procter (2003) argues, the emergence of political blackness signified a shift, riven with ambivalence, from being *black in Britain* to being *black and British*. Quoting Paul Gilroy, Procter (2003: 5) suggests that this 'involves a radical deconstruction of the idea that "blacks are an external problem, an alien presence visited in Britain from the outside"'.

Of course, the term 'black British' may not be accurate in all instances. For instance, it does not always overcome the old tendency to conflate 'England' with 'Britain'. For historical reasons, most of the black British intellectuals examined in this book have worked and written in England and in a pre-devolution context. This does not imply, however, that we should only be concerned with black English thinkers. Scottish poet Jackie Kay, the historian Ron Ramdin and academics such as Rowena Arshad have done much to extend conversations across English, Welsh and Scottish settings. Importantly, though, 'black British' is used in this book because it has remained a preferred term among many black people. In theory at least, it implies the possibility of a British identity comprising multiple ethnicities and it has allowed a creative fuzziness around the still largely unpacked limits of black 'Englishness', 'Welshness' and 'Scottishness'.

Finally, because this book comprises a history of black intellectuals and education, African-Caribbean thinkers and activists play a particularly prominent role, reflecting their profile in educational struggles. In the middle and late twentieth century Caribbean communities were the most militant drivers of the campaigns that grew around education (Sivanandan, 1982; Bryan *et al.*, 1985a, 1985b; Phillips, M. and Phillips, T., 1999). This was partly a response to the treatment meted out to the children of Caribbean migrants but also because Caribbean intellectual groupings cohered early in the post-war period, certainly in London, thrown together by forces as disparate as British immigration control, the colonial scholarship system, the shape of the publishing industry and the failure of the West Indian Federation.

Burdens of representation

Insofar as they have emerged from community activism and teaching, as well as from academia, black public intellectuals have often been, in the truest sense, organic intellectuals. Gramsci imagined organic intellectuals as those situated within a particular class or culture and whose role is to articulate its emergent identity and interests. In *Representations of the Intellectual* Edward Said (1996: 13) defines public intellectuals as, at root, individuals with 'a vocation for the art of representing ... it is publicly recognizable and involves both commitment and risk'. For Said, the public intellectual is an oppositional figure, a dissenting figure. It is this that distinguishes an intellectual from a policy-maker, who may also devote time to thinking, writing and attempting to influence public life. In contrast, Said declares, 'the challenge of the intellectual life is to be found in dissent against the status quo at a time when the struggle on behalf of underrepresented and disadvantaged groups seems so unfairly weighted against them' (Said, 1996: xvii).

So far, so heroic – but invoking the archetype of the politically engaged public intellectual does not exempt black thinkers from age-old dilemmas. Representation is, for black intellectuals, a perennial burden. Black America's arch-intellectual Henry Louis Gates (1992) describes the burden of representation as two-fold. Firstly, there is representation in the sense of depiction: offering images of black life and identity, its meanings, its subjective truths. Secondly, there is representation as advocacy, arguing for the community's interests. Black intellectuals may claim to tell 'how it is', they may claim to know 'who we are' and 'what we feel', but we should not be seduced by over-simplified notions of the organic intellectual. Nowhere does this book imply what Stuart Hall (1996b: 474) might describe as an 'innocent' notion of authentic black experience that is simply to be 'represented' in either sense by black intellectuals. Each intellectual who 'speaks for' a community also invokes a particular notion of community.

Loyalty and authenticity

Thus the relationship between black intellectuals and 'their' communities (and these are not only ethnic communities – class, gender, profession all imply certain loyalties) is always skewed, complex and deceptive. And why should it be otherwise? The American cultural historian Ross Posnock (1997, 1998) argues that black public intellectuals, such as W. E. B. Du Bois and Frantz Fanon, have often exemplified contradictions between the organic intellectual and the universal intellectual who seeks not to be bound by sectional interests but to articulate a common humanity. For Posnock, black intellectual life is, at its apex, a lived contradiction. The black intellectual is, on the one hand, a race man (sic), speaking against racial injustice from an 'authentic' black standpoint. On the other hand, the black intellectual interrogates the concept of race, critiquing the historical production of 'blackness' and 'whiteness'. In this kind of intellectual dissent Posnock (1997: 324) sees the black intellectual as a 'social type ... resisting the lure of the prevailing ideology of the authentic'.

This rejection of the burden of championing a thinly imagined authentic blackness intersects with what Said (1996) describes as the problem of loyalty to community. For black British intellectuals focusing on education, problems of loyalty apply not only to their relationships to black communities but equally to the dilemmas experienced as educators who are implicated in the sector's racialized processes and outcomes. Over the past fifty years black British intellectuals have divided in their loyalties to the education system. In the early 1970s, even as he decried the structural racism of the education sector, Bernard Coard offered guidance on how to reform and improve schooling for back pupils. In the late 1970s and early 80s black Marxists, convinced of the instability of British capitalism, argued for the rejection of a system they regarded as irredeemably complicit in capitalist domination and reproduction. In contrast, in the neo-liberal era Maureen Stone took education in capitalism as a given, arguing that black pupils and parents must work to gain advantage within an inherently unequal system. So how critical should a black critic of the education system be? Are we obliged to uproot the system or to evaluate and renew it?

Race ambivalence

Another perennial question has to be broached. Since this is a book about race, education and social justice, how does it conceive of race? Firstly, it should be clear from the earlier discussion of British political blackness that in this book race is regarded as a social construct. But so what? Anti-racist thinkers have from W. E. B. Du Bois onwards, coalesced bumpily around the sociological project to refute the conception of race as biologistic 'fact', a natural, essential condition. The salient position of this book, one that enables us to grasp most fully black British political history, is one of 'race ambivalence'. This helpful term is used often by Zeus Leonardo, a key contemporary theorist of articulations between race, class and education. It signifies that while race may be unreal in the sense that it is not a coherent scientific category, its effects, including the shaping of social relationships and the formation of our identities, are all too real:

> To the extent that race as a concept is not real, its modes of existence are real. Its racial subjects are real; likewise, schools, the workplace and families are institutional forms of race. There is good reason to believe that race is not a scientific concept, which is not reason enough to reject its study but necessitates a multiple framework that includes ideological and materialist perspectives.
>
> Leonardo (2005: 409)

In other words, it is not sufficient to regard race as a technology of other supposedly more real relationships, such as class. Race is a tool used to order political, social and economic relationships – and like all tools that we use to shape the world, those tools also shape us. Race may have its ideological origins in the government of seventeenth-century plantation societies but four hundred years on, we live with race as a social fact:

> The longevity of the race concept and the enormous number of effects of race thinking (and race acting) has produced a guarantee that race will remain a

feature of social reality across the globe ... at the level of experience of everyday life, race is a relatively impermeable part of our identity ... To be raceless is akin to being genderless.

Winant (2000: 184)

We live in ways that are informed by racialized social categories and inequalities. These modes of *race in practice* are divisive and, in terms of identification and meaning, are often arbitrary (Gunaratnam, 2003; Song, 2003). Nevertheless, we often live as if race has meaning and we live within a society in which those racialized meanings have innumerable consequences (Warmington, 2009). Race ambivalence means taking race as both unreal (as a scientific category) and real (as a social tool). For that reason, in this book the word race is not encased in scare quotes, particularly as the fad for placing race in scare quotes (but not other social constructs, such as gender or childhood) too often trivializes the experiences of black people and the real dimensions of race as a social relationship.

Aims and sources

This book's principal sources are written literature: scholarly work but also campaign literature, black journalism and educational materials. Taking encouragement from Wendy Walters' recent work on *written* black history (Walters, 2013), I make no apology for this documentary or literary take. For while oral histories have been of vital importance in tracing the experiences of black communities in Britain (Osler, 1989; Harris and White, 1999), their approach has arguably become something of a comfort zone in recent years. By contrast, too little has been said about the work of independent black journals such as *Race Today*, the writing emanating over five decades from the Institute of Race Relations, or the tensions between radical and conservative black commentators that have become ever more apparent as the consensus around political blackness has splintered in the twenty-first century.

What is the place of literary/documentary sources in social science research? To say that research is based on documentary sources does not tell us *how* those sources will be used (May, 2001). In short, the texts examined in this book are used to explore new questions about the past and its relationship to the present. These new questions arise from contemporary concerns about the hidden history of black public intellectuals' contributions to shaping education and struggles for social justice in Britain (see McKenley, 2001; Warmington, 2012, 2013). In studies of race and education black communities are often depicted as objects of social policy but their *social agency* in struggles over education is often neglected. At its basic level this book aims to give a sense of how extensive and how diverse black British thinkers' contributions to understandings of race, education and social justice have been, depicting social worlds and concerns often overlooked in writing on education. As an intellectual history, it is not about suggesting a simple correspondence between texts and events such as the placing of black children in ESN schools (schools for the 'educationally subnormal') in the 1960s and 70s. Instead it is concerned with how, within the wider flow of black intellectual history, black thinkers constructed versions of events and constructed understandings of racism, black identities, and relationships between black communities, the education system and the wider state.

The texts selected as the focus of this book are prismatic: that is, selected to exemplify shifts in thought and debate over decades, and indeed centuries, of black British intellectual life (cf. Robinson, 1983). Because this book is concerned with ideas, with intellectual production, its sources are diverse, including academic writing, campaign literature, journalism and biography; what they have in common is that they are public documents that combine theory, rhetoric and comment. They are explored in an engaged, rather than a detached fashion, in order to reflect on how black intellectuals have positioned themselves and how they are positioned in relation to my own and others' assumptions about traditions of black British thought. The sources have been selected with regard to the ways in which they exemplify contributions to the theorization of black British identities, education and social justice, principally in the period since the Second World War. The research upon which the book's arguments are based draws in considerable part upon what, in the British context, are new archival sources: recently developed independent black archives, including those housed at the George Padmore Institute, the Black Cultural Archives and online repositories, such as the Institute of Race Relations, the C. L. R. James Archive and the Tandana's Asian Youth Movement Archive. In addition, library collections and existing bibliographies have been used to identify frequently cited, landmark works and writers, in order to produce a new bibliography that covers intellectual moments in their social, political and historical contexts. These moments include early black writing; anti-colonialism; the black education movements; black Marxist critiques of education; black cultural studies; black feminism; post-racial theory; Critical Race Theory; and black social conservatism.

Structure of the book

In terms of structure *Black British Intellectuals and Education* offers a conceptual and historical account. The aim is to give a sense of chronology, while also acknowledging the complex flow of intellectual histories. History, after all, does not really fall into neat decade-long chunks. So while each chapter focuses more or less on a particular period, its aim is also to highlight thematically the debates and issues that concerned black intellectuals within that period.

Chapter 2 provides an overview of early black British intellectuals, beginning with those who emerged in the radical politics of the eighteenth and nineteenth centuries. It then focuses on the crucible of early-twentieth-century activity. Its emphasis is on how intellectual currents such as pan-Africanism and early black feminism prefigured the thought and politics that would emerge out of post-war Commonwealth migration. Chapters 3 and 4 take us to the Windrush era and the 'black explosion' in British schools that followed post-war immigration from

Asia, Africa and the Caribbean. There has long been awareness among black British thinkers that the haphazard development of education policies designed to address the needs and experiences of black children in British schools told a revealing story about the wider struggle to overturn perceptions of people of colour as an alien problem visited upon the (white) nation. The *belatedness* of race equality policies in education and the tendency of those early initiatives to pathologize black children, families and communities arguably defined race as a social relationship in Britain for decades. Chapter 3 recounts the key black educational campaigns of the 1960s and 1970s over dispersal policies, low teacher expectations and the placing of Caribbean children in schools for 'educationally subnormal' (ESN) children. Chapter 4 examines the ways in which black British thinkers theorized those grassroots struggles, severing themselves from earlier race relations paradigms, and producing elaborated analyses of race, schooling and social justice.

Chapter 5 considers how the black political and educational groundswell combined with the agendas of the British left and local government in the 1970s, 80s and 90s to be reconfigured into state multiculturalism. It examines the powerful body of educational work produced by black and anti-racist educators. It also considers the disparities between state-driven multicultural education as it emerged in the wake of the Swann Report and the critical analyses developed by radical black thinkers, who became increasingly critical of facile forms of multicultural education.

Chapter 6 looks at how, in the 1980s and 90s, black British intellectuals sought ways of moving beyond the tropes of anti-racism and multiculturalism. Under the influence of Stuart Hall and the Centre for Contemporary Cultural Studies, black British scholars transformed the social sciences and humanities, posing new questions about youth, culture and identity in Britain. Theirs should also be regarded as black educational work. Education has also been accorded a central place in black feminist thought. Black women intellectuals have figured in the British landscape from the very beginnings of black intellectual life in Britain. Chapter 2, for example, discusses figures such as Una Marson and Claudia Jones and in Chapter 7 the work of their successors is explored. Black feminists' understandings of race, class and gender as co-constituted have profoundly shaped black British intellectuals, challenging masculinized narratives of black British experience, not least in relation to schooling.

The first two decades of the twenty-first century have prompted new questions about race and education. Just as we can never return to a solid political blackness, the moment of a certain kind of state-driven multiculturalism – multiculturalism as policy – has probably passed. It is also true that some of what was championed in the 1980s as multiculturalism has become part of mainstream British culture, albeit still contested. We now arguably live, therefore, in a 'post-multicultural' society. That is not to suggest in any way that racial inequalities have been resolved or that anti-racist work is completed. Neither is it meant to chime in with voguish claims that multiculturalism is 'dead'. However, it does imply that new questions can be asked about race and British identities, and about what education in and for cultural diversity might mean. Chapters 8 and 9 examine the contexts in which contemporary black educators and intellectuals work. These twenty-first-century contexts include the impacts of the Stephen Lawrence case and the Macpherson Inquiry's definitions of institutional racism; the post 9/11 backlash against multiculturalism; and the ostensible de-racialization of public policy.

Three very different contemporary approaches to understanding race and education are examined, all of which have emerged in Britain over the past decade: post-racial theory, Critical Race Theory and what might be termed new black social conservatism. These are significant new bodies of thought: firstly, because they have defined themselves largely in relation to youth and education and, secondly, because they have become platforms for new, sometimes iconoclastic, black voices. Though in some ways analytically opposed, all address questions of how, in putatively 'post-multicultural' contexts, we might rethink race, education and social justice. The book concludes by reflecting on the state of black intellectual life in Britain at the beginning of the twentieth century. Will there be successors to James, Marson, Hall and Sivanandan? And will their voices be heard in the mainstream or on the margins?

Conclusion

There are many possible maps that might be drawn of the history of race and education in Britain. This book offers a particular introduction to oft-hidden stories, focusing principally on the literature and debates that have grown out of black intellectual activism. Above all, *Black British Intellectuals and Education* depicts black people in Britain as agents of social change – as thinkers and actors, rather than policy conundrums. In accounts of race and education, black agency is often obscured. Black communities drift into civic debate at moments of crisis – usually crises defined from outside – and, as Paul Gilroy has observed, are treated as 'objects rather than subjects, beings that feel yet lack the ability to think, and remain incapable of considered behaviour in an active mode' (Gilroy, 1987: 11).

The black British story told here is one of considered ideas and social activism: a cultural history in which the centrality of black life is presumed, not a history in which black people are other or in which black children are other people's children. This is not the same as cheerleading or advocacy; the intellectual positions examined here are too disparate, vital and contentious to be smoothed over. Instead it is an attempt to understand race, education and social justice in terms of the demands and contributions that black thinkers and communities have made, and to understand how these have shaped British social life on the grand scale. It views race and education, not primarily in terms of Acts of Parliament, policy reports or theories of race relations but through the work of black public intellectuals: scholars, educators and activists who have emerged from academia, the chalk face and the crucible of community activism.

2 Early black British thinkers

> White discourses have been constructing us as simpletons, as simple-minded primitives, as smiling country people not quite up with the fast ways of the advanced world, for centuries ... It is a reading to be refused.
>
> Hall (1984: 84)

Introduction

John La Rose (1927–2006), one of Britain's pivotal post-war black activists, was wont to remind listeners that 'we did not come alive in Britain' (John, G. 2006a: 2). His aphorism drew attention to the reserves of experience possessed by black communities. Histories of resistance in Africa, the Caribbean and Asia, La Rose insisted, offered resources for understanding black British experiences and formulating social action, so enabling us to become 'protagonists of our own fate' (Craig-James, 2006: 6). And just as we did not come alive 'here' in Britain, neither have black British communities merely come alive 'now', in some recurrent present of 'social exclusion' and 'underachievement'. In fact, black intellectuals have figured in British public life since the late eighteenth century. This chapter begins by looking at the early black British thinkers who featured in the abolitionist struggle and in the popular radical movements of the nineteenth century. Thereafter, it focuses on the development of black activism across the first half of the twentieth century, including the anti-colonial movements, but also thinkers who promoted a determinedly black British identity among the small settled communities of the 1930s and 40s, thereby prefiguring the black activism of the post-war period.

Prototypes and archetypes

In *London Calling*, his history of black metropolitan visionaries, Sukhdev Sandhu (2003: xviii) remarks that too often black Britons have been co-opted into the public sphere as 'metaphors for newness', divorced from their pasts. In order to understand how, in a relatively short space of post-war time, distinctive black British identities were asserted in and around education, it is vital to pay attention to earlier black thinkers, who in the previous two centuries were 'keen, if not always contented, observers of Britain' (Phillips, C., 1997: xv). For in these early cross-currents the spores of black Marxism, black British feminism, pan-Africanism and African–Asian alliances can all be found. Some of these early black intellectuals were directly active in education; others contributed more generally to public life. Most spoke in some fashion 'of' and 'for' nascent black communities. Some of these pre-Windrush figures are, outside of specialist circles, unduly neglected but in their own times they were highly visible, fully engaged in the flow of British and international political life.

For sure, there were times in the careers of thinkers such as Ignatius Sancho and George Padmore when they painfully resembled the 'lonely black men lost in the white London fogs' described by Richard Wright (Padmore, 1971: xxi). Just as often, however, they moved cannily within sites of power and influence. And, thankfully, they were not only men; witness the contributions of, for instance, Amy Ashwood Garvey, Una Marson and Claudia Jones. Their political concerns encompassed racial inequality, imperialism, women's rights, the welfare of children and struggles around poverty, labour and class. While some of these black intellectual pioneers were transient students and activists, laying the groundwork for independence movements from cafes and church halls in London, Cardiff and Manchester, others had begun to imagine themselves and their contemporaries as settlers, whose permanent presence would urge new definitions of what it meant to be British. In the USA by the early twentieth century black intellectual endeavour was embedded in the black universities and colleges, and in national institutions, such as the National Association for the Advancement of Colored People (Cruse, 1967; Banner-Haley, 2010). In Britain nothing comparable existed. Britain's pre-war black population did not, of course, compare in size or stability; it was ethnically more diverse and different in its class structures. Yet Britain's early black intellectuals wrought enduring influence, nationally and internationally.

Particularly important were the strands of black activism that developed across the first half of the twentieth century, culminating in the 1945 Manchester Pan-African Congress. Crucially, African, Caribbean and Asian alliances were a key feature of this black political activity. These alliances grew organically out of the anti-colonial movements and set the terms of the uniquely British definition of 'blackness' that would become a unifying principle of the post-war period. The prominence of early-twentieth-century West Indian intellectuals (they were not yet 'African-Caribbean') was also a salient factor in shaping later black British politics, hence their centrality in this chapter. Their influence could still be felt when, in the 1960s, struggles around busing, banding and exclusions were waged in London boroughs (see Chapter 3).

The slave narratives

The first black British public intellectuals rose out of one of the early crises of the British Empire: the campaign against slavery. The slaves themselves had long been unleashing periodic revolt but the abolitionist movement in Britain coalesced around the series of legal cases fought by Granville Sharp and Thomas Clarkson's circle in the mid-1760s. By the 1770s a number of former slaves had become active in the cause as political organizers, campaigning journalists and authors. Among their writing were the autobiographies that would become known as 'slave narratives'. In recent decades a robust literature has emerged that does this early black British intellectual work justice, both as historical documents and literary texts (see Edwards, 1967; Ogude, 1982; Dabydeen, 1985a; Sandiford, 1988; Carretta, 1996).

Around 1772 the first British slave narrative was published. It was a short account of the life of a 60-year-old freedman, born in northern Nigeria and transported as a child to domestic slavery in New Jersey. *The Narrative of the Most Remarkable Particulars in the Life of James Albert Ukawsaw Gronniosaw, an African Prince, as Related by Himself* was a ghostwritten account of a life (c. 1710–75), lived in all three corners of the black Atlantic. Gronniosaw's narrative used biography to educate Britain's reading public about the slave trade and the campaign for abolition. A year later in 1773 the American poet Phillis Wheatley (1759–1833) became the first black woman to publish in Britain (*Poems on Various Subjects, Religious and Moral*). Wheatley was feted during her subsequent tour of England and her letters of the time, more than the poems themselves, indicate that she had become acquainted with the British anti-slavery movement that had brought Gronniosaw and others to public attention.

Though Ignatius Sancho (1729–80) described himself as 'only a lodger' in Britain, he was in actuality a true settler (and may well have been the only black man to hold the right to vote in eighteenth-century England). Poet, playwright, musicologist and grocer, Sancho moved energetically within London's literary circles. The posthumous *Letters of Ignatius Sancho* (1782) were widely acclaimed for their pithy reflections on the Gordon Riots, Methodism, slavery, literature and electoral politics. Sancho, like Wheatley, shows that the work of early black British intellectuals was not simply an adjunct to the abolitionist campaign. As Keith Sandiford (1988: 44) has urged, their writing should be understood 'not only as a literature of social protest but, more significantly, as bearing an integral relation to the history of ideas'. The so-called slave narratives draw from sources as diverse as Christian theology, African cosmology, European travelogues, free-trade lobbying and picaresque novels, organizing them into descriptions of black life that are ironic as well as pious, tender as well as raging.

Sons and daughters of Africa

That said, it was the abolitionist cause that gave literate former slaves pulse, funding and a public platform in British life. In 1787 Ottobah Cugoano (c.1757–unknown) published *Thoughts and Sentiments on the Evil and Wicked Traffic of the Slavery and Commerce of the Human Species*. It was the first extended critique of slavery by an African writer and one which, importantly, went beyond the position of many white abolitionists of the time, by demanding not only an end to the slave trade but the complete freeing of African labour on the plantations.

Cugoano's book was possibly a joint work with Olaudah Equiano (c. 1745–97), the best known of the early black intellectuals, and today a staple of black history commemorations and school projects. Cugoano and Equiano were both members of the Sons of Africa, a London-based grouping of some two dozen black abolitionists, which agitated throughout the 1780s and 90s. Published in 1789, *The Interesting Narrative of the Life of Olaudah Equiano* remains the most durable of all the autobiographical works produced in Britain by former slaves. In short, it is a redemption song that charts Equiano's life from a free childhood in Benin (in modern south-east Nigeria) through slavery in West Africa, Barbados and Virginia, and thence, having purchased his freedom from his master in Philadelphia, to restored liberty. In form and content it is the most complete of the British slave narratives; its eloquence and sheer narrative momentum have made it a work equally accessible to specialist historians, literary theorists and schoolchildren. In Equiano's own time *The Interesting Narrative* ran to nine editions and was widely translated (Walvin, 1998).

Like Sancho, Equiano was embedded in the flow of British public life but was a far more oppositional voice. Equiano is recorded as touring the country constantly in support of the abolitionist cause (Oldfield, 1998). *The Interesting Narrative* is a prescriptive anti-slavery tract but in its descriptions of Benin, of the middle passage (the transit of captives across the Atlantic to slavery in the Americas) and of his own sensibilities, modified by his global travels, Equiano's story is also corrective of the racist defamation of African peoples. *The Interesting Narrative* begins with a lengthy account of the geographical and cultural features of Benin, immediately locating Equiano as a historical subject bearing a consciousness rooted beyond New World slavery. There is in Equiano's writing some ambivalence towards the institution of slavery, which he recognizes as a feature of African societies also. However, there is a conscious understanding that chattel slavery represents a new form of dehumanization, a *racialized* form of dehumanization. Notably, throughout his book Africans are referred to as 'black', 'negroes', 'negro-men', more often than they are referred to in ethnic or linguistic terms, indicating that a historically modern black/white worldview was already emergent by Equiano's time.

The last of the key British slave narratives, and one of the most significant, was *The History of Mary Prince*. It appeared in 1831, two years before the Abolition of Slavery Bill. Prince's ghostwritten narrative is perhaps biography rather than autobiography. Nevertheless, its stylized use of the first person form, less didactic in tone than Equiano, provides a vivid representation of the lived experience of slavery. Prince (c. 1788–unknown), the narrator, exemplifies both the descriptive and corrective registers, repeatedly invoking authenticity ('I have been a slave myself – I know what slaves feel', Prince, 1987: 214) and countering the pro-slavery lobby's myth of slave women as contented servants. The particular experiences of women slaves are apparent in Prince's references to sexual objectification and violence.

'In literacy lay true freedom'

Henry Louis Gates (1987: ix) has asserted that '[i]n literacy lay true freedom for the black slave' and in committing their argument and experiences to the page, these early black writers defied the terms of order of slaveholding society, wherein Africans were represented as either savage or infantile but never as thinkers, much less social critics. These early black British works are self-conscious, self-reflexive intellectual products. Their authors artfully construct ways of being within racialized worlds; their narratives constitute intellectual revolt. For each of the slave narratives, with greater or lesser degrees of didacticism, constitutes a form of public pedagogy: a disquisition on how human relationships – between black and white, free and enslaved – must be rethought and relearned, even within the context of social structures and intellectual conditions degraded by Atlantic slavery.

Even so, these early figures are knottier, thornier characters than any roll of 'black heroes' will admit. Wheatley, for instance, was originally sponsored by pro-slavery campaigners. Both Equiano and Cugoano became involved in (though later disavowed) the Sierra Leonean resettlement scheme, through which it was envisaged that the mass of black Londoners would be decanted to West Africa (Fryer, 1984). As for Cugoano, he disappears altogether from the historical record a few years after the publication of *Thoughts and Sentiments*, his last public scheme being an attempt to found a school for black Londoners. It is not known whether his plan ever came to fruition.

Black radicals and the black poor

However, seeing the black thinkers and activists of the eighteenth and early nineteenth centuries only in terms of 'slave narratives' risks missing the breadth of their radicalism and their immersion in Britain's political sphere (see Gundara and Duffield, 1992). Both Equiano and Cugoano worked also for the welfare and education of London's 'black poor', who comprised servants, freedmen and women, and runaways (including many children). In addition to Africans, there were growing numbers of Indian seafarers, or Lascars, cut adrift by ups and downs in the fortunes of Britain's East India Company (Gerzina, 1995). Their presence was such that by the 1780s the racialized term 'black poor' was commonly used in press and Parliament to denote a particular social problem (Walvin, 1998).

In the nineteenth century other black intellectuals entered the flow of humanitarian and radical activity that helped shape British politics. Among them was Robert Wedderburn (c. 1762–1835), a freeborn working-class Jamaican at the forefront of the socialist Spencean movement. In the 1810s Wedderburn founded the periodical *The Forlorn Hope*, in an effort to establish a free press in Britain (Dabydeen *et al.*, 2007). William Davidson (1781–1820) was, like Wedderburn, a Jamaican of mixed parentage, though of more affluent origin. Sent to study law in England, Davidson was radicalized by the writings of Thomas Paine and began to organize political reading groups. In 1820, he and four comrades attempted to avenge the previous year's Peterloo massacre, conspiring to assassinate members of the Cabinet. Turned in by informers, Davidson and the others were publicly executed (Fryer, 1984).

Later on, strains of Spencean thinking could be detected in the more radical fringes of the Chartist movement of the 1830s. Chartism became Britain's first mass labour movement, influencing all subsequent movements for parliamentary reform. Among the most militant Chartist leaders was William Cuffay (1788–1870), Kentish son of a seaman from St Kitts. Elected president of the London Chartists in 1842 (provoking numerous racist slurs in the London press), Cuffay remained, even after the rejection of the Charter by Parliament, uncompromisingly committed to full political representation and the radical redistribution of wealth. In 1849 Cuffay was drawn into ramshackle plans for a London uprising. This led to his conviction and transportation to Tasmania, where he remained after being pardoned, engaged in trade union work (Hoyles, 2013).

Indian campaigners

While activists of African descent were most visible in the British politics of the nineteenth century, a number of important Indian campaigners also made their base in London. While focusing their work primarily on political reform in India, rather than British politics *per se*, several were also strenuous in their lobbying of Parliament, and periodically made links with political reform movements in England (Fryer, 1984). The writer, educator and reformer Raja Rammohan Roy (1772–1833), one of the key figures of the Bengal Renaissance of the late nineteenth century, was based in England during the 1830s, and was perhaps the first major Indian political figure to enter the British scene. While in England in the 1840s, another force in the Bengal Renaissance, Indian industrialist Dwarkanath Tagore (1794–1846) sought out the Chartists and other campaigners (Visram, 2002).

Cambridge-educated Joseph Batista (1864–1930) was, prior to Gandhi's emergence, one of the central figures in the Indian Home Rule movement (for which he gleaned ideas from Ireland's Home Rule campaigners). In England he forged strong links with the Labour Party, converting many of its leading members to the cause of Indian self-determination (Ramdin, 1999). In contrast, Dadabhai Naoroji (1825–1917), while a declared Indian nationalist, focused his sights on the British political and cultural arena. In 1856 Naoroji was appointed as Professor of Guajarati at University College London. Immersing himself in the political mainstream, he formed the London Indian Society and, as Liberal candidate for Finsbury Central in 1892, was the first Asian MP to be elected to Westminster (Gifford, 1992).

Yet – and we would do well to remember this – these early black public intellectuals were only the most visible of those active in British politics and society. They emerged from and engaged with national movements and local clubs; they moved within streets, dockyards, chapels and salons. What their access to the press, to publishers, to influential leaders and committees enabled them to do was, like later generations of black intellectuals, record, theorize and elaborate. They constructed rhetoric designed to argue what was viscerally felt by those who signed local petitions, attended public meetings, organized charity and recruited to unions and political societies.

Pan-Africanism in Britain

By the early twentieth century Britain was not only the centre of an Empire; it was also the dutch pot in which anti-colonial movements simmered. Between the 1920s and 40s, the strand of anti-colonialism that contributed most to the shaping of black British intellectual identities was the pan-Africanist movement, the impact of which was still felt among many of those, such as John La Rose and Eric and Jessica Huntley, who were active in the black education movements of the post-war era.

For those who associate pan-Africanism only with Marcus Garvey saluting the Harlem corps of the Universal Negro Improvement Association or with the crowds of Accra carrying Nkrumah aloft, the symbiosis between black British politics and pan-Africanism may need elaboration. For despite gazing towards an imagined African future, many of those involved in pan-Africanism were also deeply concerned with the lives and welfare of Britain's settled black communities. The pan-Africanist movement was also the source of traditions of Caribbean militancy and African–Asian alliances in Britain. Pan-Africanism's origins are diverse, stretching back at least to the nineteenth century (Ramdin, 1987, and Adi, 2000, even detect precursors in the slave narratives of Equiano and Cugoano). Its influences lie in the early nationalist movements of the black diaspora, such as those led by J. A. Thorne, Edward Wilmot Blyden and Martin Delaney, as well as concepts of nationhood propagated in nineteenth-century European pan-nationalism and the pan-Arab movement. In an early attempt to map its political development from the outside George Shepperson described pan-Africanism as 'another triangular trade, a trade not of … slaves and molasses, but a commerce of ideas between the descendants of the slaves in the West Indies and North America and their ancestral continent' (Shepperson, 1960: 299).

The brilliant and imposing African-American intellectual W. E. B. Du Bois, who fathered much that black Atlantic thinkers have grappled with over the past century (see Lewis, D. L., 1993), reflected that:

> The idea of one Africa to unite the thoughts and ideals of all native peoples of the dark continent belongs to the twentieth century and stems naturally from the West Indies and the United States. Here various groups of Africans, quite separate in origin, became so united in experience and so exposed to the impact of new cultures that they began to think of Africa as one idea and one land.
>
> Du Bois (1965: 7)

In truth, pan-Africanism was both one idea and many, and is as hard to define as socialism, feminism or any other socio-political constellation. However, tenets that appear in most of its variants include: the definition of people of African descent as one people, regardless of national boundaries; the symbolic centrality of African heritage in definitions of identity and culture; the belief that African people have common history and, therefore, common political and economic concerns; the aim of securing human rights, political integrity and economic prosperity for African people across the world. There have also been varying degrees of emphasis on political and economic unification between African states.

Why, given that in important respects pan-Africanism was a less concrete and cohesive force than the Indian independence movements, was pan-Africanism so important to the development of a uniquely black British political identity? Firstly, there is the sheer range and significance of black British thinkers drawn into its orbit: among them, Dusé Mohamed Ali, Ras Makonnen, George Padmore, Una Marson and C. L. R. James. Secondly, there were strong links between local and international political activity. For example, the West African Students Union (WASU), formed in 1925 by Ladipo Solanke (1886–1958), operated as a focus for African students and activists who were concerned both with their home countries' conditions under British rule and with the grinding racism they encountered in British cities (WASU Project, 2012). Thirdly, pan-Africanism in Britain was not insular or exclusive; African–Asian solidarity was a key concern of its most progressive thinkers (Adi, 2000). At the beginning of the twentieth century Dusé Mohamed Ali (c. 1866–1945), founder of the *African Times and Orient Review*, was a committed champion of alliances between African and Asian anti-imperialist movements and an admirer of Naoroji's achievements both as an Indian nationalist and as an MP (Duffield, 1992). George Padmore (c. 1902–59), who might credibly be regarded as the chief architect of pan-Africanism in Britain, was a close friend and ally of K. D. Kumria, Krishna Menon and other London-based members of the Indian National Congress, as well as the Ceylonese activist T. B. Subasinghe, who, along with Surat Alley of the Indian Organizations in Britain Federation, attended the iconic 1945 Pan-African Congress in Manchester.

The politics of diaspora

The other reason that pan-Africanism and its intellectual tools became integral to the development of black British political identities was its understanding of *diaspora* as a political and cultural force. The African diaspora was the driver of early pan-Africanism, not its appendage. Pre-war pan-Africanism was about defining the diaspora – the scattered, the exiled – as much as the home continent. The notion of 'Africans at home and abroad', derived from the rhetoric of Marcus Garvey, was an inspired ambiguity because in pan-Africanist thought Africa was 'home' but also 'abroad'; Harlem, London and Port of Spain were 'abroad' but also 'home'. As Du Bois implied, pan-Africanism was both a kind of error, in its conception of a unitary Africa, and a form of genius – in the original sense of a presiding spirit. Because of its profound challenge to European imperialism's racialized terms of order, pan-Africanism retains a presence in the work of black

British intellectuals, even where they dissent from Garvey's 'race first' position or Aimé Césaire's belief in negritude.

It is also sometimes forgotten that London was the venue for the first ever Pan-African Conference in July 1900, organized by a local councillor from London, Trinidad-born barrister Henry Sylvester Williams (1869–1911). Conceived as an anti-colonial world conference, there were no more than fifty participants but these included W. E. B. Du Bois and other influential activists from Britain, the USA and the Caribbean (though not, it should be noted, from Africa). It was at the 1900 conference that Du Bois first offered his famous formulation of the 'color line' as the key problem of the twentieth century (Fryer, 1984). Regrettably, by the time Du Bois recounted that first 1900 conference in his major pan-Africanist statement, *The World and Africa*, Williams went unnamed, referred to only as 'a black West Indian barrister, practicing in London' (Du Bois, 1965: 7). After that first conference, Du Bois later reflected, 'the movement and the idea died for a generation' (Du Bois, 1965: 8) until after the First World War, when Du Bois helmed the 'first' Pan-African Congress in Paris, 1919. Du Bois' second (1921) and third (1923) Congresses were both held in London. The fifth, generally agreed to be the most historically significant from a British perspective, was held at Chorlton Town Hall, Manchester in 1945. Its impact is discussed later in this chapter.

Garvey in London

In the pre-war period the other major driver of pan-Africanism was Marcus Garvey's Universal Negro Improvement Association (UNIA), whose fierce wrangling with Du Bois is well recorded (Geiss, 1974; Martin, 1976). Garvey's movement was, throughout the 1920s and 30s, a popular force with a vast, international grassroots membership. Although in Garvey's lifetime (1887–1940) the UNIA did not establish extensive roots in Britain, following his death Garvey's reputation underwent some rehabilitation, even among those such as George Padmore and C. L. R. James, who were politically at odds with Garvey's racial dogma. As in most diasporan communities, Garveyism has retained some influence in the UK, albeit refracted through American-influenced cultural nationalism (Jones, V., 1986; Graham, 2001; Andrews, 2013). Certainly during the 1970s and 80s Garvey's ghost influenced the ethos of some UK supplementary schools and some conceptions of what a 'culturally relevant' black history curriculum might be (Yekwai, 1988; Jones, V., 1986). Moreover, Garvey's prescriptions for 'redeeming' black communities (a mix of black capitalism and state welfare) also have greater currency than is usually admitted in the neo-liberal mainstream, where his up-by-the-bootstraps model of self-improvement has been part-assimilated by black social conservatives (see Chapter 9).

But if Britain gave birth to important strains of pan-Africanism, in the end it also housed the demise of its pre-war modes. In 1940 Marcus Garvey died in London, his powers failing but nonetheless regularly publishing his late period journal *The Black Man*, and still hoping to reignite the UNIA (Lewis, R., 1988;

Grant, 2008). Meanwhile, the Pan-African Congress movement that Du Bois had moulded grew to maturity, passing out of the diaspora and into the hands of Africa's emergent independence movements. This shift was engineered, in significant part, by the British-based activists who helmed the 1945 Pan-African Congress in Manchester.

George Padmore: pan-Africanism and communism

The Manchester Conference was the work of George Padmore (c. 1902–59). In his introduction to Padmore's major work *Pan-Africanism or Communism*, Richard Wright (Padmore, 1971: xxi) described Padmore as 'the veritable ideological father of many of the nationalist movements in Black Africa'. Yet, at the beginning of the twenty-first century, Bill Schwarz described Padmore as 'a forgotten figure' (Schwarz, 2003b: 149). If true, then it would be a shameful erasure of a major seam of black British intellectual history. Yet Schwarz's description is not wholly correct; Padmore's influence, like that of his friend and ally C. L. R. James, persisted into the post-war period among black British educators and activists, particularly those involved with London's New Beacon Books and associated groups, such as the Black Parents Movement (see Chapters 3 and 4). Today the archive that sits above the New Beacon Bookshop, founded by John La Rose, bears the name, the George Padmore Institute. C. L. R. James, perhaps the most revered of British-based pan-Africanist elders, continued throughout his life to pay tribute to Padmore, asserting: 'I don't know *anybody else*, except perhaps Dr Du Bois and Marcus Garvey, who is worth more careful consideration' (James, 1984: 262).

George Padmore was born Malcolm Nurse in Trinidad around 1902. By the time Padmore settled in London in 1935, he had migrated physically and intellectually more than once. In 1924 he had left Trinidad, never to return. During his sojourn as a student at Fisk University, Tennessee, Nurse immersed himself in Marxist-Leninism, adopting the *nom-de-guerre* George Padmore and becoming by the end of the decade a prominent youth activist in the American Communist Party. Padmore stood out as a potential bridge between the USSR and African-American socialists. Tickets to Moscow were eagerly proffered and between 1929 and 1933 Padmore became a noted figure in Soviet politics: active in the Communist International, as head of the Red International Labour Union's Negro Bureau and, later, as editor of the Hamburg-based paper *Negro Worker* (Hooker, 1967). Padmore was lauded internationally by Marxists upon the publication of his *Life and Struggles of Negro Toilers* (1931). However, by 1933 he had broken permanently with Soviet Communism, though not Marxism itself: the cause being the USSR's withdrawal of active support for anti-colonial movements in Africa, which were abandoned as collateral damage when Stalin sought to secure wartime alliances with the western imperial powers (Padmore, 1971).

Arriving in pre-war England, Padmore became one of the architects of a pan-Africanism that was informed by socialism but had outgrown the Soviet influence, urging black self-determination' yet remaining internationalist. In England in 1937 Padmore formed the International African Services Bureau (IASB) in collaboration with C. L. R. James, Ras Makonnen and Isaac Wallace-Johnson. Through its own agitation and its communications with the British left (Padmore forged links with the Independent Labour Party but declined to join), the IASB sought to draw attention to political rights and welfare in the colonies. Padmore's pan-Africanism, which he characterized as 'an ideological alternative to Communism on the one side and Tribalism on the other [that] rejects white racialism and black chauvinism' (Padmore, 1971: 355), connected directly with the shift in the pan-Africanist movement towards African leadership. Padmore was a friend and mentor to Ghana's independence leader Nkrumah (in whose early administration he played a low-key but influential role) and to other emergent African and Caribbean leaders. Suffering increasingly poor health, George Padmore returned from Nkrumah's Ghana to London, where he died in 1959.

1945 Pan-African Congress, Manchester

In 1945 Nkrumah and Padmore also collaborated on what was to be perhaps the most important legacy of Padmore's time in Britain: the fifth Pan-African Congress. Padmore's biographer, James R. Hooker, wrote of the October 1945 Manchester Congress as 'one of the significant events of the postwar world' yet one that went 'unremarked to its conclusion' (Hooker, 1967: 98). Its full history has been uncovered in the extensive research of Hakim Adi and Marika Sherwood (Adi and Sherwood, 1995; Sherwood, 1995). What distinguished the Manchester Conference was that it had roots not just in the visionary ideas of Du Bois and the emergent class of independence leaders but also in the local, grassroots struggles of Britain's small black communities. Ras Makonnen, for instance, a prime mover in the Pan-African Federation, had long been Manchester based.

The Manchester Congress effectively signalled a shift away from Du Bois, who was largely repositioned as a venerated figurehead, to the practical control of Padmore, Nkrumah and Jomo Kenyatta. Moreover, as much as the Manchester Congress was the product of Du Bois' vision over the preceding decades, it was also the product of the Subject People's Conference that took place in London in June 1945, organized by British-based bodies, including the Pan-African Federation, the West African Students Union, the Ceylon Students Association and the Federation of Indian Students. At the end of the Subject People's Conference delegates drew up plans for a 'Colonial International' that would link trade unionists, students and progressive anti-imperialist parties across the colonized world, as well as in black communities in Europe and the USA. All of this, as Adi and Sherwood (1995) note, preceded by some years the Bandung movement that sought to unite African and Asian peoples in anti-colonial struggle. Both the Manchester and London conferences again indicate that a concept of blackness that denoted people of colour *in general* figured actively in pre-Windrush black British thought.

Pre-war grassroots activity

However, during the 1930s and 40s, political momentum was also being forged at local level among Britain's black population, growing out of small but established black communities in London, Manchester, Edinburgh and port cities such as Cardiff, Liverpool and South Shields. These communities comprised workers and their families, as well as students and a few professionals. Myriad black organizations operated in different cities, including the African Union in Glasgow, the Colonial People's Association in Cardiff, London's Communist Negro Welfare Association, the Negro Welfare Associations in Liverpool and Manchester and the Indian Seamen's Union, which was active in several major port cities (see Fryer, 1984; Ramdin, 1987; Adi and Sherwood, 1995).

Simultaneously, as MacDonald (1992) and Robinson (1983) have established, the 1930s and 40s saw an upsurge in Britain's black press. Mainly London based, they were the distant progeny of Equiano and Wedderburn. As well as Dusé Mohamed Ali's *African Times and Orient Review*, the League of Coloured Peoples' journal *The Keys*, WASU's regular journal and the *Negro Worker* (not published in Britain but published in English and available in the capital), there were other established newspapers and newsletters, such as the IASB's *International African Opinion*, *The Indian Worker* and Ras Makonnen's *Pan Africa*. In the same period the Indian Workers Association (IWA) first came into being, originating in 1937 among Sikh workers in Coventry. By the early 1940s the IWA had solidified under the influence of Marxist journalist V. S. Sastrya (Visram, 2002). While this incarnation of the IWA had largely run its course by the late 1940s, its model would be revived in the wave of migration that took place in the 1950s.

Harold Moody and the League of Coloured Peoples

Of those bodies that agitated around the concerns of Britain's pre-war settler communities, the most prominent was Harold Moody's League of Coloured Peoples (LCP). Many who invoke Du Bois and Garvey would be harder pressed to name Moody (1882–1947), although in his own time he was probably more directly influential on the everyday lives of black Britons. Born in Jamaica in 1882, Harold Moody was a product of Jamaica's Victorian middle class (like his Trinidadian near-contemporaries, George Padmore and C. L. R. James, he was a dark-skinned man in a middle-class milieu that was obsessed with skin tone). Studious and determinedly respectable, Moody's strong affinity to a colonial British identity was tested when he arrived in London in 1904 to study medicine (MacDonald, 1973). Moody's initial encounters with daily discrimination in the capital form a typical story of the disorientation experienced by members of the Anglophile colonial middle classes, who in the metropolis found themselves unceremoniously recast as black and foreign. Practising as a family doctor in Peckham, South London for over three decades, Moody regarded himself as a permanent settler in Britain. It was this vision of permanence that set the terms of his intellectual and political activity up to his death in 1947.

In the 1920s and 30s Moody developed strong networks among London's Christian charitable bodies and in 1931 he founded the League of Coloured Peoples (LCP). His concept of 'black Britishness' was fundamental to the LCP's work and its ideology. Indeed, in many ways black Britishness – that is, a rejection of whiteness as a determining criterion for being British – *was* the LCP's ideology (Rush, 2002). The LCP has often been characterized as a moderate, somewhat genteel body. Certainly, it relied upon a reading of racism as prejudice born out of ignorance and, being rooted in Christian philanthropy, bourgeois respectability, civic contribution and gradual reform were the LCP's motifs. Thus, for Moody, increased contact between communities and a determination to represent black Britons as upright and industrious were the means to create acceptance and opportunity. None of these strands, it should be said, has ever entirely disappeared from black activism in Britain.

However, the LCP was far from timid. Under Moody, the LCP was tireless at both national and local levels; Moody lobbied MPs and became a significant presence in the British press. The LCP was strident, for instance, in its defence of black seafarers in the Cardiff crisis of 1935, when the government placed quotas on the numbers of black seamen allowed to sail on British ships, rendering many unemployed and unemployable (MacDonald, 1973; Ramdin, 1987). The League also encompassed a strong sense of intergenerational responsibility to black children, for whom it regularly organized outings and Christmas parties. 'Moody's fatherly care', comments Fryer (1984: 331), 'extended to all the children born into Britain's black communities'. The LCP refused to compromise in its vision of black British communities as permanent presences, at a time when such an idea could barely be uttered; in that sense Moody and the League were radical and prophetic.

Between 1933 and 1939 the LCP's journal *The Keys* provided a forum for a diverse range of black intellectuals. As well as promoting the LCP's own ethos, *The Keys* also gave space to the views of anti-colonial activists, such as C. L. R. James (MacDonald, 1976). Indeed, the LCP's links with radical pan-Africanists were, though cautious, more extensive than is sometimes realized (MacDonald, 1973; Rush, 2002). Ramdin (1987: 123) sums up the LCP as being 'between 1931 and 1937 ... an accepted part of the structure of British race relations' while also advocating 'a Pan African brand of humanitarianism'. The LCP promoted alliances with white sympathizers but Moody was determined that, in terms of leadership, it should remain an independent black organization. Moody himself seems to have favoured a definition of 'black' as denoting those of African, rather than Asian descent, although this led to a number of tensions within the multi-ethnic LCP (MacDonald, 1973). Harold Moody has never been mythologized by black activists but the LCP was certainly archetypal of a persistent strand in black British thought and activism: church-aligned, reformist, concerned with fostering what we might now term community cohesion and with presenting itself as a 'best face' co-ordinator of race relations work.

Una Marson: too long forgotten

One of the other key drivers of the LCP was Jamaican journalist, dramatist and broadcaster, Una Marson (1905–65). Like Moody, Marson was raised in a conservative, Anglican, middle-class home. She arrived in London in 1932, becoming the LCP's assistant secretary and, after Moody, its chief spokesperson (Rush, 2002). Although an LCP stalwart, her intellectual and political trajectory was independent of Moody's. Through her editorship of the LCP's journal, *The Keys*, Marson became increasingly familiar with London-based African students' organizations and developed a strong commitment to pan-Africanism, while also moving energetically in mainstream British media and politics. Marson was the first Jamaican woman to be invited to speak at the International Alliance of Women for Suffrage and Equal Citizenship and the first black woman to attend the League of Nations in Geneva (Jarrett-Macauley, 1998). During the 1940s Marson worked with the BBC, contributing to the development of its *Caribbean Voices* series: a significant early showcase for the post-war generation of British-based Caribbean writers, such as Derek Walcott, V. S. Naipaul, Edward Kamau Brathwaite, Andrew Salkey and George Lamming, a number of whom were later associated in the 1960s with John La Rose's New Beacon circle and the related Caribbean Artists Movement. Having contributed immensely to the momentum of black British literature and politics, Una Marson returned to Jamaica, where she died in 1965.

As an intellectual, Marson was concerned with the co-constitution of gender, race and class. Donnell (2003: 126) argues that both Marson's literary work and her journalism 'testify to her capacity to synthesize the politics of feminism and anti-colonialism, translating each into the other'. Certainly, Marson's feminism meant that she was able to view both British society and the distinctive political claims of black women in ways that were beyond the reach of some of her male comrades. However, like many other black women intellectuals, Marson's feminism was often played off against her commitment to black politics by male adversaries, particularly in nationalist circles back in the Caribbean. 'Being out of step with the prevailing politics of her day', Donnell (2003: 129) has argued, '... cost Marson a place in most histories of political and intellectual change'. She remains unduly neglected in histories of black Britain.

C. L. R. James: race, class and culture

Of all the black intellectuals active in Britain in the first half of the twentieth century, it was C. L. R. James (1901–89) who retained the greatest post-war presence, being active in London up until his death. His body of writing is the most widely read and without question the most diverse in subject matter. From his first arrival in the early 1930s, much of James' itinerant life was spent in Britain. In the last decade of his life James was a visible presence in British media and political circles, and was strongly involved with London's Race Today Collective, which included activists and educators such as Farrukh Dhondy, Leila

Hassan, Linton Kwesi Johnson and James' nephew, Darcus Howe (see Chapters 3 and 4).

C. L. R. James' place in black intellectual history is monumental, yet contrary and sometimes strangely elusive. Born in Tunapuna, Trinidad in January 1901, Cyril Lionel Robert James was the son of a village schoolteacher. Before he was ten, he had won a scholarship to Trinidad's Queen's Royal College and by his twenties had made a small local reputation, both through his cricketing prowess and as a writer of short stories (Dhondy, 2001). He arrived in Nelson in Lancashire in 1931, at the behest of Learie Constantine, the Trinidadian cricketer and political activist, who like James was an agitator for West Indian independence. In 1933 James' *The Case for West-Indian Self Government* was published by Leonard and Virginia Woolf's Hogarth Press and over the next three decades James' frenetic creativity – as novelist, historian, literary critic, political theorist and Marxist-Trotskyist scholar – spawned much of his most influential work. This included the novel *Minty Alley* (1937); *The Black Jacobins* (1938), James' colossal study of Toussaint L'Ouverture's Haitian revolution; *Notes on Dialectics* (1948), a major Hegelian critique of Marxist and Trotskyist thought and *Beyond a Boundary* (1964), part bildungsroman, part dissection of Caribbean political and cultural awakening, with cricket – that eternal dialectic between English protestant discipline and anti-colonial revolt – as its case study.

The danger in looking to James for lineage – a neat contribution to black British thought – is that we lose his breadth. Thus we may end up emphasizing *Boundary* and *Jacobins* but tidying away his critical writing on Melville, or we may treat *Minty Alley* as an exemplar of the pre-war Caribbean novel but lose sight of James' abiding concern with Hegelianism as a Marxist predicate. Conversely, the danger in being intimidated by the breadth of James' intellectual work is that, since he wrote of cricket with the same acuity that he wrote of San Domingo's slave rebellion, we throw up our hands and simply declare him a kind of catch-all cultural studies prototype (Larsen, 1996, argues forcefully that the latter reading short-changes James' radical politics). James' position as both resource and conundrum is apparent from the fact that there are several first-class biographies, collections and critical studies that barely overlap in terms of the aspects of his thought that they prioritize (see, for instance, Buhle, 1988; Grimshaw, 1992; Henry and Buhle, 1992; Cudjoe and Cain, 1995; Farred, 1996; Dhondy, 2001; St. Louis, 2007). Nonetheless, *one* of the important things that James did was to map out a series of inescapable problems in which black thinkers were immersed. For James, these problems were inescapable (and one feels that, for James, this was a cause for exaltation, not mourning) because they were the very imprint of black modernity.

James' legacy

The reason that the *Black Jacobins*, for instance, can truly be called epochal is not out of what Stuart Hall has described as a misguided sense of honouring James (Farred, 1994). It is because James' recounting of the San Domingo revolution

– which is the work of a griot and a political economist and a historian 'from below' – lays out the distinctive political obligation to dissolve the false binary between the 'cultural' and the 'economic' in questions of race, class and history. Not for nothing does Paul Gilroy open *There Ain't No Black in the Union Jack* with James' famous dictum that:

> The race question is subsidiary to the class question in politics, and to think of imperialism in terms of race is disastrous. But to neglect the racial factor as merely incidental is an error only less grave than to make it fundamental.
>
> James, cited in Gilroy (1987: 15)

In short, for C. L. R. James the knowledge that had come to black Atlantic thinkers from plantation slavery, from colonialism, from diaspora, was born out of a distinctive experience of racialized capitalism, whose lesson was that no aspect of oppression or rebellion inherently divides into discrete cultural or economic categories. In short, the symbiosis between class and race in Caribbean thought – and in black British thought – is not a cultural tic. That lesson has informed black British intellectuals' sense of standpoint. As Paul Gilroy (2004) has also written:

> The political dimensions of racial discourses ... are not peripheral or decorative ideological motifs appended to colonial adventures. They shaped and still embellish the intimate, essential workings of imperial power in ways that confound any oversimple split between material embodiment on the one hand and culture, ideology and discourse on the other.
>
> Gilroy (2004: 61)

What characterizes James' work most of all is what Cudjoe and Cain (1995) describe as his audacity: the use of western culture's intellectual tools to critique and attempt to reorder that culture. With this audacity James takes up and hammers back Enlightenment thought in the form of revolution. So in *The Black Jacobins* James (1980) shows how Toussaint L'Ouverture's San Domingan revolutionaries had internalized the tools offered by the French revolution and then externalized them again in the cause of their own liberty. For James, the slaves did not merely appropriate Enlightenment thought from the outside; once Toussaint overthrew his colonial masters, western modernity itself was remade forever (see St. Louis, 2007). The political possibilities of modernity could never again be racially homogenous; the west could never again be white. From here on modernity would also be a black planet.

Interestingly, one of the other things that marks out C. L. R. James is the way his writing obsesses about his own colonial education, his childhood curiosity about literature and his auto-didacticism. In *Beyond a Boundary* James recalls the itinerant bookseller who would visit Tunapuna 'once a fortnight carrying a huge pack on his shoulders ... so I began to have my own collection of books as well as my own bat and balls' (James, 1983: 16). He goes on to recall, 'After Thackeray there was Dickens, George Eliot ... the poets in Matthew Arnold's selections, Shelley, Keats and Byron ... Hazlitt, Lamb and Coleridge' (James, 1983: 28). However, in recounting his passion for Thackeray and later Melville, or for that matter Lenin and Trotsky, he is not cleaving to the European canon for canon's sake but stating a belief, still controversial in black British debate, about powerful knowledge. In short, James' position is that there is such a thing as powerful knowledge – knowledge that is both sufficiently abstract and sufficiently useful to enable empowering critical thought among the oppressed. In taking this position, on one hand, James was tussling with the ghost of the American educator Booker T. Washington, who privileged vocational education, rather than liberal academic education, as the priority for black communities; on the other hand, he committed himself to warring, much later, with a certain kind of cultural nationalist anti-intellectualism that was predicated upon a false binary between 'western' and 'black' thought (Dhondy, 2001).

Yet for all of his wilful exploration of the contradictions of the 'black Englishman' (Farred, 1994: 21), there is a sense in which Britain's (for which, read England's) role for James was always as much ideological as it was real, a resource for his own political understanding of colonial and anti-colonial identities. James did not consistently take Britain itself as the object of his work; nevertheless, his presence in London, to which he relocated in 1981, following years in Trinidad and the United States, was highly influential among younger black intellectuals. Holding court in his small Brixton flat above *Race Today*'s offices, deep in his armchair, blanket pulled across his old legs, C. L. R. James still haunted the London fog.

Conclusion

This chapter emphasizes that black British political and intellectual activity did not originate in the post-Windrush years. Black thinkers were far from a belated presence and many of the defining concerns in black British thought – diasporan identities, multi-ethnic alliances, anti-racism and independent organization – were already present in the work of pre-war generations. Some of those today considered 'elders' in black British activism, such as Gus John, Margaret Busby, Farrukh Dhondy and Darcus Howe, had direct links with C. L. R. James and others active in pre-war pan-Africanist circles. To say so is not to make a claim for simple continuity but to emphasize again that the black educators and activists we shall encounter in Chapters 3 and 4 emerged out of a great and longstanding black Atlantic flow. Black British thought is not merely a product of latter-day race relations models or multicultural policy-making; its roots lie far deeper. This is nowhere more apparent than in the black education movements of the 1960s and 70s, to which we now turn.

3 Post-war black education movements

The school experience began as a trauma for the majority of black school children and went on to be a rallying point and a radicalising issue for their parents.

Phillips, M. and Phillips, T. (1999: 257)

Introduction

It is not such a large leap from the events described at the end of Chapter 2 to the world in which tens of thousands of black children entered British schools in the 1960s. The former troopship *Empire Windrush* has nowadays become a byword for the onset of post-war mass migration to Britain from the Caribbean, Asia and Africa. She arrived in Essex in 1948, carrying some 500 Caribbean workers, mostly Jamaican, mostly male. They would become the parents of black children who would grow up in post-war Britain. In 1948 the world was still, in all meaningful senses, a colonial world. It was less than a year since India and Pakistan had become independent states and for Britain's African colonies independence lay a decade or more away. In 1948, three years after the Manchester Pan-African Congress, Nkrumah was preparing to return to the Gold Coast to drive the liberation movement. Harold Moody had died only weeks before his Windrush countrymen docked; the League of Coloured Peoples, still the most prominent black political body in Britain, would not long survive his passing. But while the Windrush has become iconic, there are sound arguments for suggesting that it was not until the early 1960s that post-war black Britain became organic and permanent – and schooling was the site in which that permanence was established.

This chapter examines the black education movements of the 1960s and 70s, and tells how their struggles helped define black Britain. The Race Today Collective, which during its time was among the most persistent interrogators of race, racism and education, wrote of this period as witnessing a 'black explosion in British schools' (Dhondy et al., 1985). And, for better or for worse, the educational experiences of the 1960s and 70s set the tone of debate over race and education in Britain for succeeding decades, particularly among African-Caribbean communities. In one sense, the black education campaigns were highly localized, yet they also began to voice questions about race, education and national identity that were embedded in wider social antagonisms. Some of the changes and approaches for which the grassroots activists argued would become integral to education and social policy in subsequent decades; others would remain contentious, especially those that raised questions about the reproduction through schooling of racial inequalities.

In the grassroots struggles over numbers, busing, second language provision, supplementary schools and the placement of black children in schools for the 'educationally subnormal' (ESN schools) there was no rigid distinction between community activism and intellectual production. The black explosion gave rise to new, assertive intellectual activity and produced an irreversible shift from migrant to citizen politics. Relying initially on piecemeal policies around race equality and schooling, Britain struggled to grasp the consequences of its settled black population. As Henry Louis Gates (2000: 170) observed, the country was 'hard pressed to know what to do when the guests forgot that they were guests'.

Initial post-war immigration

Although this book is concerned with settlement and schooling from the perspectives of black activists and intellectuals, some context is necessary in order to help understand the dynamics of post-war immigration. The year in which the *Empire Windrush* docked was the year in which the British Nationality Act 1948 created a single category of British citizenship (for citizens 'of the United Kingdom and Colonies'), thereby weakening, in law, the boundary between white Britons and black colonial subjects. The 1948 Act facilitated the movement of workers across the Empire to meet British labour shortages. In the period between 1948 and 1953 net immigration from the Colonies and New Commonwealth totalled around 28,000. By contrast, in 1960 alone it was just over 58,000. Of those, 49,650 were from the Caribbean, 5,900 from India and 2,500 from Pakistan (Home Office, 1964). In the years between 1962 and 1972, annual net immigration from the Colonies and New Commonwealth ranged between 33,000 and 62,000 approximately. The outlier was 1962, year of the Immigration Control Act, when attempts to beat new entry restrictions saw 102,585 New Commonwealth entrants (Runnymede Trust, 1980).

The 1962 Immigration Control Act, passed by the Conservative government, and the 1968 Commonwealth Immigration Act, passed by Labour six years later, were shrouded in euphemism but both were essentially panic-driven responses to managing party political and street-level anxieties over black immigration. This was not only a control on numbers. Arun Kundnani (2007) has commented that, in seeking to control migration from the Caribbean, Asia and Africa, the 1962 and 1968 Acts re-inscribed racialized boundaries around British citizenship, identity and right of entry. In the sphere of education the significance of the 1962 and 1968 immigration Acts was that their targets were black families; both Acts limited the entry of migrant workers' dependants. The wider political and policy settings into which post-war migrants were inserted have been detailed in the work of Carter *et al.* (1993), Grosvenor (1997) and Tomlinson (2008).

Anti-immigration discourses

In the writing of black activists, both contemporaneous and retrospective, the immigration policies and the street racism of the 1950s and 60s loom large. The mid- to late-1960s, in particular, is often represented as the go-or-stay moment (Hunte, 1966; Humphry and John, 1972; Sivanandan, 1982; Wambu, 1998). A recurring theme in such accounts is that, in the absence of national political leadership on race and immigration over and above base electoral calculations, a particular form of backlash discourse emerged. It characterized black immigration as a strategy wrought by political elites to reshape Britain's labour market. It was a discourse in which the victims of immigration were a white lower-middle and working-class who had had no say about the presence or complexion of their new neighbours. The shrinkage of the British working class was apparently due to a single social force: the presence of black workers. International capitalism, Empire, a world war, the Cold War and incremental attacks on unionized labour were absolved. Needless to say, there was deep silence about the historical routes by which black people had ended up as mobile labour within the British Empire. Nostalgia for an all-white working class, still a British political motif, started here (see Chen, 2013).

This discourse was mobilized with increasing regularity through the 1960s. In his notorious 'rivers of blood' speech, delivered in Birmingham, April 1968, Conservative Shadow Cabinet member Enoch Powell warned that black immigration would bring about an apocalyptic disintegration of British life (Powell, 1968). Powell did not singlehandedly create what became known as 'Powellism' and today many passages of his speech read as a kind of kitsch jeremiad. Nevertheless, black intellectuals active in the 1960s and 70s almost invariably point to the 'rivers of blood' speech as a line in the sand. Worth noting also is the rhetorical use to which Powell put black children, his 'wide-grinning pickaninnies', in his speeches of the period. Powell's implication was that it was the children, the second generation, including those yet unborn, that Britain should fear. The 1968 Act and the further legislation that succeeded it in 1971 have led several black British commentators to reflect that while Powell's more inflammatory statements were rejected by governing politicians, 'Powellism' was incorporated into mainstream policy, 'implicitly embedded in policies which seemed to promise that race problems would have a conclusive end (returning whence they came) and protect white interests in the process' (Carby, 1982a: 186).

The shock of settlement

Reflecting on race and education policy in the early 1960s the Runnymede Trust (1980: 92) concluded that there was 'little evidence to show that government or local authorities anticipated that changes might be required to the education system as a result of the entry into British schools of the children of immigrants coming to Britain to work'. Black parents, pupils *and* their teachers negotiated the new landscape with minimal support. Faced with incomprehension, and sometimes naked hostility, black parents campaigned locally against the measures that education authorities improvised out of a tangle of poor resourcing, prejudices about the educability of black children and panic over their concentrations in particular schools.

Tomlinson (2008: 28) rightly points out that in the 1960s 'Britain was not alone in its contradictory response to migration and the incorporation of migrant children'. Global migration saw many societies negotiating tensions between assimilation and cultural pluralism, and struggling to shape the role that education would play in defining citizenship and national identity. From the perspective of the twenty-first century the mix of political evasion, racism and panicked improvisation that informed early policies can make for uncomfortable reading. However, as Male (1980) has stressed, given the piecemeal support provided, it was unsurprising that local authorities and many teachers saw the children of migrant nurses, transport staff and textile workers as a problem.

Yet it is perhaps possible to have too much 'perspective'. It is customary among educational historians to point out that the problematization of black children was not necessarily born out of malicious intent (though in the wider political world, there was no shortage of malice). However, the shock of black settlement did not only impact upon local authorities; black parents and pupils also had to make sense of the great social, cultural and economic shifts in which they were caught up. The harassed responses of local schools and the panic of education ministers too often hardened into a straightjacket from which it was difficult for black parents and children to escape.

Numbers games

Yet by the mid-1960s, the self-perception of black settlers had begun to change, as black communities realized what was at stake in every local incidence of workplace discrimination, school expulsion or false arrest. The battles over schooling in the 1960s and 70s were ultimately about the terms on which black people would continue to live in Britain. Stuart Hall has reflected:

> people coming in the 50s were coming to settle rather than just coming temporarily; they weren't just migrant workers … And it took us a long while to understand what were the long term consequences of really establishing a sizeable black presence … continuing over the generations.
>
> Hall and Walmsley (1987: 4)

So how did the make-up of British schools change in the immediate post-war period? The Commonwealth Immigration Economist Intelligence Unit calculated that between 1956 and 1964 numbers of 'immigrant' children in London schools grew from 8,000 to 38,000 (Carby, 1982a). By 1966 when the Department of Education and Science instructed schools to monitor more systematically numbers of 'immigrant' pupils (as they were officially termed), just over 131,000 such pupils were counted in state schools nationally. Of these, 43.7 per cent had origins in the Caribbean, 18.6 per cent in India, 6 per cent in Pakistan and 10.2 per cent were Cypriot. In 1966 'immigrant' pupils comprised 1.8 per cent of the total pupil population but among the under-sixes the proportion was already 2.4 per cent (Runnymede Trust, 1980). By the late 1970s 'non-white' pupils accounted for at least 4 per cent of the school population (Kirp, 1979b).

Of course, patterns of migration and settlement meant that this was not, by any means, an even spread. While in 1969 in the Inner London Borough of Hackney 'immigrant' pupils totalled 26 per cent of the school roll, half of Britain's local education authorities (LEAs) recorded no 'immigrant' pupils (Tomlinson, 2008) and only around ten schools in the entire country had a minority of white pupils (Kirp, 1979a). However, the links made by government, quasi-independent and charitable bodies between numbers of migrants, patterns of settlement and educational provision is apparent in many documents of the time, wherein authors flipped between a desire to put numbers in perspective and an anxious anticipation of the 'problem' emerging in schools. The Youth Development Trust's 1967 report, *Young and Coloured in Manchester*, stated:

> The coloured population is still largely concentrated in a few areas but nowhere near so concentrated as it was in 1951 or 1961 ... It is in the nature of "pull" migration that the first wave tends to be young unmarried adults and therefore relatively few children might be expected among the immigrant group ... (but) children account for about 18 per cent of the total coloured population in 1965; higher than the city figure of about 15 per cent. The ratio is much higher among the West Indian than among other coloured ethnic groups, as more of them are married ... A total of 20 secondary schools and 38 primary schools have more than 10 per cent immigrants on their registers ... At the eight secondary schools with more than 20 per cent immigrants, three have substantial coloured populations, the immigrants in the other five schools being predominantly Irish.
>
> Youth Development Trust (1967: 7–8)

The Manchester report typifies the ways in which families and schools became indicators of three overriding anxieties: the growth of concentrated black communities within particular cities, fears over birth rates in those communities and the consequences for schools in areas with substantial black populations. However, such documents tell us nothing about how these demographic shifts were viewed from inside Britain's black communities.

Black social movements

The political sophistication of the post-Windrush communities tends to be underestimated. In order to understand the black education movements that mobilized in the 1960s and 70s, it is vital to appreciate that they were not simply an unmediated response to the inequalities in schooling experienced by the post-war intakes of black pupils. They emerged as part of a wider wave of black and anti-racist activism. Grainy documentary footage, too, often leaves an impression of black naïfs earnestly wandering British streets in panama hats and turbans waiting to be turned away from lodging houses. What is lost, or hidden, in those bleached histories is a sense of the social agency of the new black communities.

Kalbir Shukra (1998: 9) describes the activities of black grassroots organizations in 1960s Britain as ranging 'from providing immediate support structures in the form of welfare and religious/cultural organisations to developing groups in opposition to racial discrimination'. In his study of black British social movements Max Farrar (2004) suggests that important features of these 1960s to 70s black British social movements included:

> [the] search for cultural identity ... campaigns for adequate welfare and social provision ... and, particularly in those that based themselves in specific inner areas of the major UK cities, the demand for local control of neighbourhood facilities and a recognition of their rights as British citizens.
>
> Farrar (2004: 4)

By the early 1960s there were already deep reserves of organizational experience within African-Caribbean and Asian communities. These enabled black parents to formulate educational demands. Among the new arrivals were teachers, writers, union organizers, well-travelled workers, and men and women whose political ambitions had been dashed at home. Black British commentators Roxy Harris and Brian Alleyne have argued that too little attention has been paid to the intellectual activity that was both outgrowth and shaper of the struggles of these largely working-class adult settlers (Alleyne, 2002).

However, Sivanandan's (1982) *A Different Hunger*, Ramdin's (1987) *The Making of the Black Working Class in Britain* and Shukra's (1998) *The Changing Pattern of Black Politics in Britain* have all contributed to correcting the blind spot. Other notable examinations of 'early' post-war black organizations include John, D. W. (1969) and Josephides (1991) on the Indian Workers Association; Sherwood *et al.*'s (1999) and Schwarz's (2003a) writing on Claudia Jones; Farrar's (1992, 2004) research on black British social movements; and Ramamurthy (2005, 2006, 2007) and Malik's (2012) important studies of the often overlooked Black Power-influenced Asian Youth Movements. The next sections of this chapter outline chronologically some of the currents and shifts in black community politics that were apparent between the 1950s and 70s.

Early post-war black organizations

By the time of the initial wave of post-war black immigration (1948–55) Moody's League of Coloured Peoples was defunct, the pre-war anti-colonialists had mostly scattered and the Indian Workers Association was partially dormant. This meant that when in the late 1950s the everyday experience of racism that operated under 'the twee name of colour bar' (Sivanandan, 1982: 4) was exacerbated by an increasing number of violent attacks on black immigrants, new black organizations formed. The first ones emerged in response to the riots in Nottingham and Notting Hill in 1958. They included the West Indian Standing Conference (WISC), which acted as an umbrella for various Caribbean organizations in the major cities and which, guided by the West Indian High Commission, sought to ensure the integration of Caribbean communities (Heineman, 1972). As the 1960s progressed WISC took an increasingly independent position and became active in monitoring racial inequalities in housing, employment and policing (the latter was investigated in Joseph Hunte's 1966 WISC report, *Nigger Hunting in England?*). WISC also raised early concerns about the disproportionate allocation of black children to ESN schools, issues later taken up forcefully by John La Rose's North London West Indian Association (NLWIA) and the Caribbean Education and Community Workers Association (CECWA). However, divisions over its political strategy left WISC exhausted by the 1970s.

The events of 1958 also led to the formation of the campaigning monthly newspaper *The West Indian Gazette* by Trinidadian Marxist and feminist Claudia Jones. Although Jones' time in London was short-lived (she died of tuberculosis in 1964), her impact on black British politics was considerable. Importantly, the *Gazette* gave space to other pioneering black political and cultural activists, among them veteran pan-Africanist Amy Ashwood Garvey, writers Samuel Selvon and Donald Hinds, the actor Cy Grant and educator Jan Carew (Schwarz, 2003a). Famously, in 1959 Jones instigated the Notting Hill Carnival (at least in its Caribbean-modelled form). For Donald Hinds, Jones 'was the one with her finger on the pulse of British society' and between 1958 and 1965 the *Gazette* was perhaps 'the only coherent voice from the black community in Britain' (Hinds, 2008: 92).

The resurgent Indian Workers Association (IWA) played a role analogous to that WISC did in the Caribbean community. Originally active in the 1930s and 40s the IWA was revived in the 1950s and by 1958 had become a centralized organization supported by the Indian High Commission. At this point IWA's leadership, which included Jagmohan Joshi and Rattan Singh, was strongly dominated by middle-class graduates with strong formal links to India's political parties (Shukra, 1998). These factional ties saw a series of splits and reformations but, following the 1962 Immigration Act, the IWA's attentions turned increasingly towards British politics (Josephides, 1991). In 1962 Joshi was also instrumental in forming the Birmingham-based Coordination Committee Against Racial Discrimination (CCARD), a federation including bodies such as the Pakistani Workers Association and the West Indian Workers Association. At the same time the *West Indian Gazette*'s circle of activists created a similar umbrella initiative in London: the Conference of Afro-Asian-Caribbean Organisations (CAACO).

Both CAACO and CCARD became forerunners of the better-remembered Campaign Against Racial Discrimination (CARD), which between 1964 and 1967 strove to invent itself as a broad-tent, multi-racial British civil rights co-ordinating body (Heineman, 1972). Inspired by Martin Luther King's visit to London in 1964, CARD was, in many ways, the natural successor to Moody's LCP. CARD envisaged itself as independent from the main political parties but engaged in the mainstream, aiming to influence centres of power through lobbying and hoping to bring about a robust legislative framework to counter discrimination in housing, employment and education. With regard to schools, CARD's members condemned government proposals to 'disperse' black schoolchildren, in order to prevent high concentrations of black pupils in particular schools, and also began to debate the development of curriculum content in a culturally diverse education system (Heineman, 1972). However, by 1967 CARD too had begun to dissolve; WISC disaffiliated, while the IWA had always retained a cautious distance. The centre could not hold.

Black power in Britain

Many of the fissures in the older black movements were the result of the new political mood of the late 1960s. In the USA the Black Power movement had renewed the pan-Africanism, black Marxism and black feminism that had, in part, been crafted in Britain earlier in the century. The new black radicalism influenced British activists directly (the visits of Malcolm X in 1964 and Stokely Carmichael in 1967), but also via the written word (promoted by new black British publishing outlets) and through the images of defiance glimpsed on TV, in fashion and in music. Debates continue about the degree of influence wrought on black British politics by the American movements. Hiro (1973) and Ramdin (1987) see the growth of Black Power, particularly the work of Carmichael between 1965 and 1971, as crucial to the development of black community activism in the UK, but looking back on the period C. L. R. James (1984) felt that the influence of US black radicalism was overstated. Yet, for many black intellectuals the new Black Power, with its overt use of 'blackness' as a political tool, had applications to the British context. Either way, the concerns of the late 1960s seemed, for many black activists, to consign CARD and WISC to another era.

Colin Prescod (1999a: 206), academic, broadcaster and longstanding member of the Institute of Race Relations, has described the late 1960s and early 70s as 'a hothouse of black politics in Britain'. New grassroots organizations emerged, such as the Universal Coloured People's Association (UCPA), the (British) Black Panther Party, the Black Unity and Freedom Party, the Caribbean Workers Movement, the Pakistani Progressive Party and the Black People's Alliance (a federation conjoined in direct response to Enoch Powell's rhetoric, comprising the IWA, WISC, UCPA and others). Myriad political, cultural and educational journals also came out of this period of ferment: *Black Voice*, *Freedom News*, *Spectre*, *Grassroots*, *Uhuru* and Ricky Cambridge's theoretical journal *Black Liberator*. In the late 1970s these were followed by *Bradford Black*, *Black Struggle* and *Mukti*. One of the most important developments was the spread of black women's organizations, including the Black Women's Group, Southall Black Sisters and the Organisation of Women of Asian and African Descent (see Chapter 7 of this book).

A key moment in the birth of British Black Power was the 1971 trial of the Mangrove Nine. The nine defendants were arrested during clashes that followed repeated, fruitless police raids on Notting Hill's Mangrove Restaurant, which was owned and managed by Frank Crichlow, for many years a mentor of black political and cultural activity in the capital. The acquittal of the Mangrove Nine, who included both Crichlow and Darcus Howe (at that time active in the British Black Panthers), followed a campaign that mobilized wide support in London's Caribbean community and placed the policing of black communities under scrutiny (Howe, 1988). This was arguably the point at which activists and, increasingly, sociologists began to focus on conflicts between the police and black youth as a key site in the formation of black British identity (see Chapter 6). This turn was significant, in that by the late 1970s black and anti-racist groups almost invariably came to regard policing and schooling as inextricable in the lives of young blacks in the large cities. It was an alleged police assault on young Cliff McDaniels outside his North London school that led John La Rose, in 1975, to form the Black Parents Group, which worked in tandem with the newly formed Black Youth Group and the Black Students Movement.

The Asian Youth Movements

Elsewhere, particularly in Asian communities in London, Leicester and Bradford, organized attacks from far-right groups led to the formation of new youth-led groups. The murder of teenager Gurdip Singh Chaggar in Southall in 1976 prompted the formation of the Southall Youth Movement. Over the next decade the Southall group became a model for other Asian Youth Movements (AYMs). Sikh, Hindu and Muslim parents' groups became increasingly active in the north-west in the late 1970s and early 80s, although the youth groups themselves at this time tended to remain secular and to seek broad-based alliances across communities and with a range of progressive and anti-racist activists (AYM Bradford, 1984). In documenting the Asian Youth Movements in the late 1970s and 80s, Anandi Ramamurthy notes that:

> For the AYMs, the term 'black' denoted a political allegiance between those of African and Asian origin, without denying the specific cultural differences of each group, and the term 'secular' implied a unity-in-diversity between those of different religious backgrounds, without suppressing their particular religious backgrounds.
>
> Ramamurthy (2006: 39)

The AYMs were among the most vocal advocates of Asian anti-racist activism as a form of black politics. They built on African-Caribbean and Asian community alliances of the 1960s and 70s that had agitated against official indifference to racist violence and against immigration controls, as well as being involved in joint union work and umbrella organizations, such as the Black People's Alliance (Sivanandan, 1982; Ramdin, 1987).

Among the AYMs and parts of the emergent Asian women's movements, the black idiom became a powerful strategic tool. The similarities in educational experiences between Asian and African-Caribbean young people meant that schooling became a site in which a number of young Asian campaigners took on political blackness. That is, they insisted that their struggles around schooling had racialized dimensions, akin to those experienced by all people of colour in Britain. Unsurprisingly, it was the Asian Youth Movements, comprising the generations that had been entirely or largely schooled in Britain, who most readily saw their struggles as politically black and for whom schooling was a site of struggle (Malik, Z., 2012).

Yorkshire became a particular site of secular Asian youth activism. As in many Asian communities, activism in towns such as Bradford and Sheffield during the 1960s and 70s had focused on immigration policy, threats of deportation and family separation. However, by the 1980s the experiences of Asian youth both inside and outside school had become prominent. In 1981 the young Asian leaders of the United Black Youth League were charged following allegations that they had manufactured explosives in anticipation of a large-scale attack by fascist groups. The Bradford Twelve, as they became known, were later acquitted, having argued that they had organized only in self-defence. The secular Asian youth groups had direct impacts on local education policy. Morris *et al.* (1984) suggest, for instance, that it was Bradford Council's anxieties about growing militancy among Asian youth organizations, rather than educational concerns *per se* that led the Council to formulate a race relations policy for schools that included allowing Muslim girls to dress in trousers, the introduction of non-religious assemblies, making halal food available as part of school menus, and which also required head teachers to monitor racial incidents.

Black politics: from migrants to citizens

The rapidity of change in black politics between the 1950s and 1970s helps to explain the diverse positions taken by the black education movements and by black British thinkers more widely. The key transitions in black British organizational politics might be summarized as follows. Firstly, there was a shift in focus away from the politics of 'home' to the politics of life in Britain. This was particularly apparent in longstanding bodies, such as the IWA. Secondly, there were sometimes fraught relationships with white liberal, left-wing and labour movements, whose support for black workers, families and communities was often felt to be, at best, uneven and, at worst, paternalistic (Sivanandan, 1982). There were, of course, notable black figures who worked within the trade unions, mainstream race relations bodies and the Labour Party, such as David Pitt, but many younger activists sought out determinedly independent black movements, developed at a distance from the traditional institutions of the left (Goulbourne, 1990).

Thirdly, the demise around 1967 of CARD saw a movement away from efforts to develop national black leadership along the lines of the big US civil rights blocs, and instead a shift to local campaigning and looser, more contingent co-operation between black organizations. There was arguably less dependence on middle-class black and white leadership, and a greater active role for working-class migrants, whose 'grassroots' struggles centred around immediate concerns relating to schooling, housing, childcare and the workplace. Lastly, by the late 1960s there was a supplanting of the black politics that had been rooted in post-war 'community relations' models (see Chapter 4) by more radical Black Power-derived activism. The influence of Black Power was both the result of and the incentive for the increased involvement of a younger generation of activists, most of whom had been at least partly schooled in Britain.

Sivanandan's (1982) critical account of the growth of indigenous, organic black activism, 'From resistance to rebellion: Asian and Afro-Caribbean struggles in Britain' (1982: 3–54), describes how these shifts in black political consciousness were driven by conflicts in education, campaigns against racist forms of immigration control and labour disputes involving Asian and African-Caribbean workers. The latter included, for instance, strikes led by Asian women workers at Imperial Typewriters in Leicester, 1974, and the Grunwick Film Processing plant in North London, 1976. For Sivanandan, false starts and dead ends notwithstanding, the 1960s and 70s saw an increasing employment of 'blackness' as a political colour across Asian and African-Caribbean communities.

The legacy of the post-Black Power groupings was greater than their numbers might suggest and was certainly longer lasting than the organizations themselves. Dabydeen *et al.* (2007) reflect that:

> The subsequent failure to establish a durable political or civic group embodying Black Power ideology is not to downplay the ideology's impact from the late 1960s. Instead it speaks to a diverse application of the teachings of both Black Power *and* the less radical American civil rights activists ... the long term work of gaining social justice and political empowerment for British Blacks was taken up by numerous local and regional groups.
>
> Dabydeen *et al.* (2007: 56)

In other words, the black British social movements, of which the education campaigns were a part, did not comprise stable networks, communications or terms of reference but were founded upon an emergent identity that was both a response to daily street racism and a proactive challenge to racialized definitions of Britishness. Identifying as 'black' *and* 'British' (albeit with ambivalence about the latter) became an organizing principle, not least in the site of education. Poet, journalist and activist, Linton Kwesi Johnson, a stalwart of the Race Today Collective, has said pertinently that London's Black Parents Movement organized to 'demand, as *tax payers and rate payers*, decent education for our children' (Phillips, M. and Phillips, T., 1999: 263, italics added). The Black Power-inspired groupings critiqued British society and its racism from the standpoint of both rebel and citizen movements. So what was the impact of the community struggles of the 1960s and 70s on education?

'Policies is too big a word'

The British school system did not require the presence of black children in order to reproduce social and educational inequalities. It was, as Bowles and Gintis (1976), Paul Willis (1978) and other neo-Marxists argued across the 1970s, more than capable of incorporating working-class children into their designated places in the labour process. The problem for black children and parents in the 1960s and 70s was that the education system was not even sure that it could achieve that much. In education, as in other areas of social provision, concern over numbers and distribution of black children entering the education system was the guiding principle of whatever social policy existed around race and schooling. The education sector produced arbitrary and incoherent policy responses, not least because the education of black children was one more issue stacked up in the battleground between the Ministry of Education (which in 1964 became the Department of Education and Science) and local education authorities. Best (1991), McKenley (2001) and Tomlinson (2008) have all emphasized, for instance, that the post-war arrival of black children in British schools coincided with the state system's drawn-out trauma over comprehensive education.

In the 1960s black children entered inner-city, working-class schools. These were the former secondary moderns that were struggling to recast themselves according to the ostensible comprehensive ideals of equality of opportunity, a balanced curriculum and provision of public examinations in all mainstream secondary schools. For some schools, the idea that the education of white working-class children should be transformed was disorientating enough, so where on earth would *black* working-class children fit? If parents, pupils, teachers and policy-makers were all straightjacketed, the buckles of the straightjacket were numbers, distribution, IQ testing and language. Its fibres were the residual belief in biological race, stereotypes about the educability of black children, convictions about the deficiencies of black cultures and parenting (Hiro, 1973).

There was also the insistence that the presence of large numbers of black children would impact negatively on the education of white British children. Gus John, the black British academic and campaigner whose educational activism spans the 1960s to the present day, later reflected:

> in terms of government policy in relation to education ... it was felt that if you had too many black children in one school, it would somehow contaminate the educational experiences of white kids [hence] the issue of busing and banding and so on.
>
> John and Walmsley (1988: 13)

Gus John's contemporary Sivanandan has also spoken of the racialized common sense that shaped the piecemeal responses to the new black presence:

> Policies is too big a word. There were no policies as such to begin with, except what grew out of the endemic racism in British society when labour

was recruited from the so-called "new commonwealth". After the 1962 Immigration Act, when the doors were beginning to close and the workers sent for their families, schooling became a moot question. And yet the policies were directed at what various local authorities thought was overcrowding on the one hand, and ... "under-achievement" ... on the other ... Basically, 'Blacks' were seen as the problem, meaning both Afro-Caribbeans and Asians, and the few Africans here.

Sivanandan (1989: 19)

1960s: educating 'immigrants'

Early educational provision for 'immigrant' children was often based on policy-makers' and practitioners' reactions to events in individual localities in relatively small numbers of schools (Kirp, 1979b). In 1963, for instance, the panic over the distribution of black pupils was legitimated when Education Minister Lord Boyle visited Southall in west London in response to agitation by white parents against a local school in which 60 per cent of children were Asian. The following year the DES began to collect national statistics on numbers of 'immigrant' pupils (and continued to collect data in those terms until 1972). In 1965, following continuing concern about 'segregated schooling', the DES issued Circular 7/65, advising that no school should comprise more than 30 per cent 'immigrant' children (Tomlinson, 2008). In 1966 the Local Government Act initiated Section 11 funding to support educational provision in areas with high immigrant populations.

The first explicit offer for this post-1962 generation often focused upon teaching English as a second language (with notable teacher training efforts being made in Birmingham and, later, Leeds, and at national level the Ministry of Education's recommendation to create 'reception classes'). The focus on language left black Caribbean children somewhat outside of special provision (although there were calls by some black educators to insert Caribbean children by categorizing patois or creole as a first language). For the most part, however, black Caribbean children continued to be defined primarily in terms of underachievement. Throughout the 1960s and early 70s disproportionate numbers were funnelled into schools and classes designed for children categorized as educationally subnormal (ESN) (Chitty, 2007). The ESN schools issue would become another line in the sand for African-Caribbean activists.

1970s: race in education policy

As the 1970s unfolded, the education of black children solidified as a policy object. The object of state scrutiny was a generation of young people born and/or schooled in the UK, even if they were still often spoken of, in policy discourse, as 'immigrants'. At both national and local authority levels themes of underachievement (particularly among African-Caribbean, Pakistani and Bangladeshi pupils), language (working-class Asian pupils in general) and, more contentiously, debates around self-concept and low self-esteem drove a series of reports and strategy documents. These included the DES' (1971) *The Education of Immigrants*, the DES' (1974) *Educational Disadvantage and the Needs of Immigrants* and Lord Bullock's (1975) *A Language for Life*.

In addition, by the start of the 1970s another set of issues was being generated by the rising age profile of black pupils. Growing numbers of black children were reaching the end of their formal schooling and government departments were confronted with evidence that racialized inequalities in schooling were being reproduced in the youth labour market. In 1969, following a number of local authority studies, the House of Commons Select Committee on Race Relations and Immigration (1969) had reported on barriers black school leavers faced in entering the labour market. For policy-makers and black activists alike issues of race and education were becoming conflated with broader questions about the socialization of black *youth* (as they were increasingly defined) within British society. There was a growing perception that black (particularly African-Caribbean pupils) were resisting or disengaging from aspects of schooling. Growing tensions around teachers' expectations, disciplinary processes, the 'monocultural' curriculum and employment informed documents such as the Select Committee on Race Relations and Immigration (1977) report on *The West Indian Community* and the DES (1977) Green Paper, *Education in Schools*.

Viewing these early efforts, American academic David Kirp (1979a) argued that British social policy's preference during the 1960s and 70s was to speak in terms of language and poverty, rather than explicitly addressing race or ethnicity. However, the anti-racist educator Barry Troyna (1992) subsequently took issue with Kirp's distinction between 'explicit' and 'inexplicit' efforts by the state to address race and education. Troyna (1992) argued that the key lay in trying to understand *what* educational policies were explicit or inexplicit *about*. For Troyna, the policies of the 1960s and early 70s were inexplicit about 'the realities of racism as a corrosive feature in the lives of black communities' (Troyna 1992: 74) and thus were de-racialized. Troyna contrasted these de-racialized policies with policies based on racialized analyses, which were explicit in their acknowledgement of the presence of race in the social formation. Racialized discourses and policies can be directed either towards racist or anti-racist ends but they do not remain silent about race. The history of race and education policy has arguably comprised an ever-present dialectic between de-racialized and racialized approaches, between naming racism and remaining silent about it.

The beginnings of black educational struggles

The black educational campaigns of the 1960s and 70s broke that silence, naming racism as a persistent feature of the education system and of black pupils' lived experiences of schooling. In the early 1960s the relatively established black and anti-racist bodies, such as the Indian Workers Association (IWA), the Campaign Against Racial Discrimination (CARD) and the early incarnation of the Institute of Race Relations (IRR), were slow to turn their attention to educational inequalities. Consequently, the key educational struggles of the 1960s and 70s were waged most tenaciously by a wave of new activist groups.

African-Caribbean communities tended to be first to take a militant position on their children's educational futures. This was due, in part, to the particular educational conditions that their children faced, in terms of placement in ESN schools, banding in lower streams, low teacher expectations and the increasingly fraught relationships with the police that also marked 'black youth' as an emergent category. Sivanandan (1982) has suggested also that in Pakistani, Indian and Bangladeshi communities struggles over immigration control of the entry of dependants became the primary struggle during much of the 1960s. However, Asian communities also faced racialized educational struggles that became pivotal to their experiences of settlement.

What Caribbean parents, in particular, understood very quickly was that their children were undergoing a horizontal integration into a deeply unequal education system. Don Henry and Ralph Ruddock's (1991) set of oral histories, *Thirty Blacks in British Education*, captures one sense in which black pupils were only too well integrated:

> Everybody knew the school was rubbish, a bad school ... A lot of people from my school did not achieve anything, both Blacks and Whites, but more so Blacks. The girls got wed, a couple of White lads joined the Police Force ... but that was all, the rest just drifted.
>
> Raymond Wilkie, quoted in Henry with Ruddock (1991: 58–9)

These kinds of experiences did not sit well with African-Caribbean parents, brought up to believe that a formal colonial education was *the* route to social mobility. They soon learned that in the British context their aspirational view of education was, at best, misunderstood and, at worst, derided by those in education, politics and news media, who were aghast at working-class black parents' expectations. A London paper reporting on the DES evidence presented to the House of Commons Select Committee on Race Relations and Immigration c. 1970 wrote:

> Cultural traditions, as well as language and length of stay, handicap coloured children at school and when they leave, the Department of Education and Science said ... the aspirations of coloured parents for their children's future could also be a source of tension.

The article continued with a quote from the DES' submission, suggesting that 'parental aspirations ... are far beyond the qualifications their children are likely to obtain ... which ... can give rise to disappointment and resentment'. Indeed one of the most widely remarked phenomena noted by African-Caribbean commentators, both in the 1960s and 70s and with hindsight, was that in relation to education many black parents did not willingly fit the British matrix of class and schooling. 'For the Afro-Caribbeans the business of material advancement was still paramount,' writes Mike Phillips (2001: 174) in *London Crossings: A Biography of Black Britain*. 'On the surface we were working-class people who didn't behave as working-class people should.'

Even those activists from a determinedly black Marxist tradition, such as John La Rose, who drafted the following account of the formation of the London-based Black Parents Movement, understood the very powerful aspirational strain in African-Caribbean educational values:

> The Black Parents Movement has its origins in a group of black parents in North London who in the late 1960s and early 1970s became extremely concerned about the kind of education that their children were receiving in British schools. They were, for example, disturbed and angry about the large numbers of black children who were being wrongly placed in ESN schools. The deep disappointment felt by these black parents about the British education system can only be understood if one considers their background. Most of them had come to Britain from colonial societies ... [where] education provided a clear path to upward social mobility and advancement. Naturally many black parents expected greater opportunities for self-advancement in Britain itself.
>
> Black Parents Movement and Black Students Movement
> (1976: unnumbered)

The persistent mismatches between the hopes of African-Caribbean parents and the expectations of education providers created a distinctive set of educational experiences and local flashpoints, such as that which occurred in Haringey, North London in 1968–69.

Banding in Haringey

In April 1969 a flyer was distributed in the London Borough of Haringey. Produced by the North London West Indian Association (NLWIA), it urged the following:

> ALL WEST INDIAN PARENTS ... YOUR CHILD'S FUTURE IS THREATENED. It's time to get up and NOW. We are all ambitious for our children. No mountain is too high. Some people think we are too ambitious.
>
> SO WE HAVE TO DO SOMETHING ABOUT IT. The Haringey Education Committee proposes to introduce changes which will affect YOUR child.
>
> - Children are going to be 'banded'
> - Schools are going to be 'streamed'
> - Black children will be dispersed

One of the main reasons given for this 'DRAMATIC CHANGE' by Haringey Education Committee is the HIGH PROPORTION OF BLACK

CHILDREN IN HARINGEY SCHOOLS ... UNITE AND FIGHT
FOR YOUR RIGHTS.

North London West Indian Association (1969a: 1)

The NLWIA was one of several local organizations concerned with Caribbean
social life and community welfare in London. It numbered among its members
activists such as Jeff Crawford, John La Rose, Hazel Walcott and Waveney
Bushell. John La Rose was to be a pivotal figure in black British educational
politics over the next forty years. Born in Trinidad in 1927, La Rose had, before
his arrival in England in 1961, already helped form the Workers Freedom
Movement in Trinidad and been an organizer within the Oilfields Workers Trade
Union. Settling in North London, La Rose founded New Beacon Bookshop in
1966 with his partner Sarah White. As Britain's first specialist black bookshop
and publishing house, New Beacon made available educational materials, serving
the needs of parents and students who were routinely confronted with school
books that were highly Eurocentric and sometimes crudely racist (Alleyne, 2002).

Winston Best, the NLWIA's Education Officer, has recounted the struggles
that arose in 1968 out of Haringey Council's decision to embed comprehensive
schools across the borough. Key to the reorganization was the 'banding' of
pupils. This entailed the categorization of children into ability bands ('above
average', 'average', 'below average'), in order to try to ensure that each
comprehensive school was allocated a mixed ability intake. Best (1991) suggests
that initially Haringey's black (principally African-Caribbean) community saw in
comprehensive schooling the possibility for black and working-class pupils to
gain access to those schools that were previously the domain of middle-class
children. However, as plans for the restructuring of schools were laid out, the
NLWIA accessed a confidential document produced by the Council's working
group, 'setting out the real reason for recommending banding' (Best, 1991: 17).
The Council's document stated that:

> On a rough calculation half the immigrants will be West Indians at 7 of the
> 11 schools, the significance of this being the general recognition that their
> IQ's work out below their English contemporaries. Thus academic standards
> will be lower in schools where they form a large group.
>
> Haringey Local Education Authority 1968, quoted in Best (1991: 17)

Best quotes from the concluding section of the document, which stated, in regard
to banding as a means to balance the distribution of pupils at secondary school
level, that 'while this method is not a complete solution to the racial problem, it
helps to meet it indirectly' (Best, 1991: 17).

Outraged by Haringey's treatment of their children's education as a 'racial
problem', the NLWIA formulated a response to the Council that initiated a
lengthy and eventually successful campaign to overturn the banding proposals.
In its succession of responses to Haringey's proposals, the NLWIA and its allies
recognized that the dispersal strategy was embedded in wider discourses about

the entitlement and educability of black British children. Anti-racist educators urged Haringey to abandon its proposals, quoting UNESCO's refutation of pseudo-biological theories of race and intelligence and condemning:

> the way in which the council has hinged its proposals for changes in the secondary schools on the number of so-called "immigrant" children in the schools ... many of the "immigrant" children in the primary schools and some in the secondary schools were born in England. This will become increasingly the case. This makes nonsense of the Council's arguments that future standards of achievement will be affected by the numbers of "immigrant" children in Haringey.
>
> Haringey Communist Party (1969: 1–2)

The NLWIA also recognized that the assumptions of the Haringey report were partly rooted in the revival of racialized theories of intelligence (promoted by the contemporaneous work of Arthur Jensen), combined with moral panic about 'black' schools:

> West Indians and their offspring will not be entirely satisfied until the dangerous remarks about their children's capacities as stated or implied in these documents are fully withdrawn ... There is a growing body of documentation published which constantly explores the field of the "education of immigrants", and it is noticeable that it feeds on the stereotype which it itself has been creating ... Having created a Frankenstein, we are all being enlisted in the war for his destruction by his very creators – very frequently to the extent of avoiding root problems and their solutions.
>
> North London West Indian Association (1969b: 1)

For the NLWIA the root problems were not 'racial' but an intersection of racism and class stratification. Inequalities were reproduced by the combination of under-resourcing, unstable staffing and elitism in a school system still rigidly stratified according to social class and locality:

> So long as ... class stratification in the society ensures ... good educational facilities and opportunities for the elites and largely neglects the needs, potentials and capacities of the rest, the difficulties to which we are directing our attention will persist.
>
> North London West Indian Association (1969b: 1)

Among the NLWIA's proposals in Haringey in 1968 and 1969 were calls for increased efforts to reduce high staff turnover; the employment of teacher-social workers to improve home–school relations; courses to be provided for parents to learn about proposed changes in their children's schooling; and extension of pre-school provision. The NLWIA (1969b: 2) also argued that 'the increasing deterioration in race relations in the society at large affects the sensibility of black children within the school situation. The employment of black teachers should help with this difficulty'. La Rose, Crawford and the NLWIA also urged that:

> Curriculum content should be re-examined to take into account, for example, Caribbean history and literature, and other subjects now described under the general term black studies; we should stress the value which this reconceptualization of curriculum content could have for the interest and motivation of *all* students.
>
> North London West Indian Association (1969b: 2, italics added)

Over time, debates around school–community relationships, teachers' expectations of black children, inner-city staffing and the scope for offering multicultural curriculum content would be absorbed into the mainstream. However, it should not be forgotten that later policy thinking on multicultural education, equalities and citizenship emerged from bitter disputes about racism and education in British schools.

Busing in London and Yorkshire

The banding dispute originated in local authority concerns that proportions of black pupils in particular Haringey schools would rise above the 30 per cent advised by the DES and that dispersal under the cover of banding would provide a 'solution'. The educational campaigning of the NLWIA and related groups played a large role in putting a quick end to dispersal policies directed at African-Caribbean communities. However, in several Asian communities across England local authorities pursued plans to disperse concentrations of Indian, Pakistani and Bangladeshi pupils. Early responses to busing in these communities were sometimes ambivalent, with some parents initially believing that it would aid the socialization of their children (Kirp, 1979a). However, as Asian communities became settled, opposition to busing grew and became another site upon which struggles over race and education were played out.

In the early years of post-war migration language was the area of provision among Asian pupils that tended to be acknowledged most explicitly by education authorities (Runnymede Trust, 1980; Singh, 1988). Initially, there was an assumption that Urdu, Punjabi, Hindi and Gujarati speakers would learn English by learning alongside English-speaking peers. By the mid-1960s the Department of Education and Science had recognized the need for more proactive work on language and a number of innovative second language projects began to emerge around England (in Leeds and Birmingham, in particular), supported by the new Section 11 funding made available to support schools in areas with high immigrant populations (Tomlinson, 2008).

Predictably, though, provision for Asian children soon became bound up with fears about numbers and distribution. The 30 per cent 'maximum' advised in DES Circular 7/65 did not particularly allay white parents' claims that high numbers of Asian children 'lowered' school standards, either because disproportionate resources would supposedly be allocated to second language support or simply because they were a black presence. So, while acculturation and the acquisition of English were the ostensible gains offered by the policy, the Department of Education and Science also began to speak in terms of dispersal as an end in itself (Cashmore and Troyna, 2005). In contrast to the USA, where busing between black and white neighbourhoods was designed to be reciprocal, British busing was proposed as a one-way solution.

Busing only ever became policy in a scattering of local authorities: Ealing in West London; West Bromwich in the West Midlands; Blackburn in Lancashire; Bradford in Yorkshire. However, it continued to be practised in fits and starts from the early 1960s to the late 1970s. Its relative longevity and its explicit invoking of fears about concentrations of black (particularly Asian) pupils increasingly made busing the target of parental protest and anti-racist campaigns, as covered in *Race Today*'s report 'Who's Afraid of Ghetto Schools?' (Dhondy *et al.*, 1985). In Asian communities there were persistent protests against busing from the mid-1960s onwards (Sivanandan, 1989). In Ealing by 1972 the Indian Workers Association and the Southall Communist Party had mobilized widespread community opposition to busing. Once Ealing had formally overturned its policy, Bradford phased out busing too, following the threat of investigation by the Community Relations Commission (CRC), the body set up to address racial inequalities, which was superseded in 1976 by the Commission for Racial Equality (CRE).

A history of debates about busing written from black activists' perspectives would be a welcome addition to the black British intellectual corpus. The American sociologist David Kirp (1979a, 1979b) remains the most extensive chronicler, although his interest is in policy, rather than resistance. The disparity between Kirp's (1979a, 1979b) and Dhondy *et al.*'s (1985) accounts of the demise of busing is particularly instructive. Kirp emphasizes central government's stealthy withdrawal from a policy which, by the mid-1970s, had few enthusiastic supporters, while Dhondy *et al.* remind us of the anger over the death in a gang attack on fifteen-year-old Mohammed Malik, one of six Asian boys who were bused daily from 'Asian' Southall to 'white' Ealing. Kirp's analysis of busing carries little sense of wider black British political struggles and, therefore, underestimates the kind of opposition to dispersal that Dhondy *et al.* (1985) recount. In the end, however, Kirp acknowledges that antipathy towards busing among Asian parents and students in west London was fired above all by their understanding that the busing was an undeniably racialized practice, which meant that 'predominantly white Ealing got the new schools, while non-white Southall children rode buses' (Kirp, 1979b: 282).

School strikes in Yorkshire

Accounts of disputes over busing are important, not least because they have drawn attention to black educational struggles beyond London and outside of African-Caribbean communities. As noted earlier in this chapter, Ramamurthy

(2005, 2006, 2007) and Malik's (2012) studies of the Asian Youth Movements of the 1970s and 80s have drawn attention to the breadth of black activism in the Midlands and the north of England. Lorna Chessum's research on the growth and stabilization of the African-Caribbean community in Leicester has also provided a situated, non-metropolitan account of black settlement. Covering the period between 1945 and 1981, Chessum explores the ways in which struggles against racism across sites of education, housing, faith and leisure operated in cities beyond the capital with high black populations (Chessum, 2000).

Anti-racist activist and educator Max Farrar (1992, 2004) has argued, too, that dynamics around black education in the capital sometimes differed from those played out elsewhere. An example is in regard to African-Caribbean supplementary schools, where in certain (though not by any means all) London settings, there were divisions between the designs of militant cultural nationalist activists in promoting all-black schooling and the desires of many black parents (cf. Dhondy *et al.*, 1985). In contrast, Farrar (1992) suggests that outside the capital black supplementary schools, while taking strong lines on education, racism and social justice, were rarely sectarian or separatist.

Farrar (1992) has also detailed one of the most audacious steps taken during the 1970s by black organizations, parents and pupils: the Cowper Street School Strike, which took place in Chapeltown, Leeds in June 1973. The strike was organized by the Chapeltown Parents' Action Group (formed by a coalition of African-Caribbean networks) in response to parents' concerns about teaching and facilities at the school and racist comments allegedly made by the head teacher. After parents' demands (including more black governors, improved community–school relations, improvements in facilities and staff turnover, and the dismissal of the head teacher) were rejected by Leeds Council's Education Department, parents and pupils organized a one-day strike. The impact of the strike was felt deeply in the city. Several of the Action Group's demands were subsequently met. Farrar (1992) depicts the campaign as an example of black educational struggle producing wider political and educational empowerment in black communities, noting the part played by the strike in developing black parents' organizational skills and networks. For Farrar, the Cowper Street campaign demonstrated 'the strongest possible commitment not just to education (most parents will pay lip service to the value of education for their children) but to a good education, one which will help them achieve their highest aspirations' (Farrar, 1992: 9).

Unsurprisingly, the strike was not seen in these terms by council leaders or by some white parents. Indeed, Farrar suggests, it was felt by the authorities that black, working-class parents had no business encouraging 'unrealistic aspirations' among their children (Farrar, 1992: 9). However, black parents were intent on 'challenging that supine "realism"' (Farrar, 1992: 9). It should be noted that school strikes were a tactic used later by Asian parents and pupils in the Yorkshire area, notably at Eccleshill Upper School, Bradford in 1984, where pupils protested against teachers' racism and alleged assaults on pupils (Morris *et al.*, 1984).

In the 1980s *Race Today* continued to provide commendable coverage of disputes over education in Bradford and other parts of Yorkshire. Particularly notable was the coverage in 1984 of the 'Schooling Crisis in Bradford' (Morris *et al.*, 1984). At this time Bradford had become the object of national media and government scrutiny after a local head teacher, Ray Honeyford, revived the numbers debate by claiming in a right-wing journal that white pupils were at a disadvantage at his school, where Asian pupils were in a large majority. Drawn to Yorkshire by the textile industry, Bradford's Asian families had 'been the subject of various educational experiments by the local education authority' (Morris *et al.*, 1984: 9), including school quotas, busing and other assimilation strategies. 'Schooling Crisis in Bradford' set in historical context the emergence of Bradford's Asian community, mostly Muslim and of Kashmiri origin, which by the mid-1980s accounted for 10 per cent of the city's population and a third of its pupils.

Supplementary schools

However, the black education movements did not only organize in protest against local education authorities' policies. One of the most significant products of the 1960s and 70s were the supplementary schools, which have retained a presence in the educational landscape ever since. Also referred to as 'complementary schools' or 'Saturday schools', they comprised classes that were set up, managed and staffed by black parents, teachers and activists, outside of the normal school day. In Asian communities in the 1960s and 70s additional schooling was usually attached to the work of mosques and temples, which focused on religious, cultural and linguistic learning, regarded by definition as being beyond the knowledge and resources of mainstream schools. In contrast, black Caribbean supplementary schools were not restricted to specific religious or linguistic instruction and usually provided 'a general curriculum corresponding in some measure to that of the state school and under the direction of institutions of the minority groups' (Homan, 1986: 169).

The African-Caribbean supplementary schools grew out of black parents' disillusionment with mainstream schooling: a belief that some of their basic requirements were not being met by state schools. For the creators of the supplementary schools, it was British schooling, rather than black pupils, that was in deficit. However, an area of disagreement, particularly in the 1960s and 70s, concerned the exact manner in which schools were failing black children. For the supplementary schools movement included both those with aspirational goals for black social mobility and those committed to radical cultural nationalism (although the latter tendency has fewer remnants today). Therefore, should the aim of supplementary schools be to improve black pupils' attainment in mainstream education, by offering additional tuition in Maths and English, or should they specialize in black history and culture, or provide both? Was the work of supplementary schools to feed into state schooling or to remain apart from it?

In actuality, the early post-war supplementary schools encompassed a complicated spread of aims and arrangements: in terms of the type of provision offered; their longevity and stability; the degree of formality and official recognition accorded by local authorities; and the balance of control between parents, teachers and other stakeholders. This is as much the case today as it was in the 1960s and 70s (Jones, V., 1986; Simon, 2005; Gerrard, 2013; Andrews, 2013). In fact, because of their disparity of aims and structures, supplementary schools may have limited value as a *category*. Gus John, one of the elders of the black education movement, has argued that 'the supplementary schools movement was not a mass movement of black people in education, nor did it give rise to one' (John, G., 2005: 100). However, if true, there is no doubt that such statements as do exist about their purposes tell something, not just about the dissatisfaction felt by black (particularly African-Caribbean) parents but about what it was that their founders and communities were committed to in terms of 'good education', and in terms of 'aspirations' (cf. Farrar, 1992: 9).

Supplementary schooling as ideology

While supplementary schools have become icons in the literature on black politics, the names and studies of early supplementary schools have tended to be limited to a fairly small circle of schools, usually London-based. Often listed are the NLWIA's George Padmore School; the Claudia Jones Supplementary School; the Black Unity and Freedom Party's (BUFP) South-East London Summer School; the Malcolm X Montessori Programme; Thomas Carlton School's after-school Caribbean Studies Programme; the Black Liberation Front's Marcus Garvey School; and also Birmingham's Afro-Caribbean Self-Help Organisation's supplementary school (Sivanandan, 1982; Homan, 1986; Alleyne, 2002; Simon, 2005).

Even a cursory look at the statements that accompanied calls for the creation of supplementary schools gives a sense of their diversity in aims and ethos. For instance, in a review of its activities between 1967 and 1970, the West Indian Standing Conference (WISC) called for the establishing of 'practicable classes, preferably on Saturday mornings, to assist those children still at school who need extra tuition. Demands will be made to provide facilities for West Indian Youths who have all been left out in the cold' (WISC, 1970: 2).

To aid the development of such schools WISC would lobby local authorities to fund pilot schemes, to train black youth workers and to recruit 'West Indian women as assistant teachers and welfare workers in schools' (WISC, 1970: 2). The Saturday morning schools should also promote 'West Indian history, culture, customs and traditions' (WISC, 1970: 2). Such recommendations signalled the complex agenda of mainstream educational aspirations, black identity formation and local authority patronage that would tax the energies of a number of supplementary schools over the decades.

Other bodies adopted a strict cultural nationalist line and consciously modelled a radical black pride curriculum, as exemplified in Bradford's *Black Vision* news sheet:

> He tells us that we are mentally inferior to his kind ... and uses this to put our children in the lowest streams in his schools ... That is why we need our

own educational programme because we as a people must educate ourselves to fight the man and his system, to have full control of our education.

Black Vision (Issue 1, undated: 2)

Within the black Caribbean supplementary schools of the 1960s and 70s there was strong emphasis on the teaching of black history, literature and culture. In the more radical London sites, though probably less so elsewhere, nationalist critiques of mainstream education fed into many curricula via the texts of Malcolm X, Walter Rodney and Caribbean writers and educators, such as Andrew Salkey, Sam Selvon and Edward Kamau Brathwaite (Homan, 1986; Race Today, 1988; Alleyne, 2002).

Some schools sought to combine the politics of social justice with the 'traditional' education of the upper end of the Caribbean school system. For these educators, the value of studying the literature, history and political thought of the black Atlantic was as self-evident as the value of studying the European canon. The schools orbiting John La Rose's New Beacon circle (itself influenced by the scholarship of George Padmore, C. L. R. James and Walter Rodney) exemplified this approach. For New Beacon, Alleyne (2007: 18) has claimed, education was 'perhaps the single most important process in bringing about the kinds of social transformation they desire, combining the internationalism of the classical left with the anti-colonialism of the British ex-colonial'. John La Rose explained:

> I don't mean we neglected the history of Europe, of classical Greece and Rome; that too was part of our history; it was part of my own education ... the kids were growing up here in Europe – but we wanted them to learn about and develop pride in the African parts of their heritage.
>
> La Rose, quoted in Alleyne (2002: 5)

The work of fortifying the identities and historical knowledge of black children was, as this shows, a contested field. The supplementary schools drew in those who were committed to the reform of the school system but who argued the need for changes in curriculum, home–school relations, staffing and management that would reflect and enable the democratic development of education in multiracial environments (see Stone, 1985). Others were less committed to the reform of British schooling. Some of these cleaved to 'revolutionary' class analyses of education in capitalism; others were cultural nationalists who prioritized separate black education (see Jones, V., 1986; Yekwai, 1988; Andrews, 2013). The culturalists were themselves a diverse spread: Kashmiri elders in Bradford, African-Caribbean black nationalists in London and Manchester. Moreover, what 'separatism' might mean was also contested: was it a temporary, remedial measure or a step towards a permanent withdrawal from a racist institution? Supplementary schools might occupy any of these positions, depending on who organized and attended them.

Historical readings of supplementary schooling

There are other difficulties, too, in trying to grasp what the supplementary schools of the 1960s and 70s stood for (and, equally important when considering black intellectual life, what black commentators have thought supplementary schools *should* stand for). Firstly, there is the question of ethnic definition. In particular, the term 'black supplementary schools' is often used exclusively to refer to those formed in African-Caribbean communities, despite the fact that Asian, African, Chinese and Middle Eastern communities have also produced supplementary schools (Homan, 1986). The writing that exists on the supplementary schools 'movement', therefore, often implicitly narrows the definition of black education. Secondly, there is a marked gap between the claims that have been made for and about such schools and the empirical evidence that exists about their numbers, distribution, aims and types of provision (see Simon, 2005; Myers and Grosvenor, 2009). Farrar (2011) is among those who have referred to efforts to research and report on supplementary schools in various regions of the UK during the 1970s and 80s that, due to local politics, remained unpublished. Much of the activity of supplementary schools was independent to the point of being subterranean.

The elevation of supplementary schools to iconic status has meant that myriad readings of their work have been argued: as tools for rectifying the effects of slavery and colonialism (Worrell, 1972); as a continuation of Caribbean-style 'extra lessons' (Stone, 1985); as deriving from Marcus Garvey and Walter Rodney (Jones, V., 1986; Saakana and Pearse, 1986); as creating positive respite from the racialization encountered in 'white' schools (Reay and Mirza, 2001). The claims made for the supplementary schools are not always representative of the local level but they capture something of the reorientation that took place as black parents became critical of the schooling their children received. For, as black commentators on the period have pointed out, Caribbean parents had initially often blamed their children for their poor educational performance, and young blacks had lacked an older generation experienced in British educational practices. However, as black parents began to doubt the education system, schooling became a rallying point for black families (Henry with Ruddock, 1991; Phillips, M. and Phillips, T., 1999).

Conclusion

The grassroots black education movements of the 1960 and 70s were moments of praxis. They emerged out of local concerns that required practical responses by parents, pupils and activists, and they began to evaluate and modify the terms on which black communities entered the education system. Yet, even in the midst of these struggles, those involved were conscious that what was at stake went beyond the immediate and beyond the local. In hard terms black parents were facing the consequences of settlement – and that required decisions and action on how their children would live. This is not to say that all black parents and students were politically radical in the more general sense – although Black Power, cultural nationalism and radical socialism were, for a time, significant influences among activist intellectuals. Rather, it means that many black parents understood that their relationships with schools would be marked by conflict, that they and their children would have to struggle against being marked as 'problems' for the school system and that they, as parents, would often have to become troublemakers.

Understandably, this was not a designation that many desired and in different schools, different parts of the country and among different ethnic groups, various modes of influence and agitation developed. Black commentators have suggested, for instance, that African-Caribbean groups maintained an oppositional stance longer than Asian or African parents and educators, and have argued over the consequences (Stone, 1985; John, G., 2006b; Sewell, 2009). But in the school system of the 1960s and 70s black communities, Asian and African-Caribbean, got the measure of how far they were regarded as citizens and tax-payers, and how far they were still regarded as aliens, to be assimilated and/or dispersed. For black parents and activists, the culture of British schooling (that is, state schooling for working-class children) provided one of the harshest lessons of arrival. They learned very quickly that the schools were not places to which they could, in an unproblematic sense, entrust their children or in which their children would necessarily acquire sound academic knowledge and skills or passports to social mobility. There was a frightening, racialized sense in which British schools would not act *in loco parentis*.

4 The schooling of the black working class

They knew something was seriously wrong, they didn't know how badly wrong, how it became that way, or what to do about it. They were groping for information and knowledge. They knew their individual kids had problems but they didn't have a general picture so I tried to fill in the picture.

Bernard Coard, quoted in Bergman (1971: 4)

Introduction

The distance travelled through the educational struggles of the 1960s and 70s was, in cultural and political terms, another migration for Britain's black communities. And if, to borrow Stuart Hall's formulation, 'we struggle where we are' (Gillborn, 2008: 202), then the contribution of post-Black Power intellectuals was to help us grasp exactly where we were and where our struggles might lead. In the 1970s and 80s black British thinkers drew upon their experiences of educational activism – and in many cases their own experiences of British schooling – in order to assert the place of the 'second generation' in British society. This chapter explores the ways in which black intellectuals, such as Ambalavaner Sivanandan, Bernard Coard, Hazel Carby and Farrukh Dhondy, began to build a picture of what it meant to be young, black and British by developing extended critiques of the education system.

This chapter begins by looking at how the London campaigns of the black education movement led to the publication of Bernard Coard's (1971b) *How the West Indian Child is Made Educationally Subnormal in the British School System*. Coard's book was the first by a black British intellectual to offer an extended structural analysis of racialized processes in British schooling. Coard's work has, for better and for worse, been a spectre haunting much subsequent writing by black British academics and educators. Coard's moment is then placed in its historical context with a consideration of the independent positions that black British intellectuals were already developing during the period. Central to this new phase were the ways in which black British thinkers severed themselves from the race relations paradigm that had dominated both theory and policy in the immediate post-war period. By the early 1970s independent black intellectual spaces were being carved out in the work of pioneering black sociologists such as Chris Mullard, Gus John and Dilip Hiro, the critiques developed by Sivanandan's revitalized Institute of Race Relations and the writing on education that came out of the influential *Race Today* magazine. These black commentators developed radical structural analyses of the processes of social reproduction being lived by 'second generation' black Britons. They understood education as a site of conflict for black communities, conflict that told a larger story about race and class.

Caribbean Education and Community Workers Association

Around 1963 Caribbean parents, educators and community workers in London began to become concerned at the numbers of black children who were being placed in schools for the 'educationally subnormal': ESN schools. By 1967 the statistics produced by the Inner London Education Authority were difficult to refute. Black children (in this case mainly Caribbean) comprised 15 per cent of pupils in ILEA's primary and secondary schools but 28 per cent of pupils in ILEA's special schools (Coard, 1971b; cf. Runnymede Trust, 1980). Head teachers in special schools were themselves disconcerted by what they believed was the over-referral of black children to ESN schools: the result, some heads suggested, of poor assessment of the needs and performance of black children, deriving from the misrecognition of their children's language, the perceived unruliness of black children and scrappy myths about Caribbean children's home lives and intelligence (Bergman, 1971).

The Caribbean Education and Community Workers Association (CECWA) emerged out of the same circles as the North London West Indian Association (NLWIA), members of which had become involved in setting up black supplementary schools and other educational projects. Under its first chair, NLWIA stalwart John La Rose, CECWA began to investigate the over-representation of black children in special schools and ESN streams. In 1970 La Rose invited a young Grenadian teacher, Bernard Coard,[1] to speak on the issue of ESN schooling to a weekend CECWA Conference. Coard had, a few years earlier, completed an MA at the University of Sussex, becoming a youth worker in south-east London and then a teacher in an ESN school himself. Of his initial paper on ESN placements, Coard reflected, 'I spent three weeks, eight hours a day in the Institute of Education library compiling material ... combined with my own observations and experience' (Bergman, 1971: 4).

ESN schooling

In 1971 Coard's CECWA paper was published as a book by John La Rose's New Beacon imprint, with funding scraped together from black organizations across England. Coard's *How the West Indian Child is Made Educationally Subnormal in the British School System* confirmed the fears of many black parents and educators. Its opening statement read:

1   There are very large numbers of our West Indian Children in schools for the educationally subnormal – which is what ESN means.

2   These children have been wrongly placed there.
3   Once placed in these schools, the vast majority never get out and return to normal schools.
4   They suffer academically and in their job prospects for life because of being put in these schools.
5   The authorities are doing *very* little to stop this scandal.

Coard (1971b: 27)

Coard's efforts to move from local instances of the placement of black children into the ESN system to a general picture comprised an elaboration of the critiques of British schooling that had been circulating among black community organizations over the previous decade. The ESN problem was now being fiercely debated by NLWIA and CECWA and in black community journals, such as *Grassroots* and *Black Liberator*. *How the West Indian Child* depicted a school system in which black Caribbean children who should have entered mainstream schools were being routinely placed in ESN schools, often with the consent of parents who believed these were short-term placements designed to aid children who had recently migrated in making the transition to the British system. Since most of the children found themselves *permanently* placed in special schools that were not equipped to support mainstream academic achievement, they were, in effect, filtered out of the academic system into underachievement and into unemployment or poor work. Parents rarely realized that they had any right of appeal over ESN placements.

Coard warned that black children in ESN schools were 'being prepared for *survival*, not for *excelling*, or even participating actively in the society' (Coard, 1971b: 31). Moreover, the shame, frustration and alienation experienced by these black children often gave rise to severe behavioural problems, creating a cruel self-fulfilling prophecy. For Coard, the causes of these misplacements were more complex than individual teachers' prejudices; they were a means by which the school system reproduced and maintained structural racial inequalities. His analysis referred to cultural and social class biases in assessment, schools' incomprehension of linguistic differences, their unfamiliarity with the formal, deferential modes of behaviour expected in Caribbean schools and young blacks' lack of place in the labour market.

A hostile environment

In addition, Coard suggested that teachers and parents alike often underestimated the 'temporary emotional disturbance due to severe culture and family shock, resulting from their sudden removal from the West Indies to a half-forgotten family, and an unknown and generally hostile environment' (Coard, 1971b: 35). Some thirty years later Jan McKenley (2001: 317) drew particular attention to the lack of understanding of the 'trauma of separation' that sinewed the early school experiences of children who had migrated to Britain to join their parents. While not denying the impact of some individual teachers' racism towards newly arrived black children, McKenley emphasized that the teaching profession was as 'ill equipped and unprepared for the cultural impact of black immigration as other parts of British society' (McKenley, 2001: 317).

It was also the misfortune of newly arrived black children to fall into British education's obsession with forms of IQ testing that could not possibly grasp these biases and disturbances (see Chitty, 2007). Coard condemned the impact of IQ testing on black children as 'not only a shambles but a tragedy for many' (Coard, 1971b: 37). For too many children there was little motivation to succeed in a stacked and hostile system. 'If you expect to fail,' added Coard, 'the chances are you will' (Coard, 1971b: 42). Later, some black intellectuals would see in Coard's analysis an over-reliance on self-concept theory: too much emphasis on cultivating black self-esteem at the expense of academic development and a misplaced belief that the role of the schools was to 'teach' black culture (see Chapter 5 of this book). However, Coard's work has continued to shadow black educators, even where they contest it. For some, this is a sign that debates on race and education have too often continued to re-tread old ground; for others, it is a disturbing indication of the slow progress made in addressing racial inequalities in education (see Mirza, H. S., 2007).

Sociologies of race relations

Bernard Coard's analysis of race and education had its antecedents in the black education campaigns of the previous decade, explored in Chapter 3 of this book. Those campaigns were part of the post-war reimagining of black Britain, as Asians and African-Caribbeans came to grasp the consequences of settlement. As regards independent black thought there was, between the 1950s and 1970s, a radical redrawing of understandings of blackness in Britain, one that lost all use for the 'guest' status that informed previous race relations thinking. The suggestion that the school system had failed black children, rather than the reverse was audacious; it grew out of the rethinking of questions of assimilation, integration and identity that fired the 'hothouse of black politics' described by Prescod (1999a: 206). The next sections of this chapter examine the break in sociological analyses of race, education and social justice the black education movements helped signal.

The sociology of race relations in Britain had first emerged in the 1940s with the pioneering work of Kenneth Little in Cardiff's docklands (Little, 1948). As black settlement grew in the 1950s sociological studies proliferated, notably in the work of Michael Banton, Anthony Richmond, Sheila Patterson and Nicholas Deakin. Banton's commitment to understanding race and racism in Britain has been lengthy and influential. *The Idea of Race* (Banton, 1977) was notable for its archaeological examination of shifting concepts of race in western thought. Equally important from the late 1960s onwards was the work of John Rex, whose key studies included *Race Relations in Sociological Theory* (Rex, 1970), in which he suggested sociological frameworks for understanding the persistence of racism, given the invalidity of race as a scientific concept. Rex later produced *Colonial*

Immigrants in a British City: A Class Analysis (Rex and Tomlinson, 1979), co-authored with Sally Tomlinson, who would become a leading researcher on race and education (see Tomlinson, 2005, 2008). Rex's research was particularly concerned with the injustices that excluded black communities from the political process, not least in the sphere of organized labour.

Also influential in early debates on immigration and integration was the Institute of Race Relations, set up in 1958 as an independent body in which academics, researchers and policy-makers might work together to monitor race relations in Britain. This was a very different version of the IRR from that which developed under the direction of Sivanandan, after its fractious split in 1972. The early IRR prided itself on research that aimed to furnish policy-makers with information about immigrant communities and racial tensions, promoting a residual belief that moral-rational objections to racial prejudice would gradually roll back racial inequalities. The height of the IRR's influence in its original incarnation was probably the publication in 1969 of the survey *Colour and Citizenship* (Rose, Deakin *et al.*, 1969). However, in her powerful retrospective critique Jenny Bourne of the IRR argued that *Colour and Citizenship* also represented the beginning of the end of IRR's first phase, a decline not merely due to intra-organizational disputes but to the inherent inadequacies of its race relations model (Bourne and Sivanandan, 1980). Why then did the coming generation of black and anti-racist activists, both inside and outside the IRR, increasingly regard early race relations thinking as unequal to the task of challenging racial inequality?

Goodbye to race relations

Firstly, while theorists such as Rex and Banton were concerned with understanding racism within the wider power relations of capitalism and imperialism, there was a body of less nuanced race relations work that remained focused on the size and presence of black communities in ways that rendered invisible the racialized practices of 'white' society and the historical production of racial inequalities (such as Griffith *et al.*, 1960; Rose, Deakin *et al.*, 1969). Consequently, racism in Britain was too often presented as an inevitable process of antipathy, stratification and conflict between fixed racial or ethnic blocs – hence the need for a sociology of relationships between 'the races'. For later critics, such as Bourne and Sivanandan (1980) and Gilroy (1980), there was too little recognition that 'racial differences' were the effects of political, social and economic structures – in education, occupation, housing, political representation and identity. Passing into policy in vulgarized form, there was frequent slippage at local level into a worldview in which the mere presence of black communities in Britain was the direct cause of racism.

For Bourne and Sivanandan, bodies such as the Race Relations Board, the Community Relations Commission and the earlier incarnations of the IRR 'developed a school of thinking ... which held that if racialism, seen as the cultural intolerance underlying and giving rise to racial discrimination, was educated away, equal opportunity would begin to flourish' (Bourne and Sivanandan, 1980: 336). The reference to education is not incidental; schools were frequently imagined to be a site in which to encourage the kinds of intercultural exchanges that would wither racial prejudice away. This paralleled, to an extent, the early approach of CARD and before that Moody's LCP. It is also important to note that, within the early IRR, the Race Relations Board and other official players, there was a tension between those who emphasized the need for common cultural values as a way of binding together blacks and whites and those who believed that cultural pluralism should be encouraged so long as it was accompanied by the kind of education and exchange that would counter unfortunate intercultural misunderstandings. Not least among the objections of black critics was that the logic of both these tendencies placed a heavy onus on black communities to minimize their strangeness by processes of assimilation; integration was rarely seen as a two-way street. The recent emergence of the community cohesion discourse, following the disturbances in British cities in the early 2000s, suggests that the racism-as-group-conflict model remains strongly present in British social policy (see Chapters 8 and 9).

Understanding institutional racism

What black British thinkers who had engaged with the US civil rights and Black Power movements took issue with in the old race relations model was the inadequacy of definitions that reduced racism to expressions of personal prejudice or race hate. They understood that what British sociologists of the 1950s and 60s referred to as the 'colour bar' was systemic and structural. The influence of Stokely Carmichael and Charles Hamilton's (1967) seminal American work *Black Power* is now embedded in social science but, in its time, it radically challenged the idea that racism was simply an expression of individual hatred and it profoundly influenced British anti-racists' understandings of institutional or structural racism. *Black Power*'s authors famously declared:

> Racism is both overt and covert. It takes two, closely related forms: individual whites acting against individual blacks, and acts by the total white community against the total black community. We call these individual racism and institutional racism … When a black family moves into a … white neighbourhood and is … routed out, they are victims of an overt act of individual racism, which many will condemn – at least in words. But it is institutional racism that keeps black people locked in dilapidated slum tenements … society either pretends it does not know of this latter situation, or is in fact incapable of doing anything meaningful about it.
>
> Carmichael and Hamilton (1967: 20–1)

Carmichael and Hamilton's definitions have subsequently been developed (Omi and Winant, 1986; Gilroy, 1987; Crenshaw *et al.*, 1995; Bonilla-Silva, 2006) and critiqued (Miles, 1989). However, their concept of structural or institutional racism has remained central to the practical work of addressing racism and racial inequalities. Carmichael and Hamilton's basic analysis was that overt attacks on black people, driven by race hate, were only the most obvious form of racism. Wider racial inequalities were reproduced through the everyday, taken-for-granted practices of institutions, such as schooling, policing, news media and government funding. As Paul Gilroy (1987) later argued in *There Ain't No Black in the Union Jack*, equating racism solely with far-right extremism slips too readily into a denial of the normalized place of racism in the social and political formation. Today the concept of institutional racism remains contentious, as became clear in the wake of the landmark Macpherson Report into police failures during the inquiry into the murder of black teenager Stephen Lawrence (see Chapter 8). There is still often a refusal to recognize the presence of racism unless it is knife-wielding, shaven-headed and working-class.

The 'new' Institute of Race Relations

Within the Institute of Race Relations the break with 'official' race relations thinking came to a head in the early 1970s, when a series of strident critiques of the IRR Council were made by radical academics and community workers within the IRR's staff and membership, among them Robin Jenkins and Ambalavaner Sivanandan. These concerned the IRR Council's apparent lack of independence from government departments. The stark divisions that followed were subsequently recounted by Alexander Kirby (in Mullard, 1973) and Sivanandan (1974). By 1972, under the aegis of Sivanandan, the IRR declared a new position, independent of government policy-makers: one that stressed a commitment to race-conscious sociology and transformative politics. Much as the International African Services Bureau had done in the 1930s, the reconstituted IRR declared itself 'a catchment area for the Third World intelligentsia, its radicals and political activists' (Sivanandan, 1974: 29). Henceforth, the IRR's mission would focus around critical education:

> Seminars and meetings ... would bring these minds together, the Institute's Library would feed them ... [its] publications would infiltrate the cloisters of academe and generate an insurgent sociology and an insurgent politics – designed not to obliterate but to understand and change reality.
>
> Sivanandan (1974: 29)

In 1975 IRR's journal *Race* was re-launched as *Race and Class*. It has remained one of the principal spaces for the work of international black and anti-racist intellectuals, including many of the most important voices of the late twentieth and early twenty-first centuries. Its British contributors have included a wide range of academics and educators, such as Chris Searle, Paul Gilroy, Liz Fekete and Stella Dadzie. Mention should also be made of another IRR-related work that explicitly argued for a break with the race relations model. Chris Mullard's (1973) *Black Britain* was the first book-length attempt by a British-born black academic to take stock of the implications of the post-war black presence. It was part sociological analysis, part polemic, part autobiographical reflection: 'not yet another race relations book: it is a book about crisis written from a black's point of view' (Mullard, 1973, unnumbered). It contains impassioned critiques of *Colour and Citizenship*, of the Race Relations Board and the politics of immigration control. Mullard's book also recounted the growth of independent black activist groups as a feature of black settlement, critiqued the rhetoric of assimilation and proposed reforms in teacher training and curriculum development. Today it is too rarely cited and yet many parts of it lay out the key areas of departure from race relations approaches that were pursued by later black British intellectuals.

Race Today collective

In addition to the launching of *Race and Class*, the IRR's regular newsletter, *Race Today* also became an independent political journal. While the outlook of *Race Today* was Marxist and internationalist (strongly influenced by C. L. R. James' example), it was driven by the transformations in Britain's black communities and, in particular, by a young generation of activists with roots in community campaigning, education and publishing. In 1974 Darcus Howe (former member of the British Black Panthers, Mangrove Nine defendant and nephew of C. L. R. James) assumed its editorship. *Race Today*, like *Race and Class*, became a major forum for black British voices in politics and the arts until its demise at the end of the 1980s. A single issue might incorporate reporting on homelessness in east London, black trade unionists in the National Health Service, Tariq Ali in conversation with Rajiv Gandhi, tributes to James Baldwin or a review of new Latin American women writers. The Race Today Collective drew upon diverse and sometimes fractious currents in black British left-wing thought; its value lay not in the propagation of an agreed socio-political line but in the expansiveness and often downright cantankerousness of the voices contained in its pages.

Importantly, throughout the 1970s and 80s *Race Today* maintained independent, critical commentary on the experiences of black communities within the education system. Its contributions to theorizing race and education proved influential among black and anti-racist educators and activists (Dhondy, 2001; Farrar, 2011). Many of *Race Today*'s earliest reports on education conveyed scepticism about efforts among race relations officials to make schools a site for national 'intercultural' campaigns. Contributors' objections were often rooted in the Marxist belief that schools could not compensate for society, schools being themselves an effect of social inequality. Even before *Race Today* took a more radical position under Darcus Howe, David Stephen (1970: 218) had queried the implication of race relations projects in schools that 'if only immigrants could be made to learn our ways all would be well' and questioned the tendency of race relations work in schools to restrict its focus to the impacts of individual, openly expressed prejudices of white teachers and pupils, rather than seeking to understand the role of schooling itself in reproducing social inequalities.

Coard's impacts and contradictions

Set against the dissatisfaction of the early 1970s, the impact of Bernard Coard's *How the West Indian Child is Made Educationally Subnormal in the British School System* was immediate among black communities and anti-racist educators; it was, after all, a distillation of the concerns many had raised over several years. Veterans such as Gus John and Max Farrar have both remembered selling Coard's book door-to-door in carrier bags or from trestle tables at parents' meetings. Its publication was also accompanied by mainstream coverage in the *Guardian*, *New Statesman* and *Times Educational Supplement*. It was, therefore, the first extended, independent black British commentary on education to pass through the hands of black parents, teaching professionals, academics, news media and some of the more forward thinking policy-makers. However, it is important to note some of the complexities and contradictions in Coard's analysis and his proposed solutions. Understanding these helps illuminate some of the positions and oppositions that have emerged among black educators in the decades since.

Firstly, Coard offered a structural analysis of how schools reproduced racial inequalities. In the terms used by the Critical Race Theorist David Gillborn (2008) almost four decades later, Coard argued that British schools operated not to create the kind of education that would counter racial inequalities, but to maintain racial inequalities at manageable levels. The idea that schooling reproduced social inequalities was hardly peculiar to Coard. Radical sociologists of education had long been concerned with the political character of education, drawing on Althusser's Marxism and on Michael Young's 'new sociology' of education. In Britain and America the 1970s would be the decade of Bowles and Gintis, Basil Bernstein, Madan Sarup and Paul Willis (see Cole's, 2008, overview of Marxist educational theory).

In Britain, though, the shift from focusing on the reproduction of class inequalities to the reproduction of *racial inequalities* represented a marked sociological and political break. At heart, what Coard argued was an inversion of the cultural deficit theses that had informed much British thinking on race and education; for Coard and CECWA the deficit lay in the schooling of black children, not in black children themselves. However, Coard did not shift blame from black children to their teachers. His analysis was structural in that it rejected the notion that black children would thrive if white teachers were simply encouraged to be less prejudiced; the intersection of black migration and a deeply unequal educational system had produced a compact deeper and wider than that.

Yet while Coard drew attention to the relationships between the schooling of black children and post-imperial labour processes (including the suspicion that educational gains for black children were blocked because they would deny Britain the cheap labour that was the original 'purpose' of the black presence), he did not abandon a belief in what British schooling *might* offer. Like the NLWIA and the New Beacon grouping, even as Coard decried what he regarded as the structural racism of the education sector, he offered guidance on how to improve schooling for black pupils. For schools, these included a set of recommendations around

ESN referral processes and IQ testing, effective home–school relationships, increasing the recruitment of black teachers and the incorporation of black history and culture (Caribbean, American, African and Asian) into the curriculum 'for the benefit of the Black *and* white children' (Coard, 1971b: 52). Under the heading 'Things we can do for ourselves' Coard called upon black communities to open nurseries and supplementary schools, to increase parental contact with teachers, to provide children with educational materials and a listening ear at home.

Coard and black self-esteem

Coard's book offered what was, at the time, a radical prescription. By the 1980s some of the basic conditions he and the black education movement as a whole urged would become increasingly taken for granted in state schooling. Yet, while *How the West Indian Child* is often hailed as a breakthrough *structural* analysis, Coard's reading of educational inequalities arguably retained a certain kind of deficit thinking. Like many educators working in urban settings in the early 1970s, his approach was noticeably informed by self-concept theories that stressed the need to build black children's self-esteem as a prerequisite to improving their educational performance. In Coard's book black children are described as being trapped in 'a vicious circle of self-contempt' (Coard, 1971b: 52). He also refers at some length to 'black self-hatred' (Coard, 1971b: 47) and to the black and white doll self-esteem experiments of the period.

In an article written in the *Guardian* to accompany the publication of *How the West Indian Child*, Coard asserted that the Eurocentric images and curriculum of 1960s British schools had made black children 'neurotic' (Coard, 1971a, unnumbered). He concludes that:

> The black child acquires two fundamental attitudes ... in the British school system; a low self-image and consequently, low self-expectations in life. These are obtained through streaming, banding, bussing, ESN schools, racialist news media, and a white middle class curriculum; by totally ignoring the black child's language, history, culture and identity.
>
> Coard (1971a, unnumbered)

Coard's comments draw on mid-twentieth-century self-concept theories (such as Radke and Trager, 1950; Goodman, 1964) but also upon Frantz Fanon's anti-colonial social psychology – particularly those parts of Fanon that spoke of colonial subjects' potential for internalizing the oppressor's gaze, for seeing themselves as they were seen by whites: not just as inferior but as 'other' (Fanon, 1963). In the early 1970s partial readings of Fanon's anti-colonial social psychology were a growing influence on radical black British educators and one sees a particular reading of Fanon (not always a nuanced one) in Coard's bringing together of structures and actors, and in his gloss on black pupils as racialized subjects, who had internalized their low streaming and were alienated not just from schooling but from self. In the 1980s Maureen Stone (1985) decried forms of multicultural teaching that she believed were reliant on outdated self-concept theories and promoted deficit models of black education. Whether the multicultural education that Stone damned can be laid at Coard's feet is open to question.

The remainder of this chapter examines the radical structural critiques of schooling, race and class that dominated black intellectual work in the 1970s and 80s, post-Coard. These commentators might be termed black conflict theorists, in that they drew upon conflict models of educational stratification (Collins, R., 1971), on analyses of institutional racism in education (Carmichael and Hamilton, 1967) and on neo-Marxist critiques of functionalism in schooling (Bowles and Gintis, 1976). They sought to explain why, regardless of emergent race equality policies, the education system effectively reproduced racial and class inequalities.

Race Today and education in capitalism

Across the 1970s and 80s *Race Today*'s contributors produced a series of reports and think pieces that were critical of both black cultural nationalism and liberal multiculturalism. These joined the flow of 1970s Marxist educational theory, rejecting Dewey's conceptions of 'democratic' schooling. Dewey and his descendants had argued the liberal case for schooling as an egalitarian and democratic process: one that ideally facilitated the integration of young people into adult roles, ensured their moral and cognitive development and lessened economic extremes, thus enabling self-fulfilment. For Marxist educators, theorization of schooling *as it existed* could logically only comprise a theory of education in capitalism. Therefore, they emphasized schooling as a site of class conflict, a process of socialization into the wider relations of capitalism, wherein the majority of working-class pupils were, regardless of the principled efforts of individual teachers, fitted for subordination and exploitation.

Race Today's writing on education included several special issues, material from which was later collated in Farrukh Dhondy, Barbara Beese and Leila Hassan's (1985) *The Black Explosion in British Schools*. Dhondy *et al.* (1985) had the effect of making *Race Today*'s coverage of education look a little more consistent than it perhaps had been in real time: voices such as Keith Worrell (1972), who advocated all-black schooling as a means to correct the racial trauma of colonialism, or those that had been influenced by earlier race relations models, were excised. However, Dhondy *et al.* (1985) powerfully summarized the campaigns and the critiques that had, since the early 1960s, driven those black British intellectual analyses of education that were rooted both in the new social movements and in the politics of James and Padmore.

Black conflict theories

The central arguments asserted in *The Black Explosion in British Schools* were these. Firstly, Dhondy *et al.* (1985: 11) reclaimed hidden histories of post-war black activism, identifying a 'black movement in education in this country from the time that our children began to be schooled here'. Moreover, while Dhondy *et al.*

(1985) acknowledged the adult campaigners who had agitated in the late 1960s, their main concern was with what they believed was a shift to activism among pupils themselves, particularly strikes and protests, not least in response to schools' apparent lack of support for pupils caught up in conflict with the police. More common still than these youth protests, which Dhondy *et al.* (1985) characterized as spontaneous and outside the direction of 'parental' organizations such as NLWIA, were day-to-day acts of disengagement and refusal. Dhondy *et al.*'s (1985) depiction was one in which sections of black working-class youth (both African-Caribbean and Asian) had come to regard schooling as simply one part of a web of what we now term social exclusion. As such, it was the class function of schooling that was most keenly felt by black pupils, not the supposed Eurocentricity of the curriculum or low self-esteem:

> black students in schools will more readily concentrate on the interference of police in their lives and educational institutions than they will on the quality of the curriculum. I know of no committee, no strike, no demonstration from Asian or West Indian youth which demanded that world geography be taught, that slavery replace Tudor history as part of the syllabus, or any other tinkering with the subject matter of schooling. That doesn't mean that I find students apathetic or uncaring about curricular change [but] it doesn't seem ... to be a political obsession. ... Work and police and money and the relative strength of black gangs and white gangs, self-defence against whites who attack them, feeling against racist teachers and an opposition to the boredom and routine and discipline of schooling seems to be.
>
> Dhondy *et al.* (1985: 12)

Among those marginalized were, the authors argued, large numbers of black pupils excluded from schools for non-attendance and indiscipline, who were now deemed unplaceable within the system and were beyond any possible disciplinary pact between parents and the schools. In further education colleges disruption was caused by unemployed friends of students who, with no prospect of work or training, gravitated towards the canteens and common rooms. The upper end of the secondary system, in particular, seemed less a place of education and more a holding container for adolescents who were becoming 'fully fledged independent members of the unruly section of the working class at the bottom of the British ladder of labour' (Dhondy *et al.*, 1985: 13).

There is no doubt that this was a partial view (albeit one drawn from Dhondy's own teaching experiences in south London), and a summoning of what the authors imagined to be a potentially radical underclass. However, it contained several elements that, stripped of the romantic hopes that black youth would emerge as an oppositional force, perhaps even a radical vanguard, were prescient and critically observed. Indeed, their depiction of the schooling of the socially excluded and their doubts about the kind of multicultural education that promoted cultural diversity for its own sake have now become standard motifs among commentators.

Hazel Carby: schooling in Babylon

The influence of Marxism also pervaded, at least for a while, the writing of younger black thinkers emerging in the early 1980s, including those associated with the Centre for Contemporary Cultural Studies, at the University of Birmingham, which since 1968 had been directed by the Jamaican-born social theorist Stuart Hall. As Chapter 6 of this book shows, those associated with the CCCS would soon turn sharply away from the previous generation's melding of Black Power and Marxism but in the book that announced their arrival, *The Empire Strikes Back: Race and Racism in 70s Britain* (CCCS, 1982), Hazel Carby's chapter 'Schooling in Babylon' followed on directly from the analyses proffered by Dhondy and Sivanandan.

Like them, Carby (1982a) began by rejecting the race relations discourse. Carby critiqued what she saw as the pathologization of black families and communities that had ensued in the scramble to 'account for' poor educational outcomes among black pupils (Carby's analysis referred principally to African-Caribbean children). For Carby, race relations discourses that prioritized assimilation as a panacea may have been depicted as beneficial to black and white alike but because they began from the belief that black and white interests were materially opposed (hence the need to cultivate race relations), their real intent was the promise to protect the interests of white communities in which blacks had settled. That is, while the race relations bodies opposed explicit racial prejudice and discrimination, racist 'hostility was seen to be the result of whites' justifiable fear of the very presence of blacks' (Carby, 1982a: 186).

Thus the frantic political juggling of the race relations bodies was not, for Carby, the result of incompetence or naivety but rather was embedded in the profound contradictions inherent in British social democracy, 'notably in the attempt to balance the perceived needs of the working class and the demands of capital' (Carby, 1982a: 184). One means of rhetorically resolving this contradiction was for the British state to manufacture a national interest: a 'we're all in it together' view of education, work and economy. However, for the state, the place of blacks within the 'national interest' was always ambiguous (did they belong, were they welcome); so, when it suited, the 'national interest' could be constructed by the state as being *in opposition to* the interests of black 'immigrants'. For Carby, therefore, the educational interests of black pupils as a fraction of the working class were distinct from (but not opposed to) their white peers. This was evident in the fact that black communities' demands over schooling often lacked even the shaky support of the Labour Party, the trade unions and employers that made sense of parts of schooling for white working-class youth (Carby, 1982a, 1999).

Reflections on black conflict theories

What was it then that these black conflict theorists succeeded in elaborating and why was it that vital parts of their messages were lost from debates on race and education as the 1980s progressed into the 1990s? First of all, as for other radical sociologists of education writing in the 1970s, education in capitalism was, for the black Marxists, nigh irredeemable, though forms of social democracy might, if they addressed racialized and pro-capital assumptions, create some spaces for black agency in the field of education. In general, though, black Marxists' conflict analyses of race and education did not offer detailed local prescriptions because solutions would only come with radical social overhaul ('As a teacher, I don't want to contain indiscipline, I want to do away with the system that causes it,' Dhondy *et al.*, 1985: 20).

If the role of intellectuals in education is taken to be the design of new practices, this retreat from practical solutions was a failing. In Dhondy *et al.* (1985) there is also much rhetoric about 'pupil power' and 'black pupil revolt'. From the vantage point of the twenty-first century the emphasis placed upon black schoolchildren as an oppositional force seems incredible. However, to focus only on this is to miss the point. For, following on from the early work of Gus John and Chris Mullard, Carby, Dhondy and Sivanandan were among the first black British intellectuals to understand that there was a coherent history of black educational activism that needed to be drawn upon in order to avoid the errors of superficial multicultural education, and in order to understand that the relationship between black communities and the education sector was more than a form of welfare service provision. Secondly, these black thinkers emphasized that while it was necessary to form immediate opposition to practices such as busing and banding, approaches to racism in education and to the experiences of black children which focused only on 'within classroom' solutions were inadequate. To see the experiences of black children only through prisms of a multicultural curriculum or teachers' prejudices or intercultural exchange was not enough; educational inequalities, they insisted, could only be understood within the context of the wider social antagonisms in which schooling was embedded.

The black Marxist analyses of schooling were not just elevated theory but rooted in the everyday concerns around unemployment, policing and racist violence that were leading black youth in Britain's inner cities to resist, or at least refuse, what they were offered in schools. Crucially, Dhondy, Sivanandan and Carby credited black students with the ability to read their own situations, to read the social role of schooling and their own marginalization; they were not ungovernable or uneducable but living out a depressing logic. Black parents of the 1960s and 70s felt a fundamental disappointment in and disillusionment with the British school system but it was their children who lived the consequences. In this context the emphasis upon the oppositional potential of black pupils was not mere radical chic but optimism of the will balanced against pessimism of the intellect.

Conclusion

For the black Marxist theorists, even to focus on systemic flaws, as Coard had done, was only to grasp part of the picture; they turned to the bleak probability that black and working-class children did not fail because of flaws in the system; race and class inequalities *were* the system. To paraphrase Diane Reay (2006) in her impassioned call to reclaim social class analyses in education, a cultural analysis of race and class rested upon the understanding that they were everywhere and nowhere within the education system, 'denied yet continually enacted' (Reay, 2006: 289).

The downsides of the influence of conflict theory were the deferral of work on immediate reform of schooling (or, more accurately, a split between those who devised race/class critiques and those black and anti-racist educators left in the classroom) and, arguably, an over-focus on the most charged areas of conflict: those affecting young African-Caribbean males in the big cities. In addition, the valid refusal of state and academic scrutiny on the supposed failings of black families and communities in the 1960s, 70s and 80s also ruled out of bounds for many years examination of the agentive role of black parents and communities in education, in favour of focusing on education's structural inequalities.

The black conflict theorists also pointed in directions other than those they imagined. The focus on the wider experiences of black students, particularly their experiences of policing and unemployment, led away from examination of black pupils as pupils only and towards the study of 'black youth' as a social phenomenon in itself. As Chapter 6 explains, in the 1980s and 90s the study of black youth would become the nub of black British cultural studies and attendant subcultural theory. However, the impact of the black education movements reached far beyond the field of sociological theory. Chapter 5 considers how approaches drawn from the black education movements entered the mainstream during the 1980s and 90s, reshaping schooling and culture and being incorporated into state multiculturalism.

Note

1   It would be disingenuous to avoid mention of Bernard Coard's subsequent political life, which has made him a controversial figure in black British politics. In 1986 Coard was convicted of involvement in the 1983 coup that deposed the government of Grenada and led to the killing of Prime Minister Maurice Bishop. Released in 2007, Coard has continued to protest his innocence but remains a divisive figure.

5 Multicultural and anti-racist education

...within a society, that is cohesive not uniform, cultures are respected, differences are recognized and individual identities are secure.

'Multi-Ethnic Education' (ILEA, 1977),
quoted in Troyna and Williams (1986: 36)

...integration, in the Home Secretary Roy Jenkins' classic 1966 definition, was 'equal opportunity accompanied by cultural diversity in an atmosphere of mutual tolerance.' But equal opportunity and mutual tolerance never got off the ground – so that all you were left with was cultural diversity.

Sivanandan (1989: 20)

Introduction

At its high watermark in the 1980s and 90s multiculturalism had a thousand parents, black and white; today it is the orphaned child of British social policy, repeatedly declared at the highest political levels, from left as well as right, to be irrelevant, dead or responsible for undermining social cohesion (Doward, 2011; Goodhart, 2013). Nowadays multiculturalism is so deeply mired in a discourse of derision that few public intellectuals rise to defend it and its critics rarely seek to understand its complex history. This chapter explores a particular part of its genealogy: how, during the 1970s, 80s and 90s, educational approaches drawn from the black education movements combined with the agendas of local and national government in developing multicultural education as a central feature of what is sometimes termed state or municipal multiculturalism. How did the work of black educators enter the multicultural mainstream and why were black British intellectuals deeply ambivalent about state-driven multiculturalism? This chapter examines black educators' contributions to multicultural education as an aspect of the wider struggle for social justice, their critiques of multiculturalism and the impact that the politics of diversity and difference had upon the black movements that had, indirectly at least, spawned them. It begins, however, by defining multiculturalism and the culture wars that shaped black British thought and activism in the 1980s and 90s.

What is multiculturalism?

One of the genuine difficulties in unpacking what the multiculturalism of the 1980s and 90s meant to black thinkers, campaigners and pupils is that the term connotes a bundle of phenomena. Kenan Malik has explained why multiculturalism has been paradoxical:

> The term 'multicultural' has come to define both a society that is particularly diverse, usually as the result of immigration, and the policies necessary to manage such a society. It has come to embody, in other words, both a *description* of a society and a *prescription* for managing it. Multiculturalism is both the problem and the solution...
>
> Malik, K. (2009: 70)

Questions of how societies should manage difference are ancient ones. Black immigration did not originate social diversity in Britain, although we sometimes speak as if it did. However, post-war immigration gave new inflections to questions of social management. So it is that multiculturalism came to signify both a social challenge and the policies designed to address that challenge. We might talk of these two dimensions in terms of *factual multiculturalism* and *state multiculturalism*.

Factual multiculturalism refers to demonstrable shifts in population demographics and the consequent diversification of language, tastes, belief, family structures and other cultural forms. However, because cultural diversity is also lived in relation to institutions, resources, rights and morality, it raises questions of social policy. As a dimension of social policy, 'state' or 'municipal' multiculturalism is concerned with how institutions, including schools, should recognize cultural diversity, ensuring fairness and legal equality but also addressing cultural pluralism. As such, it exists within the overlap between politics of recognition and the politics of redistribution.

Cultural diversity

In order to understand both the growth of and resistance to multicultural education in Britain, we need to consider what kinds of cultural diversity exist in a multicultural society. Struggles over multiculturalism in Britain were local struggles but also took place in a global context of post-war population shifts and social reconfiguration; late-twentieth-century politics across the world were informed by 'multiculturalism' in the broadest sense. New forms of pluralist social activism included feminism, gay rights, disability rights, indigenous peoples' movements and minority faith, ethnic and linguistic struggles. These 'multicultural' movements were politically diverse, geographically scattered, and they informed the social mainstream in different ways. What they had in common was a belief that social justice entailed acknowledging difference as well as sameness: that there was more than one valid way to live and that a just society necessarily comprised negotiation between those ways.

The work of black British political theorist Bhikhu Parekh, which draws upon both western liberal traditions and 'non-western' philosophies, has proven influential both on policy-makers and on scholars. Parekh's (2006) heuristic definition of multiculturalism suggests that cultural diversity in contemporary societies takes three broad forms. Firstly, there is 'subcultural diversity', wherein particular social groups (for example, lesbian, gay, bisexual and transgender [LGBT] people) seek to carve spaces to live out their own lifestyles, while still generally adhering to the wider society's dominant political values. Secondly, there is 'perspectival diversity', wherein particular groups (they might be Maoists, evangelistic Christians or jihadist Muslims) hold oppositional views and call for radical reconstruction of the social formation (Parekh, 2006: 3). Thirdly, there is 'communal diversity', wherein cohesive and longstanding groups – usually defined by ethnic origin, faith or linguistic grouping – seek to maintain distinctive cultures (Parekh, 2006: 4). In a multicultural society all three of these kinds of cultural diversity exist and in some instances overlap. At any given time, they might be distinguished according to the extent of the challenge that they present or are *perceived* to present to the social order.

The ethics of multiculturalism

One of the most lucid efforts to map out the basic *ethical* problem of living with cultural diversity, at the global as well as the local level, is contained in Kwame Anthony Appiah's (2007) *Cosmopolitanism: Ethics in a World of Strangers*. A quintessential black Atlantic intellectual, Appiah was born in London to Ghanaian and British parents, and while studying at Cambridge was mentored by Henry Louis Gates. Appiah remains sceptical of the term multiculturalism, describing it as 'another shape-shifter, which so often designates the disease it purports to cure' (Appiah, 2007: xiii). Drawing upon both Parekh and Appiah helps to show why the variants of state multiculturalism that emerged in Britain in the 1970s and 80s were not necessarily faddish, wrong-headed or cynical (although they could be), but an attempt, among many being advanced worldwide, to address the ethical problems of living with cultural diversity.

Parekh (2006) has argued that multiculturalism implies an equality of difference predicated upon understanding human beings as cultural, as well as natural, beings. In short, while nature imbues us with things in common, our diverse cultures imbue us with difference, so human beings share:

> common human identity but in a culturally mediated manner. They are different and similar, their similarities and differences do not passively coexist but interpenetrate, and neither is ontologically prior or morally more important. We cannot ground equality in human uniformity because the latter is inseparable from and ontologically no more important than human differences.
>
> Parekh (2006: 239)

However, knowing this at the abstract level does not tell us how issues of difference and similarity, plurality and commonality are to be resolved in any particular instance. Appiah (2007) argues that much of the time fuzzy pragmatism is our day-to-day mode: we may not accept our neighbours' beliefs and values as 'true' but we accept that they do and we are often happy for them to persist with different modes of family, faith, custom, leisure or artistic expression. Beyond this make-and-mend cosmopolitanism, there may be little need to try to construct a more permanent, codified balance. At this level, it could be argued, multiculturalism or cultural pluralism does work fuzzily and pragmatically as both 'problem' and 'solution'.

But what happens once we reach those instances in which modes of social life are incompatible, instances in which one section of society simply and unbendingly regards another as wrong or bad? In such instances, Appiah (2007) states, there is an objective clash of values and desires. Moreover, clashes of values will often be bound up with struggles over material resources and representation. What price then multiculturalism as 'solution'? The limitation of state multiculturalism was not always in its motive, which was to acknowledge and address the ethical challenges of cultural diversity. However, multiculturalism-as-solution often proved less able when faced with objective contradictions between values and tensions over resources. And, as its black British critics argued, while multiculturalism addressed 'horizontal' differences between social groups, it was ill equipped to deal with the 'vertical' contradictions of power. It is unsurprising that the contradictions of multiculturalism were repeatedly tested in the field of education.

Neo-liberal education

Of course, the story of race, education and social justice in the 1980s and 90s was not simply about multicultural education. Throughout these decades, schooling remained, as always, a site of struggle between central government and local education authorities. In 1979 Margaret Thatcher's Conservative government came to power producing additional tensions between left-wing local authorities (including many of the urban centres with the largest black populations) and the right-wing Conservative administration. In the ferment of Conservative education reform multicultural education was only one area of contest. As Tomlinson (2008) notes, ten Education Acts were passed between 1980 and 1990. If the introduction of comprehensive education had formed the backdrop to the black education movements of the 1960s, its partial rolling back was evident once Margaret Thatcher's government took office in May 1979.

In the succeeding years the 1980 Education Act introduced quasi-markets into the school system, emphasizing the right of parents to express school 'preferences' and in 1986 the Conservative government signalled its intention to reduce the role of local authorities in the management of schools (Benn, 2011). These, and other elements of what is often termed neo-liberal education, were reinforced by the 1988 Education Reform Act, trumpeted as the most significant reimagining of state schooling since the 1944 Education Act (Ranson, 1988). Schools were now given the right to opt out of local authority control; those remaining within local authority control were given their own budgets and schools published their exam results as an aid to parental 'choice'. Alongside these neo-liberal market elements, Tomlinson (2008) also notes a conservative impulse: in, for example, the introduction of the first National Common Curriculum and the explicit statement that religious education was to be 'of a broadly Christian character' (Tomlinson, 2008: 74). In the post-1979 context multicultural and anti-racist education efforts were not the only bout in town but they were, needless to say, politically contentious.

Multiculturalism in education

By the late 1970s most black children in the British education system were 'second generation', born in Britain and/or schooled here. They could no longer be managed simply as an immigrant presence. What this shift meant in terms of race and education remains, even now, fiercely contested among black thinkers. One tidy reading of the period is that social policy swept out of an era of 'assimilationism' and into a phase of 'multiculturalism' or 'anti-racism' (cf. Mirza, H. S., 2007). In such readings assimilation is defined as the state-driven injunction for minority cultures to absorb into an 'unchanging', monolithic majority culture, as contrasted with the multicultural embrace of pluralism and diversity, promoting integration but not cultural uniformity. However, as Mullard (1982) cautioned early on, those discrete categories sometimes conceal how far the principles of assimilation remained in place even amidst the rhetoric of multiculturalism.

Multiculturalism in British education had developed tentatively since the mid-1960s. Early post-war race relations policy, while often subsequently described as assimilationist, also contained a cultural pluralist strand. In addition, there were also pragmatic forms of multicultural education, regarded as fundable by local and central government. These included second language and other Section 11 resourcing. However, the state's commitment to multicultural education was qualified. Hazel Carby remarks that when guidance on cultural pluralism first began to appear in teacher training handbooks and other local education authority resources in the late 1960s, '[i]t was clear ... which cultural factors were to be encouraged to contribute to the "enrichment of our society and its culture" and which were viewed as threatening to the British social fabric' (Carby, 1982a: 193).

It was not until around 1977 that the Inner London Education Authority (ILEA), which schooled almost half of all the country's black pupils, initiated explicit multicultural approaches in its schools, prompted by fears about educational disengagement, unemployment and social disruption among African-Caribbean young people in particular (Troyna and Williams, 1986). While this showed some responsiveness to the black education campaigns, ILEA's first reports such as *Multi-Ethnic Education* (1977) tended to be framed by a conviction that increased cultural recognition might raise the self-esteem of black children and thereby improve their educational performance. ILEA was initially more circumspect regarding black activists' claims that it was structural racism within the education system that produced poor outcomes for many black pupils, rather than pupils' cultural differences *per se* (Troyna and Williams, 1986). However, by the early 1980s documents such as *Anti-Racist School Policies* (ILEA, 1982) signalled a shift in ILEA's perception of race and education.

'Second generation' black Britain

So what did multicultural Britain look like by the start of the 1980s? By 1981 black ethnic minorities comprised 3.8 per cent of the total British population: 2,092,000 out of a population of 53,700,000. By 1988 Britain's black communities constituted 4.9 per cent of the total population. The largest black groups were now Pakistanis, Indians, African-Caribbeans, a growing mixed race population, plus sizeable West African, Bangladeshi, Sri Lankan, Chinese and Arab communities. Yet by the 1980s these ethnic designations were merely shorthand; almost half the black population had been born in Britain.

How did these population changes translate into Britain's schools? Between 1971 and 1980, the proportion of black pupils in primary and secondary state schools had risen from 3.3 per cent to around 7 per cent (Runnymede Trust, 1980). However, the distribution of black communities across the UK meant that 'in some areas black children are not a small proportion of the population but a significant element: this has serious implications for the authorities ... they come from different cultural backgrounds and thus have different experiences and needs' (Runnymede Trust, 1980: 93). In the late 1970s around half of these children were in London schools; high concentrations could also be found in cities such as Birmingham, Manchester, Bradford, Bristol, Leicester, Liverpool and Leeds. Dilip Hiro (1973: 311) commented that by the early 1970s 'there were already scores of schools with more than 60 per cent black and Asian pupils'.

Black youth and the state

In addition, in the 1970s and 80s, increasing numbers of black school-leavers found themselves entering a shrinking youth labour market. There was a sharp rise in the numbers of unemployed black people aged between sixteen and twenty-four. In 1979 the total unemployment rate rose by 2.5 per cent but among African-Caribbeans it rose by 13.5 per cent and among Pakistanis by 10.1 per cent (Runnymede Trust, 1980). Over the following year total unemployment rose nationally by around 66 per cent but increased by 82 per cent among black workers (Runnymede Trust, 1980). In early 1981 when large-scale riots erupted in Brixton, south London, unemployment among black males aged sixteen to nineteen in Brixton stood at an estimated 55 per cent (Scarman, 1982). For many young black people the shape of 'multicultural' post-war Britain was distorted and uncertain.

By the mid- to late-1970s, young African-Caribbeans had become the most visible category of black youth, in terms of both sociological analysis and policy deliberation (Hall *et al.*, 1978; Pryce, 1979). In 1976 and 1977 street conflicts exploded at the Notting Hill Carnival. While mainstream news media offered graphic coverage of the 'riots', a generation of black thinkers who had been educated in Britain described them as community 'uprisings': rebellions provoked by years of police harassment and street racism. Brixton was followed by disturbances in Bristol in 1980, and in London, Liverpool, Birmingham and other major cities in 1981 and 1985. As the 1980s unfolded, black thinkers critiqued the ways in which those in charge of planning schooling and other aspects of youth policy were now scrambling to address what educators and policy-makers increasingly perceived as a 'second generation' crisis, one that encompassed education, employment and policing.

Youth and education policy in the 1980s

Indeed, it is difficult to consider race and education in this period without becoming overwhelmed by the proliferation of policy that had emerged from the mid-1970s onwards, in response to government and community concerns about 'second generation' African-Caribbean youth. Among the reports that appeared were the 1977 Green Paper *Education in Schools* (DES, 1977) and the same year's Select Committee report on the *West Indian Community* (SCRRI, 1977). A number of local authorities also published reports on multicultural education: a landmark effort being the collaboration between Redbridge Council and the Black People's Progressive Alliance, *Cause for Concern: West Indian Pupils in Redbridge* (1978).

In 1979 just prior to the exit of the Labour government (the party would not be returned to power until 1997) the Rampton Committee was set up to investigate the causes of poor educational performance among Caribbean pupils. Its interim report, *West Indian Children in Our Schools*, was published in June 1981, making over eighty recommendations. Shifting the emphasis away from cultural deficit theses, the Rampton Report concluded that low teacher expectations and racism within both schools and wider society were primary factors in the underachievement of African-Caribbean pupils. By this time, however, policy had been overtaken by the Brixton riots of April 1981. Lord Scarman's report on the riots/uprisings was mercilessly disparaged by commentators such as *Race Today*'s Darcus Howe, who regarded Scarman's recommendations as failing to confront the structures and assumptions that underlay heavy-handed policing of black communities (Benyon, 1984; Howe, 1988). For community activists such as Howe, the riots were uprisings of communities that refused to be policed as if they were an alien presence.

However, the Scarman Report did, at least, make some reference to the role of education in reproducing social exclusion. It referred to the range of work with black pupils being developed in parts of the Inner London Education Authority but it also identified shortcomings in educational provision as a key factor contributing to the riots. Scarman acknowledged that schooling in areas such as Brixton was bound in 'deprivation and alienation' and quoted the 'careful words' of an earlier Select Committee, opining that 'it has long been evident that we have not got ethnic minority education right' (Scarman, 1982: 26). Given that a decade and more had now passed since the warnings of CECWA and the NLWIA, it was little wonder that Howe regarded the Scarman Report as too little, too late.

Rampton and Swann

Following the publication of *West Indian Children in Our Schools*, Lord Swann took over from Anthony Rampton as Chair of the Committee of Inquiry into the Education of Children from Ethnic Minority Groups. The Swann Report of 1985, titled *Education for All*, has often been identified by black and anti-racist educators as the marker of multicultural education becoming mainstream policy (Haydon *et al.*, 1987; John, G., 2006b). Over the coming decade the Swann Report became the official incarnation of multicultural education policy (and, thereby, state multiculturalism in the broader sense, too). Although its definitions and recommendations drew from the practices and debates developed over the previous decade by community groups, schools (both mainstream and supplementary), particular local authorities and academics, Swann declared that multicultural education could no longer be left up to scattered LEA or community initiatives. It described Britain as a multiracial and multicultural society, in which all schools should seek to combat racism and respond to cultural diversity. No school, whether multiracial or 'all-white', was to be left untouched. A Runnymede Trust commentary summarized Swann's vision:

> multicultural understanding has to permeate all aspects of a school's work ... only in this way can schools begin to offer anything approaching the equality of opportunity for all pupils which must be the aspiration of the education system to provide.
>
> Runnymede Trust (1985: 10)

Swann emphasized that education for all would necessitate reforms to the inspectorate, school governance, the curriculum, teacher training and recruitment. Despite this, many black and anti-racist observers regarded Swann as a much softened version of the preceding Rampton Report. Nevertheless, the Swann Report seemingly signalled that multicultural education was now incorporated into national policy.

Multicultural education as settlement

Ultimately, multicultural education policy was neither the gift of enlightened politicians nor cynical social engineering nor simply a response to the successes of grassroots black education struggles, but rather an example of what Avis (1993) has termed educational settlement:

> The notion of settlement refers to the balance of forces in and over education. Settlements are inherently unstable, having to be continually resecured. They do not unequivocally serve the interests of a particular class or faction but reflect the work of compromise and negotiation expended in their construction.
>
> Avis (1993: 4)

The concept of settlement defines policy-making not as a coherent ideological space but as a site of struggle. Parekh (1992), for example, outlines the way in which competing interests came to constitute the Swann Report's version of multiculturalism. The position taken by Swann-era proponents of multi-culturalism and anti-racism was that Britain was now, as a consequence of post-war migration, multiracial and multicultural; this logic carried with it an expectation that schooling should prepare children to live and work in culturally diverse settings. How to put this expectation into practice, in turn, became a site of struggle in itself (see, for instance, Gus John's [2006b] critique of anti-racist initiatives in all-white schools). Those on the radical left, for instance, often drew a severe distinction between what they saw as superficial *multicultural* approaches and the *anti-racist* education that they saw as necessary to tackling structural inequalities. Meanwhile, the political right might deny altogether the proposition that Britain was a multicultural society or that state multiculturalism was a valid option, lobbying instead for schooling that reinforced a sense of a common culture based upon a 'traditional' British way of life. The 'soft' right, on the other hand, might acknowledge Britain's increasing diversity but deny that it had significant implications for the design and practice of schooling (Parekh, 1992).

As Parekh (1992) points out, it is easy for political commentators to see these positions as discrete and firmly opposed camps but in any given institution or committee all of these positions on multiculturalism might weigh influence. Multiply this across every interaction between central and local government, across the bargains struck within each layer of government and it becomes apparent not just why policy relating to race and education was unpredictable at the time, but also why there is continued disagreement over the rationale behind particular approaches to multicultural education. This continual negotiation and compromise also helps explain why the period for which Stuart Hall coined the term 'Thatcherism' has also been invoked as the high watermark of state multiculturalism. Hall's neologism was a gift to social theorists but it has also sometimes obscured the highly evolved local sites of resistance and negotiation that generated much black and anti-racist activism in Britain during the 1980s.

Anti-racist activism

Its black and anti-racist proponents understood multiculturalism and anti-racism in terms of institutional design, governance and management, and curriculum change. Varied and quarrelsome as the multicultural approaches of the 1970s and 80s may have been, what they shared in terms of principles usually included:

- determination to combat racism and discrimination within schools and in wider society;
- disatisfaction with British schools' reproduction of racial inequalities and the schools' role in the poor educational experiences and outcomes of many black pupils;
- the conviction that post-war migration had altered Britain not only demographically but culturally, and that these new cultural realities required an educational response;
- belief in both the intrinsic and extrinsic value of multicultural education, the extrinsic value being the preparation of all pupils for life in a culturally diverse society;
- the need to embed multicultural and anti-racist strategies across all schools, not only those with high numbers of black pupils.

At a minimum, this would certainly entail changes in curriculum and classroom materials, but also shifts in the hidden curriculum, in pedagogy and in institutional arrangements, including teacher training, inspection, management and governance of schools and home–school relations.

For the most politically attuned campaigners of the 1970s and 80s, multiculturalism was not an end in itself but a dimension of wider struggles for social justice. Indeed, a distinction was sometimes made between 'multiculturalism', which defined problems and solutions in terms of difference, and 'anti-racism', which was held to offer a fully structural analysis of power, labour and institutions (Troyna, 1992). Those who defined themselves primarily as anti-racists were often contemptuous of what they saw as facile versions of multiculturalism. The samosas, steel pans and saris approach certainly existed but not all aspects of multiculturalism or multicultural education fit that tag. Moreover, this distinction was probably exaggerated; in the 1980s the key division was not between 'multiculturalists' and 'anti-racists' but between those who defined Britain as a changing, multicultural society whose institutions needed to respond to that fact and those who did not accept at all the premise that Britain was multicultural. By its opponents on the right multicultural education is usually represented as a powerful, monolithic force that would overturn all that was properly British. Conversely, radicals on the left often derided what they saw as facile multiculturalism precisely because they believed it to be entirely lacking the potential to restructure society along more socially just lines. Both of these lines arguably credit multiculturalism with greater cohesion as a 'movement' than was perhaps the case. It is doubtful whether multiculturalism or anti-racism in the 1970s and 80s were movements in that sense, as opposed to many instances of educators and activists challenging racism where they encountered it (Sivanandan, 1989).

Beyond protest

These local instances produced protests organized by parents, pupils and teachers, but protest campaigns were not the only activity. There were myriad home–school liaison initiatives; the development of resources for teacher training and for classroom projects; collaborations around curriculum development; interfaith initiatives; as well as action against far-right groups attempting to recruit around schools. In addition to black-led groupings, such as the Black Parents Movement, the Black Students Movement and the Afro-Caribbean Educational Resource Project, there were multiracial organizations steered by teachers, unions and churches. These included the National Association for Multiracial Education (NAME), Birmingham's All Faiths for One Race (AFFOR), All London Teachers Against Racism and Fascism (ALTARF), the Campaign Against Racism in Education and on-going campaigns sponsored by the National Union of Teachers (NUT).

Within this activity, there was the work of black and white anti-racist educators whose concern with diversifying the curriculum applied to class as much to race, and whose concern was with knowledge and history 'from below' as a means of combatting what they saw as the alienation of the aims of state education from the lives and imaginations of black and working-class children. Among these were many pioneering figures, such as Len Garrison, Stella Dadzie, Ansel Wong, Ann Dummett, Gillian Klein, Ali Rattansi, Cecile Wright, Mike Cole, Bob Carter, Clive Harris, Andrew Pilkington and Chris Searle. White Londoner Searle exemplifies this vein of grassroots anti-racism. Searle had taught in Tobago in the late 1960s amidst the stirrings of Black Power. Returning to England, he unwittingly became a national figure when sacked from his East London school in 1971 for publishing a striking collection of poems by his pupils, *Stepney Words*. The successful campaign to reinstate Searle included an eight-hundred-strong pupil strike and support from ILEA, the NUT and then Education Secretary, Margaret Thatcher. In 1973 Searle published *The Forsaken Lover*, an exploration of literature, colonialism and children's identities, based on his experiences of working with black children, in both the Caribbean and England (Searle, 1973). Searle's work as an educator, journalist and author has tackled intersections between race and class in schooling from theoretical and practitioner perspectives, developing one of the most influential bodies of multicultural and anti-racist work in education.

Writing for the classroom

Some of the most significant and innovative black intellectual work of the 1980s and 1990s came out of the scholarship that emerged among black and anti-racist educators. In the 1980s and 90s writing on black history, literature and art, on pedagogy and educational philosophy flowed into schools, colleges, community libraries and resource centres. This was organic intellectualism in the truest sense. Teachers were able to draw on a growing corpus of classroom resources produced by educational publishers and anti-racist campaigning bodies (White *et al.*, 2005). Among the important writing that made its way into classrooms was work that set out to reclaim hidden histories and to emphasize the longevity of the black presence in Britain. This approach was exemplified by Nigel File and Chris Power's (1981) landmark *Black Settlers in Britain 1555–1958*. File was Head of History at south London's Tulse Hill School, which had pioneered black studies in British schools; Power was Adviser on Multicultural Education for the Borough of Haringey. The book's approach drew on the work of the supplementary schools, ILEA and the scholars who had begun to uncover histories of black Britain. Its combination of photographic material, archive documents and concise biography introduced key figures and events and, in doing so, rethought British history in a style that was accessible to secondary school pupils and parents alike.

Black Settlers in Britain paved the way for other books aimed at schools, such as the Institute of Race Relations' (1982) *Roots of Racism*; Liz Curtis' (1984) *Nothing But the Same Old Story: The Roots of Anti-Irish Racism*; Tony Sewell's (1990) *Garvey's Children*; David Bygott's (1992) *Black and British*; Hakim Adi's (1995) *The History of African and Caribbean Communities in Britain*; and Susan Okokon's (1998) *Black Londoners 1880 to 1990*. Important critical and theoretical books were also published for teachers beginning to work with black literature, such as David Dabydeen and Nana Wilson-Tagoe's (1988) *A Reader's Guide to West Indian and Black British Literature* and Suzanne Scafe's (1989) *Teaching Black Literature*. In addition, publishers Heinemann and Longman revitalized their African and Caribbean Writers series, making widely available the work of a vast range of authors.

Community education networks

Informal learning sites were also integral to the development of multicultural and anti-racist education. As well as the supplementary schools, there were community centre meetings, study circles, arts festivals and black history events. Of tremendous importance, but all too rarely commented upon, was the role of black publishers and bookshops. Chapter 3 recounted the founding by John La Rose of New Beacon Bookshop and publishing house. The years following New Beacon's arrival saw an upsurge in black publishing activity. In 1967 Ghanaian-born Margaret Busby formed Allison and Busby, with partner Clive Allison, publishing work by C. L. R. James, Roy Heath and Rosa Guy. In 1969 Eric and Jessica Huntley formed Bogle L'Ouverture Books, which promoted, in particular, the work of the radical Guyanese historian Walter Rodney, whose *How Europe Underdeveloped Africa* (Rodney, 1972) remains one of the most influential works of the black Atlantic. In 1970 Arif Ali founded Hansib Publications, which produced the *West Indian Digest*, *Asian Digest*, *Caribbean Times* and *African Times*, before moving into book publishing, with the work of black British academics, such as David Dabydeen and Mark Christian.

By the 1980s there was a dynamic network of independent black publishing houses and bookshops. Publishers included Karnak House, Dangaroo-Rutherford

Press, Karia, Trentham, the African-Caribbean Educational Resource Centre, Peepal Tree and Black Ink. In London, alongside New Beacon, were Soma Books and the Africa Book Centre; in Leicester there was Raddle; in Sheffield I and I; in Birmingham Harriet Tubman, Tree of Life and Third World Publications; in Liverpool there was Source Books. Such was the energy of the time that Dangaroo Press was able to publish Prabhu Guptara's (1986) *Black British Literature: An Annotated Bibliography*, which listed hundreds of current titles, many produced by small, independent black publishers.

Adding to the library

Teachers also benefited from well-produced journals aimed at practitioners that combined educational debates on multicultural and anti-racist education, accounts of experiences of teaching and learning, policy critiques, reviews of literature and resources. These included Gillian Klein's *Multicultural Teaching* and Birmingham LEA's *Multicultural Education Review*, as well as frequent publications by the Runnymede Trust, the Inner London Education Authority and Manchester's Development Education Project. In addition, there were black arts journals such as *Wasafiri* and Race Today's *Review*.

In this period several major academic works began to recover strands of black British thought and history. These included Amrit Wilson's (1978) *Finding a Voice: Asian Women in Britain*; Sivanandan's (1982) *A Different Hunger*; Peter Fryer's (1984) *Staying Power*; Buzz Johnson's (1985) biography of Claudia Jones, *I Think of My Mother*; and Ron Ramdin's (1987) *The Making of the Black Working Class in Britain*. The great American scholar Cedric Robinson's (1983) *Black Marxism: The Making of the Black Radical Tradition* was also part-conceived in Britain and included illuminating critical histories of Padmore, C. L. R. James, Claudia Jones and other figures politically active in mid-twentieth-century Britain. These books and authors found their way via teachers, parents, lecturers and librarians into many classrooms and lecture halls. Publishers and bookshops alike arguably reached a zenith in the 1980s, supported in part by local authority and Arts Council funding but also forming independent networks around the International Book Fair of Radical Black and Third World Books, which was initiated by the New Beacon circle. Sarah White, Roxy Harris and Sharmilla Beezmohun (2005) have amassed a magisterial history of the Book Fair and, in doing so, gone some way to uncovering the spread and educational influence of the network of black British publishers and bookshops during the 1980s and 90s.

Arts and education

There is limited space here to explore the considerable overlaps that also existed between the black art scenes and educational initiatives but their importance should be noted. In the late 1960s and early 70s the Caribbean Artists Movement, which included Pearl Connor, Alex Pascall and James Berry, had been among those who had followed the initiatives in community arts and education trailed by Claudia Jones (Walmsley, 1992). In the 1980s and 90s Yvonne Brewster's Talawa Theatre Company, the Black Theatre Co-operative and the Black Audio Film Collective were also active in the field. Educators often worked in tandem with young writers, musicians and film-makers who sought to explore the experiences of young blacks in Britain, including their schooling, relationships with peers and parents, and the antagonism felt on British streets. This work included the poetry of Linton Kwesi Johnson, who was active in the Race Today Collective. Johnson's early work was built in equal parts upon celebration, reportage and critique, depicting the lives of black youth, their family relationships and encounters with authority.

Johnson's themes were paralleled in the militant, Rastafari-influenced British reggae made by Steel Pulse, Aswad, Black Roots and others who had grown up and been schooled in Britain. Elsewhere glimpses of the lived experience of the 'black explosion' were apparent in the literature produced across the 1980s and 90s by Caryl Phillips and Hanif Kureishi. Notable also for depicting the lives of young black Britons was the photographic work of Dennis Morris and Vanley Burke, very young photographers, who documented their peers' worlds: schools, weddings, churches, dances and political rallies in London and Birmingham.

In film the work of Horace Ové and Menelik Shabazz depicted starkly scenes that sociologists of the time sometimes struggled to grasp, including transitions from school to unemployment and parent–child relationships in African-Caribbean homes. Horace Ové's 1975 film *Pressure* is particularly notable for its scenes in which the exasperated and uncomprehending mother of school leaver, Anthony, chastises him for being unemployed despite having gained educational qualifications ('You have an English education so nothing should stop you!'). Later at a community meeting we witness what had by the mid-1970s already become an archetypal figure in black British culture: the black community activist who calls for independent black schools, berating the:

> schools that only prepare us for menial tasks in this society ... try getting a job on the basis of your certificates ... We can't depend on white people for our education anymore. What we need in Ladbroke Grove, brothers and sisters, is to open our own supplementary schools whereby we can give our own children the help they need.

That speech and the frustration of Ové's central characters give a sense of how far poor schooling and subsequent unemployment formed the tapestry of life for black youth in British cities. Meanshile, Menelik Shabazz's (1982) *Blood Ah Goh Run* notably recorded March 1981's Black People's Day of Action organized by New Beacon. The Day of Action saw 20,000 people join together to protest the lack of official response to the death of thirteen young African-Caribbean people, mostly aged between sixteen and eighteen, in a house fire at a birthday party in New Cross, south-east London. The causes and subsequent investigation of the fire remain ill explained to this day (see La Rose, 1984; Howe, 2011). Still barely mentioned in mainstream social histories, Linton Kwesi Johnson has described the day's march, which was joined by many black schoolchildren and students, as 'a watershed moment in our struggle for racial equality and social justice'. For Johnson, the Day of Action for the New Cross Thirteen:

> Gave black people up and down the country a new sense of our power to resist racial oppression and fight for change. It became clear for all to see that second- and third-generation black people … were no longer prepared to endure what our parents had. We were the rebel generation, a politicised generation.
>
> Johnson, L. K. (2012: 34)

It should be noted, however, that Ové and Shabazz's depictions of street confrontations were not the only cinematic images being produced about growing up black in Britain. Gurinder Chadha and Meera Syal's (1993) *Bhaji on the Beach* portrayed young Asian women's experiences of family, sexual relationships and generational tensions. Meanwhile Isaac Julien's (1991) *Young Soul Rebels* explored homophobia, love and the burgeoning musical subcultures of second generation black Britons.

Black critiques of multicultural education

However, black educators, artists and activists should not be absorbed into unequivocal celebration of a new multicultural post-war Britain. As we have seen in Chapter 4, in the 1970s, 80s and 90s black intellectual positions were defined also by their critiques of multicultural education. The most vocal black critics were grouped around Sivanandan's Institute of Race Relations, *Race Today* and New Beacon. These black left critics were particularly concerned with developments in multicultural education. They argued that schools had become the focus for a form of multiculturalism that evaded the wider social antagonisms that produced differential cultural experiences and which body-swerved questions of the role of education in reproducing and maintaining racial inequalities. Recurrent black left critiques included the argument that much of what passed for multicultural education was a retooling of old race relations models that reduced racism and racial inequality to questions of prejudice and ignorance, often by implication the 'prejudice' and 'ignorance' of black pupils' white working-class peers (see Dhondy *et al.*, 1985).

The assumption that racism was simply a form of personal prejudice that could be educated away through intercultural initiatives was a denial of the structural and economic processes that reproduced disadvantage among black communities. Worse still, it could be locked into a depiction of racism solely as a within-school problem, in which white pupils were constant aggressors. This form of 'symbolic, moral and doctrinaire anti-racism' (Macdonald *et al.*, 1989: xxiii) was condemned by the Macdonald Inquiry's (1989) Burnage Report. In September 1986 thirteen-year-old Ahmed Ullah was stabbed to death by a white peer at Burnage High School, south Manchester. The Macdonald Report by Ian Macdonald, Reena

Bhavani, Lily Khan and veteran anti-racist Gus John, into the tragedy was critical of what it saw as the school's lack of a practical anti-racist strategy: one that involved the whole school community in tackling racial violence and bullying among pupils. Instead, the Macdonald Inquiry felt, Burnage had concentrated its efforts on high profile, symbolic gestures towards anti-racist practice. Macdonald was insistent that the report was not an attack on or dismissal of the need for anti-racist strategies in schools:

> [W]e are clearly not saying that racism does not exist ... or that anti-racist policies have no place in schools. Nor do we suggest that because anti-racist policies were applied in a senseless and counter-productive way in that particular school, all anti-racist policies should be abandoned or considered suspect ... We urge care, rigour and caution in the formulating and implementing of such policies because we consider the struggle against racism and racial injustice to be an essential element in the struggle for social justice which we see as the ultimate goal of education.
>
> Macdonald *et al.* (1989: xxiii)

In Britain's national press, however, the Burnage Report was mostly editorialized as if it held anti-racism to be directly responsible for conflicts within the school and for Ahmed Ullah's death. The popular depiction of multiculturalism and anti-racism as doctrinaire and counter-productive, as something that needed to be abandoned, took strong root post-Burnage.

Tackling culture or tackling inequality?

Black critics of multicultural education were sceptical about 'symbolic' anti-racism but like Macdonald *et al.* urged a coherent social justice-based approach to anti-racism in schools. There was, for instance, scepticism among black critics towards superficial curriculum change as a panacea for unequal educational outcomes, as with the introduction of black studies-type courses into schools (Carby, 1982a; John, G., 2006b). They argued that, scaled down to primary and secondary school levels, 'multicultural' curriculum content was often shaped by spurious judgements about what subject matter was 'relevant' to black pupils, fetishizing the 'exotic' surface of African, Caribbean and Asian cultures, in ways divorced from the histories of struggle that had produced those cultures. For Dhondy *et al.* (1985) the products of diverse black cultures were, of course, intrinsically worthy of study but worth more than mere assimilation into the curriculum as a safety valve within a deeply unequal education system:

> If the state, the educational authorities and inspectors of schools are serious about what they say ... teachers will have to examine what working class values and cultures are and begin to feed into the curriculum the primary fact of working class life – the struggle against the ownership ... and distribution of wealth in a capitalist society. If I, as a teacher, want to

represent black culture, black values, histories ... I am determined to start from the fact that young blacks fight the police, they refuse dirty jobs; their forms of culture and gathering always bring them into conflict with the rulers of this society ... antagonism to school and society as it is.

Dhondy *et al.* (1985: 18)

In comparable terms Gus John, speaking in 1985, claimed that early efforts in the 1960s by some schools to incorporate black studies programmes into their curricula foundered as soon as schools realized that black pupils and communities were not content merely to derive 'self-esteem' from admiring the black heroes of the past. When they began to bring their own contemporary experiences of race, class and education to the table, '[t]eachers took fright, charged those school students and the communities that supported them with seeking to politicize schooling and education ... and, before very long, the in-school variety of Black Studies gave way to multicultural education' (John, G., 2006b: 109).

Cultural theorist Hazel Carby criticized forms of multicultural education that had become 'totally absorbed with issues of black ethnicity at the expense of examining institutionalized racism' (Carby, 1982a: 194). These forms of multiculturalism, argued Carby, 'reacted to racism as if it were limited to a struggle over representation – a struggle over images – in an attempt to disguise the social relations of domination and subordination' (Carby, 1982a: 197). At root, Carby claimed, celebrations of cultural diversity barely concealed approaches that still positioned black children as an 'alien group that present problems to "normal" schooling' (Carby, 1982a: 205). Moreover, much of what passed for multicultural education and black studies was constrained by a double bind. On one hand, efforts to capture living, vibrant black and working-class cultures were soon commodified and made routine by multicultural teaching. On the other hand, adding black studies to the list of what the curriculum offered children in inner-city schools did not transform the system of curriculum and credentials in which black, working-class children were disadvantaged. Among black parents, as much as political activists, there were practical concerns about whether multicultural education would become a kind of alternative provision, wherein black pupils would be turned out into the job market with low-level qualifications, instead of the gold standard certificates.

Maureen Stone: radical or conservative?

In the mid-1980s there was another significant critical voice that could be categorized as part of neither the black Marxist left nor the emergent field of black British cultural studies. Maureen Stone's book, *The Education of the Black Child*, first appeared in 1981. A former social worker and school liaison officer, Stone was, by the time of its publication, based in the University of Surrey's Department of Educational Studies. Stone drew upon the theories of social class reproduction advanced by Bernstein, Bourdieu and Brian Simon, plus the relatively new translations of Gramsci. Her book also examined the influence of Garveyism and

Rastafari upon the black supplementary schools. Stone's core argument was that multicultural education remained tied to deficit models of the education of black children: models rooted in the research on self-concept and ethnicity that had been developed in the UK by Milner (1973) and Weinreich (1979) under the influence of US research into the role of low self-esteem in the underachievement of black pupils. For Stone, the problem with multicultural education as it had developed in Britain was that it drew uncritically on self-concept theory, albeit decked out in the language of anti-racism.

Stone depicted mainstream multicultural education as being too often a form of compensatory education; it sought to compensate black children for not being white and middle class by concentrating on building relationships between black children and their (white) teachers, and on building self-esteem by 'teaching' elements of black culture, as filtered through the sensibilities of white liberals. But, Stone asserted, white middle-class teachers were not, and were never likely to be, 'significant others' for most black children. Moreover, black culture, insofar as it was formed in part as a dynamic resistance to schooling and other radicalized structures, could hardly be sold back to black pupils by those same schools (here she concurred with Dhondy and Carby). As such, Stone concluded, multicultural education failed at a political level because it ducked the actual power relations that structured educational inequalities in class-stratified society; it failed at a cultural level because it dismissed the formal pedagogy that black Caribbean parents understood and valued; it failed in pragmatic terms because it had had no proven effect on raising black children's attainment:

> [T]he idea that middle-class schools and teachers can influence the self-concept of the majority of working-class or black pupils could only have arisen in a theoretical vacuum. Those teachers of working-class children who believe they can provide an environment for ... the development of positive self-concept within schools, without reference to the social structure which ultimately determines their pupils' role in society and thus their ultimate life chances, are operating within a philosophical tradition which says that the aims of education should include the free development of personality in a society which is hierarchically structured along fairly rigid class lines and where schools are explicitly or implicitly charged with socializing children (of whatever social or racial background) into the cultural values of the dominant groups.
>
> Stone (1985: 22)

Stone (1985: 35) was in no doubt that 'the social structure [was] operating through schools to reinforce the low status of black pupils' but, for her, multicultural education contributed to that low status, rather than countering it. Instead, she urged, black parents and children had to equip themselves as best they could to play the game of credentialism, even if the cards were often marked.

Stone's depiction of multicultural education perhaps overplayed its hegemonic nature and underplayed its local nuances. She gave little acknowledgement to how the work of multicultural educators like Len Garrison and Grace Nichols located black cultural voices within their social struggles, rather than abstracting them. Instead, in *The Education of the Black Child* Stone presents the 'Saturday schools' (that is, African-Caribbean supplementary schools) as possible models for reorganizing schooling to meet the needs of black pupils. The Saturday schools, according to Stone, were organized around principles of hard work and intellectual effort but could also explore black history and identities in ways that mainstream schools could not because they were the organic, historical products of black communities. They encouraged an instrumentalist commitment among pupils, who appreciated the educational advantages they offered, but because the Saturday schools were democratically run by parents alongside professionals, they demystified schooling and also offered creative approaches that offered children both improved attainment and enjoyment. Thus the Saturday schools could both contribute to raising black achievement in mainstream settings and become spaces in which black parents, teachers and pupils sustained and developed black cultural identities. Stone's book was a curious melding of Gramsci, the black education movements and the exam boards. Nevertheless, her influence persists; vulgarized versions of Stone have become a key element in new black 'conservative' readings of education in the twenty-first century (see Chapter 9 of this book).

Conclusion

Debates over the impacts of state multiculturalism and its beacon, multicultural education, have continued to perplex black British intellectuals and activists, way beyond questions about schools' structures and practices. Rightly or wrongly, the rise of state multiculturalism has often been implicated in the retreat of the independent black politics that fired the black education movements in the first place. At the level of individual schools, some said, multicultural initiatives might be well-meant attempts to draw uninterested pupils back into education. At a broader level, as part of a wider municipal multiculturalism in which projects with designated ethnic value were funded by and competed for local authority budgets, state multiculturalism arguably served to contain and buy off the discontent that had fuelled black community activism in the 1960s and early 70s (Dhondy *et al.*, 1985; Prescod, 1999b; Phillips, M., 2001). A related claim has been that the resourcing of ethnically specific projects in schools and other parts of local authorities dealt a near fatal blow to the political blackness that had emerged in the latter part of the 1960s. Accessing these pots was dependent on grant-worthy projects that emphasized distinct *ethnic* identities and this produced a generation of funding-savvy black community leaders and managers who had motive to shift away from campaigns against institutional racism and social inequalities, towards initiatives around cultural diversity (Sivanandan, 1983; Prescod, 1999b; Phillips, M., 2001).

In truth, attributing the decline of political blackness to local authorities' multicultural policies is probably too large a claim. This is particularly apparent from the perspective of schooling. For by the early 1990s different black communities' educational (and class) interests were pulling apart and there were sometimes valid sociological reasons to avoid umbrella definitions of blackness when considering schooling, higher education, employment, income, faith and language. Differences in black experiences of education did not, of course, suddenly spring into being in the 1980s and 90s but educational trends that have continued to the present became increasingly apparent. Indian and Chinese pupils started to outperform Pakistani and African-Caribbean children, and ethnic 'patterns' were further complicated by intersections with social class and gender (Gillborn and Mirza, 2001; Pilkington, 2003). Issues around language, faith in schools, exclusions and special educational needs impacted differently on different 'black' communities. In short, political blackness fractured from the inside as well as from the outside.

Yet, for all its myriad contradictions, multiculturalism helped shape political blackness, as well as eroding it. Multicultural and anti-racist education have long fallen out of favour as policy buzzwords but their history – vastly different from approaches developed in other parts of western Europe – has continued to inform British approaches of cultural and ethnic diversity. This has been apparent in twenty-first-century policy drives around citizenship (Ajegbo *et al.*, 2007; Osler, 2008; Race, 2011), community cohesion (Ouseley, 2001) and human rights (EHRC, 2009). Moreover, in wider British culture factual multiculturalism – street multiculturalism – is lived day in, day out. To paraphrase Gary Younge, its absence, not its presence, is now unimaginable.

6   Black British cultural studies

Hall's field of influence is less in the establishment channels of the quality press and the portals of government, and more in the lecture theatres and seminar rooms of the redbrick and new universities and, of course, the late night broadcasts of the Open University. Stuart Hall has operated throughout his career very much as a teacher...

McRobbie (2000: 212)

Introduction

One of the effects of the problem–victim depiction of black British life has been the downplaying of links between the various black intellectual spaces. Thus the campaigns around schooling are often thought of as protests but not intellectual movements, while the work of black academics is not always thought of as part of the educational movement. This applies, in particular, to the generation of black cultural theorists who transformed British scholarship from the late 1970s onwards. The intellectual routes taken by theorists such as Stuart Hall and Paul Gilroy were different from those of Sivanandan or John La Rose but their cultural studies work was also created out of post-war black British flux – and their scholarship played its part in transforming understandings of race, youth, schooling and identity.

This chapter explores the emergence of black British scholarship from the late 1970s to the 1990s. It focuses on what is sometimes termed black British cultural studies: the work of Stuart Hall, Paul Gilroy, Hazel Carby and their contemporaries at the University of Birmingham's Centre for Contemporary Cultural Studies (CCCS), the literary theorist and historian David Dabydeen and others who reshaped academic disciplines. These black academics were also public intellectuals. They made it increasingly possible to speak of black *British* cultures, histories and identities, while also problematizing notions of blackness, the idea that there is a single black experience. The 'elite' academics and the 'grassroots' activists shared many concerns but there were also schisms that emerged with the cultural turn taken by Hall. This chapter reflects, in particular, on the extent to which black cultural studies' fascination with the broader categories of 'black youth' and 'cultural identity' signalled a shift away from the positions established in the black

Marxist analyses of schooling and social reproduction. The cultural theorists' innovations are another reminder of the breadth of black British contributions to the field of education.

Stuart Hall and the Centre for Contemporary Cultural Studies

At the outset of this book it was suggested that Britain has disregarded many of its black intellectuals. Stuart Hall is the chief exception. Of all the contemporary figures included here, Hall's status as an internationally recognized intellectual is the most secure. But, if, as suggested in Chapter 2, the richness and cussedness of C. L. R. James' work has produced wildly differing portrayals of his life and ideas, almost the opposite has occurred with Stuart Hall. For as protean as his work has been, it has become the custom to portray Hall as the 'father of British cultural studies', alongside Richard Hoggart and Raymond Williams. This fixity has led to an under-emphasis of the fact that many of the great, early strides in Hall's work came out of conditions and concerns akin to those being confronted by grassroots black activists. These included the limitations of British models of race relations; the policing of black communities (in both the literal and the representational sense); the marginalization of black histories and cultures; the processes of diaspora and the new identities that black settlement in Britain produced.

Stuart Hall arrived in England from Jamaica in 1951 to study at Oxford as a Rhodes Scholar. As Hall has frequently remarked, when he arrived in Britain the first Caribbean community he encountered was that of expatriate students and artists (Hall and Chen, 1996). That community was eclipsed very quickly by the new working-class migrants and families of the late 1950s and early 60s. The rapid change in what being 'West Indian' in Britain signified, in terms of class and permanence, arguably infused Hall's subsequent work with a sense of both the limitations and the potential of academic scholarship in relation to the political struggles of the wider community.

Hall's academic prominence came through his leadership, between 1968 and 1979, of the Centre for Contemporary Cultural Studies (CCCS), the postgraduate research centre at the University of Birmingham that became the institutional home of British cultural studies. Founded in 1964 by Richard Hoggart, CCCS was from its beginning a volatile hybrid. It was of the left but emerged out of the crisis in Marxism that followed the Soviet invasion of Hungary (Hall, 1996a; Hall and Chen, 1996). Its concerns were sociological but also rooted in Hoggart and Hall's backgrounds in literature. Its concept of culture and the forms of culture regarded as fit for study upset academic distinctions between 'elite' and 'popular' culture, and between culture and politics. Under Hall's leadership the CCCS pulsated with multi-directional influences: the Frankfurt School of sociology, Freudian psychoanalysis, Saussure's models of language and linguistics, Althusser's Marxism and Fanon's troubling philosophy of race and identity.

In critical terms what CCCS, under both Hoggart and Hall, sought to do was to counter economistic forms of Marxism. CCCS questioned at every turn conventional Marxist distinctions between the 'cultural' and the 'economic'.

Moreover, Hall, drawing on Edward Said and other post-colonial thinkers, explored the tensions between Eurocentrism and universality in Marxist thought. As an emergent discipline, cultural studies resisted policing but for Hall, what connected its unruly strands was its awareness of:

> [t]he question of the great inadequacies, theoretically and politically, the resounding silences, the great evasions of Marxism – the things that Marx did not talk about or seem to understand which were our privileged object of study: culture, ideology, language, the symbolic … the things which had imprisoned Marxism as a mode of thought, as an activity of critical practice, its orthodoxy, its doctrinal character, its determinism, its reductionism … In my own case, it required a not-yet-completed contestation with the profound Eurocentrism of Marxist theory … the most developed parts of Marxist theory … suggested that capitalism evolved organically from within its own transformations. Whereas I came from a society where the profound integument of capitalist society, economy, and culture had been imposed by conquest and colonization.
>
> Hall (1996a: 265)

Here Hall's words contain traces of generations of wrestling over what Marx's tools offer to those who have approached him via histories of colonialism and slavery. For societies, such as Hall's boyhood Jamaica, that were shaped by empire and slavery, and in which labour and class were profoundly racialized categories, provided the lesson that no dimension of human life is either intrinsically 'cultural' or 'economic'. This was the lesson found in the writing of Caribbean historians such as C. L. R. James, Eric Williams and Walter Rodney and it would find new expression in the questions that Hall asked in Britain about articulations between race and class and what it might mean for the generations schooled in Britain to be black *and* British.

Black British cultural studies

The historian Bill Schwarz (2003b) once queried the reasons for young black British intellectuals' engagement with cultural studies, rather than his own discipline. Hall's definitions of the cultural studies project provide answers (see Morley and Chen, 1996). What cultural studies did was to speak profoundly and historically to young diasporan minds that knew London, Birmingham and Bristol better than they knew Mirpur or Kingston. Under Hall's stewardship, CCCS offered powerful analyses of intersections between race, gender, class and sexuality, and of emergent black British identities.

There is also another plain fact about CCCS' role. It did what British academia has so often failed to do: support and promote the work of black academics who wished to explore race in Britain. Before its closure in 2002 the CCCS provided a platform for, among others, Paul Gilroy, Hazel Carby, Gargi Bhattacharyya, Errol Lawrence, Pratibha Parmar, Anoop Nayak and Kuan-Hsing Chen, as well as white British scholars, Angela McRobbie, Paul Willis and Dick Hebdige. In doing so, it arguably created a new field, what Owusu (2000) has termed 'black British cultural studies'. Owusu (2000) argues that the period coinciding with Hall's stewardship of CCCS witnessed an identifiable rift within British cultural studies and that it is possible to speak of black British cultural studies as distinct from the earlier work of Richard Hoggart, Raymond Williams and E. P. Thompson: work that, for all its strengths, had little to say about race or empire *per se*. Others, though, have seen the idea of black British cultural studies as too weighty a category (Sivanandan, T., 2001). It might be preferable perhaps to view black British cultural studies not as a field *per se*, but more loosely, as a *moment* in which a critical mass of young black intellectuals found voice.

Tracing the genealogy of black British cultural studies is a huge and contentious task. In recent years a number of edited collections have tried to convey the momentum and eclecticism of the work of the CCCS-inspired cultural theorists who emerged between the late 1970s and the 90s (see Morley and Chen, 1996; Gilroy *et al.*, 2000; Owusu, 2000; Procter, 2000). In addition, the influence of CCCS was international, both because of the breadth of its postgraduate intake and because, particularly in the USA, Hall and others suggested pathways through the American culture wars of the 1980s and 90s, wherein feminist, LGBT, African-American, Latino and indigenous scholars battled what they saw as a neo-liberal retreat into monoculturalism. Scholars such as Judith Butler, Michele Wallace and Henry Giroux have credited the influence on their own work of, for instance, Hall and Jefferson's (1993) *Resistance through Rituals*, and Hall and du Gay's (1996) *Questions of Cultural Identity*.

Black academia, black education

As suggested at the start of this chapter, the *educational* impact of the black British voices within cultural studies is often underestimated. In its heyday black British cultural studies did not just produce a new generation of black academics; it also informed the learning, in further and higher education, of generations of students of sociology, politics, literature and media studies. Cultural studies was also fundamental in validating multidisciplinary approaches in higher education and, through its frequent engagement with post-colonialism, in reinvigorating fields such as African studies and Asian studies. There were respected research and teaching centres influenced by CCCS at institutions such as the University of Warwick, Goldsmiths College London and Middlesex University.

In 1979 Hall left Birmingham and continued his teaching and research at the Open University, contributing to a series of study texts that were widely used across further and higher education, including *Formations of Modernity* (Hall and Gieben, 1992), *Modernity and its Futures* (Hall *et al.*, 1992) and *Representation: Cultural Representations and Signifying Practices* (Hall, 1997). These took cultural studies into the lives not just of traditional undergraduates, but access students, distance learners, mature students and others included in the drive to widen participation in higher education.

Black youth studies

Towards the end of his tenure at CCCS Hall collaborated with Chas Critcher, Tony Jefferson, John Clarke and Brian Roberts on *Policing the Crisis: Mugging, the State, and Law and Order* (Hall *et al.*, 1978). Today it is hard to convey (and, for some, uncomfortable to remember) the force of the media panic around 'mugging' in the mid-1970s. Mugging was a neologism favoured by the British press to describe violent street robbery. The term had no special legal status but was taken up by the news media in a way that was explicitly racialized. Mugging became a crime associated in the public mind with young black men. As much as anything Hall has written, this book marked out the distance between conventional British sociology, which in the 1970s still tended to examine race through the prism of race relations, and the Gramscian thought that increasingly informed CCCS' work, wherein the state was understood as a cultural project.

Hall *et al.*'s (1978) concern was with political constructions of mugging as a 'black' crime. The authors examined the ways in which media, politicians and the police made racialized use of mugging to promote a hard-line, crisis approach to law and order, and to justify the resourcing of intensive policing of black communities. The discourse around mugging ensured that both street crime and the law enforcement response were abstracted from their social and political contexts. *Policing the Crisis* initiated a pivotal shift in the coverage of racism and black communities. Firstly, it was followed by a raft of work that focused on the policing of black communities, specifically the fraught and often violent relations between the police and young African-Caribbean men, including Ken Pryce's (1979) *Endless Pressure*, Peter Ratcliffe's (1981) *Racism and Reaction*, CCCS' (1982) *The Empire Strikes Back* (particularly Paul Gilroy's chapter 'Police and Thieves'), Darcus Howe's (1988) *From Bobby to Babylon* (which collected several years' worth of *Race Today*'s reporting on policing, youth and racism) and later Michael Keith's (1993) *Race, Riots and Policing*.

Secondly, it produced a 'new' sociological category, or at least rebranded an old one. Sociologists and cultural theorists became increasingly focused on the status of 'black youth' as the measure of racism in Britain and the country's failure to educate and employ the children of the black explosion. By the early 1980s Cecil Gutzmore was able to write in *Race and Class* about the sociological coverage of black youth and crime as a phenomenon in itself. Gutzmore (1983) traced the construction of black youth as a sociological category, and as a policy object, not only to the then current work of CCCS but to British sociologists' older post-war obsession with youth studies and to the state scrutiny of the 1960s and 70s, wherein the Home Office, the CRC, the Select Committee on Race Relations and Immigration and other reporting bodies had attempted to grasp the implications of migration, settlement and the black presence in schools (see Chapters 3 and 4 of this book). Like Hall *et al.* (1978), Gutzmore (1983: 13) also explored the 'specially nurtured relationship' between media and the police, which, in his view, had reduced the lives of British-born and schooled blacks to a few 'deviant' motifs: parental conflict, unemployment, rootlessness and street crime. This focus diverted attention from the less frequently noted conflicts with schools and police that Asian youth in both London and the northern towns were living out, and inevitably marginalized the experiences of black women. Yet in these depictions there was a residual truth about daily confrontations that became a way of life for many young blacks in major British cities in the 1970s and 80s.

Critiques of black cultural studies

However, Gutzmore, Sivanandan and others from the IRR's circle became increasingly critical of what they saw as the cultural theorists' fascination with black youth. For Sivanandan (1983: 4), 'a certain politics of the black left itself was beginning to romanticize the youth, separating their struggle from those of their elders – and destroying the continuum of the past, the present and the future'. Tellingly, the same year also saw *Race and Class* publish Lee Bridges' (1983) review of CCCS' *The Empire Strikes Back*. Bridges pounced, in particular, on Hazel Carby's chapter 'Schooling in Babylon' (see Chapter 4 this book), arguing that while Carby and her co-authors critiqued multicultural education for treating racism as a struggle over forms of representation – negative and positive images in the classroom – CCCS had succumbed to the same kind of idealism, approaching the daily racism with which young blacks lived 'not as a set of systematic practices aligned with deeper economic and political structures but as an outcome of constantly shifting "articulations" and "conjectures" of racist ideas' (Bridges, 1983: 100). Increasingly the response of *Race and Class* to CCCS-inspired 'cultural' work drew attention to the schism opening up on the black left – as elsewhere in the British left of the 1980s – between those who tended towards conventional Marxism and those who tended now towards cultural theory.

Cultural studies' representations of black youth tended to take as paradigmatic black British working-class African Caribbean men in their teens and twenties, unemployed or excluded from school and in conflict with the police (although CCCS did attempt to counter this gender-blindness). Perhaps the most thorough critique of this prism was voiced by veteran anti-racist Roxy Harris (2000) in his paper 'Openings, absences and omissions: aspects of the treatment of "race", culture and ethnicity in British cultural studies'. For Harris, CCCS and other chroniclers of black British youth prioritized:

> analysis of the highly visible, overtly rebellious, reactive section of black youth, accompanied by an absence of sustained work on the actions and perspectives of the adult black population in shaping black culture in Britain … the main focus has been on black youth in relation to policing, crime, youth style, music, language and schooling … the adult population where it is mentioned, is deprived of any sense of agency and becomes a conservative counterpoint to the radical youth.
>
> Harris (2000: 399)

For Brian Alleyne (2002), too, the focus on black youth contributed to the erasure from historical accounts of the experiences and organizational strategies of black adults, such as the New Beacon and NLWIA circles (of which Roxy Harris was part) that had formed the bedrock of the black education movement. What is apparent is that between the mid-1970s and the 1990s policing and youth, rather than schooling *per se*, became the prism through which 'second generation' experiences tended to be understood in leading-edge academia.

Culture clashes

It sometimes appeared then that during the 1980s black British intellectuals were engaged in two culture wars: one a struggle to establish in British political soil principles of multiculturalism and anti-racism; the other, a struggle over the 'culture' of black British thought and political practice. Moreover, the positions taken around black cultural production were not always predictable, as made apparent in the disagreements between Salman Rushdie, Stuart Hall and Darcus Howe over the Black Audio Film Collective's 1986 film *Handsworth Songs*, in a series of letters printed in the *Guardian* in early 1987.

John Akomfrah's film depicted Handsworth (one of the centres of Birmingham's African-Caribbean and Asian communities) in the aftermath of the previous year's rioting. Rushdie, an icon of high literary culture (and still a couple of years away from becoming the vastly different signifier of multicultural contradictions that he became post-*The Satanic Verses*) sympathized with the film's aims but felt it had failed to give voice to the lived experiences of the people of Handsworth, accusing it of recycling hackneyed media images of black youth 'in the dead language of race industry professionals' (Rushdie *et al.*, 2000: 262). The 'literary' Rushdie's language on this occasion was the language of black activism: 'It isn't easy for black voices to be heard. It isn't easy to get it said that the state attacks us, that the police are militarized. It isn't easy to fight back against media stereotypes' (Rushdie *et al.*, 2000: 263). In contrast, the 'cultural' Hall took issue with what he saw as a misunderstanding on Rushdie's part of the 'new language' for which the film grasped: 'whose originality is precisely that they tell the black experience as an *English* experience' (Rushdie *et al.*, 2000: 264). In response the 'activist' Howe aligned himself with Rushdie, arguing that Rushdie's analysis of the film's flaws paved the way for a much-needed 'critical tradition in the field of black arts and culture ... Without it we are left with nothing but cheer-leaders on the one hand and a string of abuses on the other' (Rushdie *et al.*, 2000: 265).

The lines dividing and linking cultural production, cultural critique and political activism in black Britain in the 1980s and 90s were dynamic and contested. Seen in this context, the exploration of 'black youth' within black British cultural studies was not a fetish but a search for answers to the biggest question prompted by the children of the post-war migrants. In short, what was the impact of the black British presence? What did black Britain amount to beyond being, among antagonists, a 'problem', and, among allies, the site of anti-racist campaigning? How were young black Britons, in the schools and in the streets, defining themselves and their worlds?

Difference and identity

Therefore, one way in which black British cultural studies can be understood is as a critique not just of the old tropes of the sociology of 'race relations' but of the residual understanding of young black people as second and third generation 'immigrants' and a certain kind of reductionism that framed their worlds entirely in the binary of 'racism' and 'anti-racism'. What Hall initiated was a profound reading of black British life in terms of cultural production. For Hall this entailed rejecting notions of black identities as homogenous, stable, continuous and authentic – whether those notions were held by policy-makers, race relations experts, multicultural educators or black thinkers themselves.

In pieces such as 'New ethnicities' (Hall, 1988); 'Ethnicity: identity and difference' (Hall, 1989) and 'Cultural identity and diaspora' (Hall, 1990) Stuart Hall wrestled with blackness and Britishness in the knowledge that the logics of the great collective identities of class, nation and race had faltered. It was not, Hall argued, that it was possible to do *without* identity, as if 'wandering in an endlessly pluralistic void' (Hall, 1989: 22), but that identity had to be recognized as a:

> cover story for making you think you stayed in the same place, though with another bit of your mind you do know you've moved on. What we've learned about the structure of the way in which we identify is not one thing, one moment. We have now to reconceptualise identity as a process of identification, and that is a different matter.
>
> Hall (1989: 22)

In 'Ethnicity: identity and difference' Hall (1989) addressed the processes of identification through his own story of migration to Britain and the story of his British-born son. Here Hall conceptualized identity and difference in ways that draw upon academic schemes but also upon an intimate knowledge of the questions and conversations that sinewed the lives of those black British children who, in more than one sense, 'can't really go home again' (Hall, 1989: 25). Their journeys negotiated identity and difference in two forms: the difference between contingent blocs, such as 'black' and 'white', but also the differences produced across time by identities that were continually in motion:

> There we are, inside the culture, going to their school, speaking their language, playing their music, walking down their streets, looking like we own a part of the turf, looking like we belong. Some third generation Blacks are starting to say, "We are the Black British." After all, who are we? We're not Jamaicans any more. We have a relationship to that past, but we can't be that entirely any more … Debates around questions of identity are at the center of political life in England today.
>
> Hall (1989: 24)

Hall (1996b: 472) forced these questions about 'cultural positionality, a different logic of difference' again in his essay 'What is this "black" in black popular culture?' Referring to the questions of 'second generation' identity that 'Paul Gilroy … so vividly put on the political and cultural agenda of black British politics in the United Kingdom', Hall insisted:

> blacks in the British diaspora must, at this historical moment, refuse the binary black or British … the aim of the struggle must be to replace the "or" with the potentiality or the possibility of an "and". That is the logic of coupling rather than the logic of a binary opposition. You can be black and British, not only because that is a necessary position to take in 1992 but because even those two terms … do not exhaust all our identities. Only some of our identities are sometimes caught in that particular struggle.
>
> Hall (1996b: 472)

This notion of identity, of *identification*, as a dynamic account of social selves was the recurrent theme of black British cultural studies. Black British cultural theorists were acutely conscious that when identity was regarded as in process, in production rather than static, black communities were confirmed as historical agents, actively reimagining black subjectivities, reimagining British social and cultural life.

The Empire Strikes Back: young black British commentators

The protagonists of black British cultural studies were the 'second generation' children of the black explosion. This was apparent in the book that became emblematic of CCCS' post-Hall approach to the study of race and racism: *The Empire Strikes Back: Race and Racism in 70s Britain* (CCCS, 1982). This collection, which took as its theme the symbiosis between authoritarian state racism and popular, common-sense racism, was produced by a group of CCCS' rising stars, black and white: Hazel Carby, Paul Gilroy, Pratibha Parmar, Errol Lawrence, John Solomos, Bob Findlay and Simon Jones.

The book's opening statement was an assertion of the centrality of 'issues raised by the study of "races" and racisms … to the concern of cultural studies' (Gilroy, 1982b: 7) and it reasserted CCCS' oppositional space: impatient with race relations theory, sceptical of Eurocentric Marxism, critical of race-blind feminism and gender-blind anti-racism. Its analyses of the co-constitution of street racism and state repression of black communities was announced by the book's cover, taken at a march by the far-right National Front, which pictured a senior police officer escorting a Union Jack-brandishing 'vanguard'. What, it asked, was the relationship between law enforcement and boot-boy intimidation? What was the relationship between 'wogs out' graffiti, the myth-making of the news media, and social policy?

The authors surveyed education, policing, immigration policy and the labour process but also the perceived failure of anti-racists, the labour movement and white feminist groups to grasp the racialized dynamics of state power, culture and identity in Britain. Its landmarks included Pratibha Parmar's (1982) critique of the marginalization of Asian women's struggles in race relations sociology, in mainstream feminism and also in the representations favoured by black male activists. She warned that accounts of black British experiences risked becoming atrophied if they ignored the gendered character of the processes of migration, settlement and work. Black struggle, Parmar (1982) argued, could not be understood without reference to the role of Asian women workers in industrial action (such as 1976's Grunwick strike) and without reference to the pathologizing of Asian and African-Caribbean parenting or the pervasive portrayals of Asian women as passives.

Prescient too was Errol Lawrence's critique of forms of sociology that remained locked into race relations and ethnic studies paradigms. For Lawrence, these approaches 'failed to question all but the most obvious common-sense racist assumptions' (Lawrence, 1982: 95) and failure to grasp forms of racism that were not accompanied by violence or verbal abuse led sociologists to absorb and recycle too many pathologizing depictions of black communities. One of the things that Lawrence focused upon was the increasing pop-sociological distinction made between Asians and African-Caribbeans: 'the sense that the different communities pose different problems for the state and for "British society"' (Lawrence, 1982: 97). This tended to take the form of a discursive contrast between Asian communities, who it was often claimed had integrated 'better' because of strong bonds of family, faith and cultural continuity and African-Caribbean communities, or more precisely, African-Caribbean youth who, it was said, had emerged from culturally broken societies, had failed to appreciate how 'alien' they were and who had become a 'rootless' burden on education and social policy. The pathologization of black youth, and their conflicts with teachers, employers and police became (despite the book's historical spread and gender analysis) the motif of *The Empire Strikes Back*.

What was significant and powerful about *The Empire Strikes Back* was that, while it took pains to construct its theory out of the work of black Atlantic thinkers, alongside Marx and Gramsci, it was unapologetically British and 'second generation'. Like Sivanandan's (1982) *A Different Hunger*, published in the same year, *The Empire Strikes Back* was historically grounded in black British life. Like the youth it described, it belonged uneasily but it belonged nowhere else.

No black in the Union Jack

Published in 1987, Paul Gilroy's *There Ain't No Black in the Union Jack* (subtitled 'the cultural politics of race and nation') continued the CCCS project of grounding high theories of race and racism in local British materials: the municipal multiculturalism of the Greater London Council (GLC); the anti-racist campaigns of Rock Against Racism; the late 1970s fascination among both black and white youth with Jamaican roots reggae; the controversy created by Bradford head teacher Ray Honeyford's attack on multiculturalism (see Chapter 3 of this book).

Where Gilroy brooked no compromise was in his analysis of race and racism as *central* to the social and political formation. In that sense, *Ain't No Black* reasserted, in black British terms, what bell hooks and Cornel West (1991) were restating in contemporaneous American sociologies of race:

> Racism is not akin to a coat of paint on the external structures of social relations which can be scraped off if the right ideological tools and political elbow grease are conscientiously applied ... Seeing racism in this way, as something peripheral, marginal to the essential patterns of social and political life can, in its worst manifestations, simply endorse the view of blacks as an external problem, an alien presence visited on Britain from the outside.
>
> Gilroy (1987: 11)

This theoretical position should not be severed from the lessons of the black educational struggles described in Chapters 4 and 5 of this book. For Gilroy's critique went beyond the frequently voiced distinction between 'soft' multiculturalism and 'radical' anti-racism. In fact, it was a critique of the blind spots of anti-racist politics as they were then developing in the GLC, in ILEA and the Anti-Nazi League. In *Ain't No Black* Gilroy addressed tensions between forms of 'anti-Nazi' anti-racism that emphasized the need to combat neo-fascism and those which proposed 'an anti-racism of a more diffuse nature focused on state agencies and popular politics' (Gilroy, 1987: 148).

Gilroy's argument was that to equate racism simply with the activities of far-right groups 'inevitably pulls discussion of "race" away from the centre of political culture and relocates it on the margins' (Gilroy, 1987: 148). The forms of anti-racism that viewed racism as aberrant and extreme, the work of cranks and fascists, risked concealing the contours of racism as they marked the wider social and political structure. In short, while Gilroy acknowledged that 'anti-Nazi' activity was often necessary at a tactical level, its firm sense of what it was against was often matched by a silence about what it was for. This returned Gilroy to the black cultural studies project: to questions of what the black British presence was actively producing in terms of culture and identity. This was cultural theory felt viscerally.

Critiquing ethnic absolutism

Importantly, given the terms in which multiculturalism was sometimes being implemented in schools, Gilroy also began to critique essentialist notions of culture that were, he argued, steering multiculturalism and multicultural education back into a racialized cul-de-sac. For Gilroy, as for Hall, increasingly voguish usages in policy and education of terms such as 'ethnicity' and 'culture', which were meant to acknowledge diversity while shifting away from fixed biological notions of race, did not circumvent the old problems of the race concept at all. As a category, ethnicity was becoming as rigid as the old notions of race. Hall (2000) memorably described uncritical concepts of 'race' and 'ethnicity' as merely two different registers of racist discourse.

Since the early 1990s, Gilroy has argued against the dangers of 'ethnic absolutism', which he defined as:

a reductive, essentialist understanding of ethnic and national difference ... separating people off from each other and diverting them into social and historical locations that are understood to be mutually impermeable and incommensurable.

Gilroy (1993b: 65)

Paul Gilroy has continued to map the production, shifts and tensions in black British culture: in his work on black intellectual histories (*The Black Atlantic*, 1993a); in his development of 'post-racial' theories, which have questioned the continuing usefulness of race identities as the basis of liberation politics (*Against Race*, 2000); and in his reflections of post-multicultural living in Britain, and 'conviviality' as a way to live with cultural diversity, a form of street praxis (*After Empire*, 2004). In *After Empire*, in particular, Gilroy returned to the distinction between state multiculturalism and the lived multiculturalism that had emerged dynamically and imperfectly in schools, colleges, workplaces, high streets and dancehalls – not through political gift but through the friction provided by protest, education, art, neighbourliness and trial-and-error pragmatism. The 'cultural turn' as understood by Hall and Gilroy was not, therefore, a turning to culture as a refuge from political struggle but the turning of a critical gaze on to black culture as it emerged out of political struggle.

The cultural turn in education research

In the 1980s and 1990s the post-CCCS field pulled away from viewing schooling as the frontline of race in Britain. However, cultural studies was still influential on an important strand of educational research that emerged during that period. This included cultural sociologies of race and education such as Máirtín Mac an Ghaill's (1988) *Young, Gifted and Black*, Heidi Safia Mirza's (1992) *Young, Female and Black* and Tony Sewell's (1997) *Black Masculinities and Schooling*. While these texts were based upon classroom ethnographies, their concern was not primarily with pedagogy, rates of achievement or the impacts of education policy. Instead their explorations of black pupils' educational experiences treated schooling as a site of cultural struggle. Their analyses of power, institutional regulation and the intersections between race, gender and class drew upon CCCS, upon Foucault and upon bell hooks. They were influenced, in particular, by the subcultural resistance analyses developed by CCCS alumni Paul Willis and Dick Hebdige (Willis, 1978; Hebdige, 1979).

Mac an Ghaill (1988), for instance, focused on how different expressions of pupil resistance were produced across divisions of ethnicity and gender, with different levels of visibility and accommodation. Thus the 'Black Sisters' (both Caribbean and Asian), well understood the racialized, classed and gendered divisions present in education, and saw little intrinsic value in the schooling they were offered but used the education system instrumentally, to gain qualifications. There were similarities here with Mirza's (1992) critical ethnographies of African-Caribbean girls, which also focused on their educational instrumentalism. Among Mirza's African-

Caribbean girls, education was valued as a means to gain qualifications and, thereby, labour market standing. Their cynicism about aspects of schooling was balanced by a faith in meritocracy (albeit meritocracy qualified by racism and sexism). Mac an Ghaill's Asian 'Warriors', meanwhile, negotiated teachers' stereotypes of conformist, passive Asian students by developing anti-school practices that remained largely invisible to the school authorities, whose scrutiny was perched on the more overt resistance of African-Caribbean boys (Mac an Ghaill, 1988).

Tony Sewell's (1997) study focused on African-Caribbean masculinities as they were negotiated in school settings. The African-Caribbean boys' behaviour was constantly reified: caught between, on the one hand, myths of cool and physical/sexual prowess and, on the other hand, myths about black male aggression and resistance – what David Gillborn (1990) had termed the myth of an African-Caribbean challenge. In Sewell's analysis, black boys and their teachers were both implicated in the production of a power-deprived/power-hungry black masculinity that undermined the boys' educational outcomes. For both Sewell and Mac an Ghaill, black male pupils and their white teachers and schools tended to lock into a cycle in which black pupils' experiences of school racism, particularly disproportionate punishment and marginalization in the classroom, encouraged forms of resistance that, in turn, led to further punishment and marginalization, leading to greater resistance (see also Pilkington, 1999, on this 'vicious cycle'). Much of the context of Sewell's analysis lay in African-Caribbean communities' anger at the disproportionate rates of school exclusions among African-Caribbean communities, exclusions that, as Sewell's own case study suggested, bore no relation to the achievement or commitment to education shown by African-Caribbean boys. The issue of school exclusions has, for African-Caribbean communities, remained a persistent point of protest (Blair, 2001; Christian, 2005; Wright *et al.*, 2005; Weekes-Bernard, 2010; Gosai, 2011).

With regard to changing the *practices* of schooling, Sewell (1997) argued the need to question normative whiteness and to rethink superficial school policies around diversity that tended to relegate black (that is, African-Caribbean) experiences and culture to 'special' celebrations. Sewell argued instead for the everyday incorporation of black history and art into the curriculum, drawing upon models provided by supplementary schools. Other aspects of Sewell's proposed toolkit focused on conflict resolution, peer mediation, and encouraging what he termed ego-recovery among black pupils. He spoke of the latter in terms of the abandonment of rigid black nationalist identities, the refusal of a mind–body split and engagement in critical learning. Importantly, Sewell recognized the dangers of anti-racist approaches that located racism in education entirely with the behaviour of black pupils' white peers. Sewell stressed that both black and white boys should be encouraged to rework their racialized and *gendered* identities.

Black masculinities and subcultural analysis

Yet questions remained about how far Sewell's efforts returned to the self-concept theories that Stone (1985) had critiqued ('Black ego recovery must be about healing the body and mind wounded/divided by slavery, colonialism and cultural racism', Sewell, 1997: 210). In addition, for Mirza, 'Sewell's dependency on phallo-centrism and subcultural analysis limit[ed] his ability to move the theoretical debate on black masculinities forward' (Mirza, H. S., 1999: 145). Sewell had, she argued, fallen foul of the dominant tendencies of subcultural theory in education research, becoming entranced by the most visible aspects of rebellion at the expense of understanding the diversity of raced, classed and gendered identities.

Moreover, claimed Mirza, Sewell had ultimately objectified black masculinities by scrutinizing them, while leaving the question of white masculinities mostly untouched. Mirza (1999) saw in Sewell's ethnography a persistent strain of deficit analysis. Across the course of the book there was an under-estimation of structural inequalities and an inflation of the power wielded by black boys within the school system, so that while Sewell credibly described some hyper-masculine traits, he exaggerated the boys' role in their own educational failure.

The art of being black

Mirza's (1999) claim that Sewell had reduced African-Caribbean boys to objects of a racialized social scientific gaze was a significant one because what the black British cultural theorists prioritized was the understanding of black people in Britain not as objects but as social *agents* who were producing new ways of being black and British. One of the cultural ethnographies that built upon Hall and Gilroy with real originality was Claire Alexander's (1996) *The Art of Being Black: The Creation of Black British Youth Identities*. Alexander focused precisely on the *art*, the *creativity* and the sense of *becoming* that was at the heart of second (and third) generation life. This approach was both a response to Hall and Gilroy and also a dashing away of the residue of early British sociologies of race, which held that while Asians had culture, African-Caribbeans, the progeny of slavery and forced diaspora, had been left only with colour. Alexander (1996) wrote:

> I am concerned not with generalized external pronouncements about the 'problems' or 'crises' of black identity, but with its form and content as it is lived in everyday experience. I thus move away from a predominantly macro-structural approach, in which black youth constitutes a social category considered only in its relation to institutions ... far from constituting a culture of despair and nihilism, I hope to show that black youths are concerned with the construction of new cultural alternatives, in which identity is created and re-created as part of an ongoing and dynamic process.
>
> Alexander (1996: 17–18)

Interest in the identities and cultural production of the second (and third) generations infused even those sociologies of education that took a more traditionally ethnographic line, and which were concerned with education policy and the inequalities it produced in terms of examinations, exclusions and transitions to employment. These included AFFOR's (1982) *Talking Chalk*, Gibson and Barrow's (1986) *The Unequal Struggle*, and also the work on race, identity, youth and education being developed by educators such as Ann Phoenix, Lola Young, Barry Troyna and Maud Blair. However, Alexander's (1996) reference to moving away from considering black youth only in relation to institutions provides an indication that while there was not a rigid separation between black cultural theorists and educators, a gap had emerged. In contrast to Alexander, Modgil *et al.*'s (1986) *Multicultural Education: The Interminable Debate*; Singh's (1988) *Language, Race and Education*; Pumfrey and Verma's (1990) *Race Relations and Urban Education*; and Bourne *et al.*'s (1994) *Outcast England: How Schools Exclude Black Children* placed their focus on the impact of policy, on systemic inequalities and on the political economy of education. In addition, there was work, such as Saakana and Pearse's (1986) *Towards the Decolonization of the British Educational System*, Jones' (1986) *We Are Our Own Educators!* and Yekwai's (1988) *British Racism, Miseducation and the Afrikan Child* that explored black (that is, African-Caribbean) culture and education within a very different concept of culture. Their aim remained the affirmation of a cultural nationalist narrative as the basis for future black educational programmes.

David Dabydeen: black cultural histories

However, Hall, Gilroy and the cultural theorists inspired by CCCS were not the only significant black British academic forces of the 1980s and 1990s. Another strain of black scholarship emerged that focused on black British cultural histories, on the black presence in literature and art, and on hidden 'histories from below'. It drew on the approaches of C. L. R. James, E. P. Thompson and Richard Hoggart, on the contemporaneous work emerging in the USA on early black writing and pan-Africanist movements, but also on emergent post-colonial theory and, importantly, on the legacies of the groupings of Caribbean, Asian and African artists and cultural historians that had maintained a vigorous presence in Britain since the end of the Second World War.

Among the field's pioneers was David Dabydeen, Guyanese-born historian, novelist and poet. Dabydeen's progress was as picaresque as the eighteenth-century novels that inspired his fascination with literature. Migrating to London as a teenager, Dabydeen briefly ended up in care and attended a south London comprehensive school before going up to read English at Cambridge. Dropping out of academia after a PhD on Hogarth, Dabydeen worked in community education in Wolverhampton, West Midlands. Wolverhampton had been Enoch Powell's parliamentary constituency and Dabydeen, who arrived in Britain at the height of Powell's influence, claims to have been drawn to the city by a sense of idealistic challenge (Arnott, 2008).

Dabydeen entered academia in 1984, via the Centre for Caribbean Studies at the University of Warwick (and later Warwick's Centre for British Comparative Cultural Studies). By his own admission, when first employed to lecture in Caribbean literature, he knew relatively little Caribbean literature. It is perhaps the combined experience of rapidly devouring Caribbean writers, a background in canonical English literature and art, and an education that spanned Guyana's colonial system, English comprehensive schooling and Cambridge that shaped Dabydeen's contributions to black British scholarship. Dabydeen's critical and historical works include *The Black Presence in English Literature* (as editor, 1985a), *Hogarth's Blacks: Images of Blacks in Eighteenth-century English Art* (1985b) and *The Oxford Companion to Black British History* (co-edited with John Gilmore and Cecily Jones, 2007).

Importantly, Dabydeen's audience has not been restricted to academia. Co-authored with Nana Wilson-Tagoe, *A Reader's Guide to West Indian and Black British Literature* (1988) explored in highly accessible fashion post-colonial themes in Caribbean literature, histories of black British writing and representations of race in English literature. Dabydeen's (1988) *Handbook for Teaching Caribbean Literature* was aimed at teachers working at upper secondary level. However, Dabydeen was not a lone pioneer in bringing black voices into both academia and schools. As indicated in Chapter 5, his work joined that of Suzanne Scafe, Chris Searle, John Agard and Benjamin Zephaniah on the library shelves of schools and colleges. In the sphere of higher education Dabydeen's rediscovery of hidden black British histories sits alongside the work of Bill Schwarz, Robert Beckford, Jagdish Gundara and Ian Duffield.

Conclusion

This chapter underlines the fact that black British movements in education have not been restricted to schooling or to specific campaigns against educational inequalities. The work of scholars such as Hall, Gilroy, Dabydeen and others has, over the past four decades, helped reshape the very nature of academic disciplines, pedagogy and methodological inquiry. If British higher education has never become a home to black studies, in the sense that it would be understood in the USA, the wave of black British cultural theorists that emerged in the 1980s and 90s did work on race, culture and identity that has exerted influence beyond academia and beyond Britain. Their cultural analyses of race and education opened up spaces in which to address contemporary practices of race and young people's negotiations of multiple identities. It is, however, essential to understand that the work of Hall, Gilroy and other cultural theorists did not develop in isolation from the contests and crises explored in Chapters 3, 4 and 5. It is not just that black British cultural studies has *influenced* educators; the cultural work itself emerged out of the black explosion and the questions of identity, nation and multiculturalism prompted by black settlement. Chapter 7 looks at another body of black intellectual work that has been central both to the coalescing of black British intellectual activism and to its decentring: black British feminism.

7 Black feminism and education

It is only in the writings by black feminists that we can find attempts to theorize the interconnection of class, gender and race as it occurs in our lives and it has only been in the autonomous organizations of black women that we have been able to express and act upon the experiences consequent upon those determinants.

Carby (1982b: 213)

Introduction

Black women intellectuals have figured in the British landscape since the abolitionist movement – which is to say from the very beginning of black intellectual life in Britain. The development of black British thought, particularly in relation to education, cannot be adequately grasped without understanding the contributions of black feminism. This bears restating because so many of the categories through which black British narratives have been recounted have been implicitly male. Slavery, colonialism and migration have often been inscribed as male experiences. The field of black education, too, has routinely been mapped in masculine terms. Indeed, the fact that education is not always regarded as a sufficiently masculine site may account for its under-representation in some of the standard accounts of black British history (see Fryer, 1984; Ramdin, 1987). Moreover, insofar as education *has* been addressed as a site of black agency, accounts invoke histories of school exclusions, rebel boys and crises in black masculinity.

In addition, black British women intellectuals have not only had to fight for visibility amidst their male counterparts; they have routinely been passed over in media and academic circles in favour of the black American feminist canon. There is no doubt that the influence of African-American feminists has been powerful. However, as Lola Young notes, while 'black British women have found a rich source of intellectual sustenance and networks for support and debate in African-American feminist scholarship' (Young, 2000: 48), they have also had to consider carefully 'the extent to which black American feminism is applicable in a British context' (Young, 2000: 48). Reasons for this include the greater institutionalization of social class in Britain and the histories of Empire and migration. Young (2000: 49) concludes rightly that 'there needs to be much more by way of encouragement, awareness and validation of the work, experiences and opinions of black women in Britain'.

Black women, black feminism

This chapter examines the role of black British women thinkers in the development of political blackness and the central place given to education in their work. 'Black feminism' is employed in this instance as a broad, provisional category. Collins, P. H. (1990) and Young (2000) have both written extensively about the problems of labelling all black women intellectuals as feminists. This chapter does not reiterate those arguments but it acknowledges that, while much of the work discussed in this chapter can justifiably be described as black feminist work, debates persist among black women intellectuals over feminism as a political identity (Bryan *et al.*, 1985b; Brah and Phoenix, 2004). Nor does this chapter suggest that black women intellectuals have been preoccupied with gender as a discrete category; indeed, the insistence among black feminists on understanding race, class and gender as *co-constituted* has profoundly shaped black British intellectual concerns.

Mirza (1997) and Young (2000) have both given comprehensive coverage to movements in black British feminism. In contrast, what this chapter does is contextualize three particular facets of black feminist work around education. Firstly, it focuses on the ways in which black feminists have challenged sociological inattention to black women's particular experiences of education, state, work and family. This includes discussion of black feminists' critiques of the pathologization of black families and their scepticism towards the kind of subcultural theory that remains fascinated with romantic effigies of black boys. Secondly, it considers the importance black women thinkers have placed upon *historicity*: the need to understand genealogies of black feminism and shifts in conceptions of gender, race and identity over time. Thirdly, it looks at ways in which black feminists have contested colour-blind feminism and gender-blind forms of anti-racism, refusing 'parallel' understandings of race and gender as separate political spaces and instead developing analyses of education based on what is nowadays often termed 'intersectionality'.

Black feminist writing on education

So how have black British feminists re-conceptualized articulations between gender, race and education? From the late 1970s onwards a wave of literature emerged from black feminist activists and academics who had grown up in Britain and had been influenced by grassroots community campaigns. Much of the initial literature that addressed education did so within broader sociological examinations of first and second generation women's experiences in Britain from the 1950s onwards. Education was addressed within writing on black families, relationships between black women and the state, black political organization and the labour market.

Landmark texts included Amrit Wilson's (1978) *Finding a Voice: Asian Women in Britain*; Margaret Prescod-Roberts and Norma Steele's (1980) *Black Women:*

Bringing It All Back Home; and Valerie Amos and Pratibha Parmar's (1981) chapter 'Resistances and responses: the experiences of black girls in Britain'. CCCS' (1982) *The Empire Strikes Back* included chapters by Hazel Carby and Pratibha Parmar. A few years later these were followed by Beverley Bryan, Stella Dadzie and Suzanne Scafe's (1985b) *The Heart of the Race: Black Women's Lives in Britain*; Ann Phoenix's (1987) chapter 'Theories of gender and black families'; Audrey Osler's (1989) *Speaking Out: Black Girls in Britain*; Nira Yuval-Davis and Floya Anthis' (1989) *Woman-Nation-State*; and Gita Sahgal and Nira Yuval-Davis' (1992) *Refusing Holy Orders*.

Their approaches varied from oral history (Osler) to advocacy (Wilson) to critical ethnography (Prescod-Roberts and Steele) and social psychology (Phoenix). Some, such as Osler and Carby, cleaved to British political blackness; others focused specifically on either Asian or African-Caribbean experiences. The flow of work produced by black women intellectuals in the 1980s and 90s on youth and education often took a cultural turn, insofar as it was concerned with the absence of self-defined representations of black women in sociology and social policy. Particularly notable was writing on gendered experiences of schooling and adolescence (Amos and Parmar, 1981; Osler, 1989). These black feminist critiques of education recovered the hidden stories of black girls, mothers and families, mature female students, supplementary schooling and black women educators.

Black feminist histories: thrown away women

The marginalization of black women intellectuals in accounts of British history was not accidental but the consequence of history written 'from above', in terms that maintained patriarchal narratives and denied the independent experiences and consciousness of women, working-class Britons and imperial subjects. One response by black feminists was to reclaim neglected histories of black women's thought and activism. Recovering early black female voices has been a key project within black British, as well as American, feminist scholarship. African-American academic Patricia Hill Collins refers to the 'painstaking process of collecting the ideas and actions of "thrown away" Black women' (Collins, P. H., 1990: 5). Invoking the lives and work of 'thrown away' women has had a central intellectual significance among black British feminists, too.

One purpose of this historical work has been to emphasize that, even though their influence has often been neglected, black women thinkers are not a belated presence in black British intellectual history. In the British context 'thrown away' women include abolitionists and authors of slave narratives, such as Mary Prince and Phillis Wheatley; activists in the pre-Second World War pan-African and anti-colonial movements, such as Amy Ashwood Garvey and Una Marson; and those who helped cement post-war black British settlement, among them Claudia Jones and Olive Morris. As Chapter 2 has shown, Marson and Jones, in particular, were pioneers of mid-twentieth-century black British activism. Both sought to carve out political intersections between feminism, pan-Africanism, cultural politics and, in Jones' case, Marxism. Both were concerned with youth and education in the broadest sense. In the 1930s and 40s Marson and the League of Coloured Peoples worked with black children, organizing welfare and social events (Jarrett-Macauley, 1998) and Jones' promotion of London's Notting Hill Carnival grew out of her work with local black youth (Sherwood *et al.*, 1999).

Black feminism and political blackness

However, within half a decade of Claudia Jones' death in 1964, black British politics had been transformed by changing demographics, the influence of Black Power and bitter struggles around schooling, policing and immigration policy (see Chapters 3 and 4). In the late 1960s and 70s black women's organizations – and again it must be stressed that 'black' here refers to political blackness – were an integral but frequently underestimated part of the hothouse of black politics (Bryan *et al.*, 1985b). The post-Black Power upsurge included the Black Women's Liberation Movement; Southall Black Sisters, whose members included Pragna Patel and Gita Sahgal; and the Black Women's Group, co-founded by young Brixton activist Olive Morris, who also worked with Manchester's Black Women's Co-operative. Their emphasis on the commonalities between African-Caribbean, African and Asian women's experiences shaped British political blackness and arguably maintained the ties of political blackness, even as that unifying concept began to decline elsewhere (Sivanandan, 1983).

The commitment to political blackness was exemplified in the work of the Organisation of Women of Asian and African Descent (OWAAD). Initially formed as an African and African-Caribbean grouping, by summer 1978, OWAAD had adopted the broader political definition of blackness:

> Despite differences in our histories and our culture, the racism in this society affects the Black community as a whole. Afro-Caribbean as well as Asian women are victims of deportations ... Asian youths as well as Afro-Caribbean youths are harassed and victimised by the police ... there's the racism of the Health Service ... when dealing with reproduction, fertility and family planning. We're fighting the issue of racism and sexism in British institutions – we're all victims of that oppression, even though we may experience it in different ways.
>
> Bryan *et al.* (1985b: 171)

OWAAD offered a critique of institutional discrimination that foregrounded gendered experiences of racism. Its campaigns against, for example, virginity-testing of Asian women migrants and the NHS's neglect of sickle-cell anaemia, drew attention to dimensions of black British experience that had received scant attention in male-dominated activist circles (Bryan *et al.*, 1985b; Ramdin, 1987). Like the Race Today Collective and the British Black Panthers, OWAAD's influence persisted long after its demise in 1983 through the subsequent activism of former OWAAD members, such as educators Stella Dadzie and Beverley Bryan.

Gender, race and class: triple oppression

In order to appreciate the departures made by OWAAD and other black British feminists, it is important to consider some of the ontological shifts made by black feminists in relation to gender, race and class. In Britain, as in the USA, a key claim among black feminists was that their experiences of cross-cutting oppressions offered a unique initial standpoint from which to renew social justice movements (Smith, 1983; Collins, P. H., 1990; Wallace, 1990; Young, 2000). This involved rethinking concepts of patriarchy, family and reproduction, but it also necessitated rethinking Black Power's definitions of conflict and resistance. The next sections of this chapter outline some of the ways in which black feminists addressed the 'triple oppression' of gender, race and class. These are exemplified by two of the most influential black British feminist statements, both of which made schooling a key focus: Hazel Carby's chapters in the CCCS' (1982) *The Empire Strikes Back* and Beverley Bryan, Stella Dadzie and Suzanne Scafe's (1985b) *Heart of the Race: Black Women's Lives in Britain*, a book that emerged out of the work of OWAAD.

In the post-Black Power period the concept of 'triple oppression' was used to signify that understandings of black women's lived experiences had, at minimum, to take account of gender, race and class as co-constituted. As such, the notion of triple oppressions was a counter to both the gender-blindness that had afflicted Black Power politics and colour-blindness of 'white' feminism. For bell hooks Black Power's confrontationalism too often atrophied into an 'obsession with viewing racism as being solely about a masculinist phallocentric struggle for power between black men and white men' (hooks, 1994: 161). African-American feminist Barbara Smith (1983: xxvi) regretted that too often: 'Black men didn't say anything about how poverty, unequal pay, no childcare, violence of every kind … translated into "liberation".'

Blind spots were evident also in relationships between black feminists and the wider, whiter feminist movement. Black feminists such as Carby (1982b) and Smith (1983) argued that feminism's colour-blindness was produced by the failure of white feminists to interrogate the historically and culturally specific nature of concepts such as patriarchy, and denial of the racial and class biases of the feminist movement's political priorities (see also Brah, 1996). Barbara Smith reflected, in terms that have resonated among black British women intellectuals, that:

> [h]eading families, working outside the home, not building lives or expectations dependent on males, seldom being sheltered or pampered as women, Black women have known that their lives in some ways incorporated goals that white middle-class women were striving for, but race and class privilege, of course, reshaped the meaning of those goals profoundly.
>
> Smith (1983: xxvii)

For British thinkers, too, black feminism required interrogating colour-blind notions of childhood, family and education. Ann Phoenix explored how, as black children learn or acquire gender and race, they come to understand that, in a racialized society:

> black women and black men are in a qualitatively different position from white women and white men ... black people and white people occupy different structural positions ... They learn that their parents, and hence they, are excluded from positions of power within society. From this they learn that gender differences between black males and black females are qualitatively different from white female–male differences. Hence black children learn about racism as well as gender differentiation.
>
> Phoenix (1987: 63–4)

Writing in the 1980s Phoenix argued that in 'ignoring issues of race and class, current theories ... actually address the development of gender in the white middle-classes. This means that black children (and white working-class children) are rendered invisible in the processes of normal gender development, but visible in pathological categories like "father-absent" households' (Phoenix, 1987: 65). Unsurprisingly then, black British feminist work has focused repeatedly on the pathologization of black families within the education system (Bryan *et al.*, 1985b; Rhamie, 2007) and on the stereotyping of black girls, which is itself ethnically differentiated (see Osler, 1989; Archer and Francis, 2007).

Against parallelism

In struggling against political marginalization, black British feminists have been vigilant against gender, race and class being interpreted as parallel oppressions, emphasizing instead that these forms of oppression intersect and co-constitute one another. The first implication of this approach is that black women's lived experiences cannot be partitioned out: the struggle against racism here, the struggle against sexism there, the struggle against homophobia somewhere else again. In *The Empire Strikes Back* (CCCS, 1982) Hazel Carby's 'White woman listen! Black feminism and the boundaries of sisterhood' urged that black women's political self-definitions must resist 'parallelism':

> Much contemporary debate has posed the question of the relation between race and gender, in terms which attempt to parallel race and gender divisions ... The experience of black women does not enter the parameters of parallelism. The fact that black women are subject to the simultaneous oppression of patriarchy, class and 'race' is the prime reason for not employing parallels that render their position and experience not only marginal but also invisible.
>
> Carby (1982b: 213)

Carby's was among a body of work that debated black feminism in the British context from the late 1970s onwards, and which characterized the black intellectual work of the period as much as debates over multiculturalism did. Carby stressed that colour-blindness could not be countered merely by giving greater visibility to black women; there was also a need to challenge some of the 'central categories and assumptions of recent mainstream feminist thought' (Carby, 1982b: 213). Carby's (1982b) analysis was based upon the emergent black Atlantic feminism of the post-Black Power period and upon critiques of Eurocentric and masculinist forms of Marxism, but also on the specifics of education, family and work in post-Windrush Britain.

Patriarchy, family and reproduction

Hazel Carby's analyses of patriarchy, family and reproduction would become pivotal to subsequent writing on black women's experiences of education. Firstly, Carby argued that for black women the family was a source of gendered oppression but also 'a site of political and cultural resistance to racism' (Carby, 1982b: 214), insofar as it generated social networks and some respite from the norms of whiteness. Mainstream feminism, Carby argued, overlooked black women's experiences of family and had done little to counter the pathologization of black family structures that informed British social policy.

Secondly, Carby problematized the concept of patriarchy, arguing that mainstream feminism's definition of patriarchy was historically inadequate. In feminist circles this was a contentious position, one strongly influenced by African-American feminists and by Fanon's theorization of colonialism and domination. In this vein Carby argued that slavery and colonialism had racialized patriarchy, producing different and uneven forms of gender domination between white men and black women, as well as between black men and women. Thirdly, Carby turned her critique to Marxist-feminist concepts of labour reproduction. The role of women in post-war recruitment of Commonwealth labour, Carby noted, was unexplored in British feminism, and the particular gender patterns of migrant labour had rarely been taken into account in white feminists' analyses of education, family and work structures (Carby, 1982b).

Heart of the race

Like Hall and Gilroy, Hazel Carby was based at the Centre for Contemporary Cultural Studies and thus at the centre of black British academia in the 1980s and 1990s. Other black feminists drew more directly upon their experiences of grassroots community politics. Published in 1985, *The Heart of the Race: Black Women's Lives in Britain* by Beverley Bryan, Stella Dadzie and Suzanne Scafe was published by British feminist imprint, Virago. *The Heart of the Race* was a landmark in that it provided a historically grounded account of black British women's experiences in the site of empire, migration, education, health, state welfare and autonomous political organization. The authors' politics were strongly shaped by their involvement in OWAAD, a body Bryan *et al.* (1985b: 164) described as 'one of the most decisive influences on Black women's politics in this country' (although it should be noted that, writing after OWAAD's demise, Bryan, Dadzie and Scafe chose to restrict their book to the struggles of African-Caribbean women in Britain, rather than black women defined more broadly).

Bryan *et al.* (1985b) offered a detailed account of OWAAD's efforts to draw together a national network of black women's groups and of the ideological debates that circulated within OWAAD over whether feminism was to be kept at a distance or reclaimed but in terms that spoke to the race–class locations of OWAAD's members. The authors debated whether, for instance, it was valid to hold to the position that 'if you're a Black woman, you've got to begin with racism' (Bryan *et al.*, 1985b: 174). However, the argument for race-first/gender-second was queried by other black feminists, with Young (2000) being particularly sceptical of the bias evident in *The Heart of the Race*. Certainly, Bryan *et al.*'s (1985b) coverage of schooling appeared to prioritize racism as the determinant of black women's educational experiences:

> For black schoolgirls sexism has, it is true, played an insidious role in our lives. It has influenced our already limited career choices and has scarred our already tarnished self-image. But it is *racism* which has determined the schools that we can attend and the quality of the education we receive in them.
>
> Bryan *et al.* (1985b: 58)

In many ways *The Heart of the Race* also forms a historical bridge between the black conflict theorists of the 1970s, who highlighted the correspondence between working-class schools and a racialized and classed labour market, and the position that Critical Race Theorists, such as Gillborn (2008), took in the twenty-first century, in portraying what they regarded as the conspiratorial nature of a racialized school system. For Bryan *et al.* (1985b) the under-achievement of black Caribbean children was not accidental:

> [E]ducation has been a crucial issue for the Black community, for it has highlighted the true nature of our relationship with the State. The education system's success can be measured directly in terms of Black children's failure within it. By institutionalising the prejudices and the undermining assumptions we face in our everyday lives, the schools have kept our children at the very bottom of the ladder of employability and laid the blame on us. The schools' ability to churn out cheap, unskilled factory fodder ... may have served the economic needs of this society; but it has not met the aspirations of a community which has always equated education with liberation from poverty.
>
> Bryan *et al.* (1985b: 58–9)

Bryan *et al.* (1985b) recounted, in terms redolent of Bernard Coard, the traumatic impact of migration and separation on the first wave of African-Caribbean children entering British schools in the 1950s and 60s. They examined the disparity between the educational aspirations of the Windrush generation and the actuality of Britain's urban working-class schools and recalled the black education movements' campaigns over ESN placements and busing. However, Bryan *et al.* (1985b) brought to the fore analyses largely unexamined by Coard or Dhondy. These centred, firstly, on correcting representations of black families that underpinned the cultural deficit accounts of black pupils' school performance and, secondly, on drawing attention to the political maturity of the new breed of British-born black schoolgirls, including those who, influenced by Black Power politics, had agitated for curriculum change and against low expectations and tokenistic multicultural education.

Black mothers and families

In fact, *The Heart of the Race* returned repeatedly to the ways in which schools' misrecognition of family and gender in black communities disadvantaged black girls in the education system. There was salient discussion of the 'bewilderment, anger or bitterness' (Bryan *et al.*, 1985b: 77) experienced by black Caribbean mothers in fraught home–school relationships. It was, after all, mothers who dealt with much of the fall-out of their children's suspensions from school or placement in 'sin bin' units for disruptive pupils or the disappointment of exiting school into unemployment. What Bryan *et al.* (1985b) emphasized was a paradox also noted in Amrit Wilson's seminal *Finding a Voice: Asian Women in Britain* (1978), which was that in social policy, academia and media coverage, black mothers were simultaneously depicted as marginal but also as powerfully responsible for the 'deficits' that led to their children's educational failure.

During the period in which OWAAD and other black British women's organizations flourished Jan McKenley was also prolific in her analysis of the ways in which race, class and gender were lived out by black women in education, as pupils and as mothers. Born in Brixton in 1955, McKenley was herself one of the 'second generation', schooled in both London and Manchester. Entering higher education in the mid-1970s, McKenley became immersed in the women's movement. Active in both OWAAD and in the Brixton Women's Group, she taught in London schools and further education colleges and by the early 1990s had become part of Ofsted's inspectorate and school improvement team (Black Cultural Archives, 2010).

Writing in the early days of OWAAD, in a draft speech for a conference on Black Women in Britain, McKenley (who, unlike Bryan *et al.*, retained the umbrella definition of blackness) conveyed the sense of black mothers as the unacknowledged frontline in the fraught relations between young blacks and the state:

> Where education is concerned it is we black mothers who have to go down and take on the schools and the teachers, who were never prepared for our arrival and who even today have done little to accommodate our needs and

those of our children ... it is the black mother who suffers most when our youth are picked up and harassed by the police on trumped up charges like SUS, and many a black mother has come under the attack of the police when she rose in defence of her child.

McKenley (undated: 3)

In a late 1970s paper titled 'Black women and education', McKenley focused on the historic role of mothers in the black education movements:

Black parents, especially Black mothers, have also fought against the miseducation of our children. Because we know that our children are not subnormal we have fought and won the battle against ESN. Because we know that they do not lower standards we have resisted bussing to white areas ... we have set up supplementary schools. From Southall to Lewisham to Brixton, supplementary schools have flourished with Black people giving time and effort to correct racist indoctrination and encourage the confidence needed to assert oneself in this racist society.

McKenley (c. 1978: 1)

But McKenley was also keenly aware that in both policy studies and the sociology of education, insufficient attention was given to the specific, racialized, classed and gendered educational experiences of 'second generation' black girls. 'How', McKenley asked, 'do black girls fare in this set up ... black female figures are conspicuous by their absence. We are not even abused; we do not exist' (McKenley, c. 1978: 3). The marginalization that McKenley described was a gendered one. The black conflict theorists, in particular, had tried to understand the tensions lived out by black children in British schools in terms of refusal and direct confrontation – but these were often depicted by recounting masculine acts of resistance. What was still lacking was the kind of ethnographic work that would point to the daily patterns of school life experienced by black girls.

Rewriting race, gender and identity

From the late 1970s onwards sociological fascination with 'black youth' engendered a wave of subcultural analyses of second generation African-Caribbean boys (Pryce, 1979; Ratcliffe, 1981; Dennis, 1988; Sewell, 1997). In educational research this produced normative depictions of the lived experiences of black pupils; their emphasis was on visible conflict between black Caribbean youth and the state. Sociologist Heidi Safia Mirza observed:

There has clearly been a black and male monopoly of the 'black subject' ... In the masculinist discourse on race and social change the assumption is that 'race' is contested and fought over in the masculine arena of the streets ... urban social movements, we are told, mobilize in protest, riots, local politics and community organizations ... This is the masculinist version of radical social change; visible, radical, confrontational, collective action, powerfully expressed in the politics of the inner-city, where class consciousness evolves in response to urban struggle.

Mirza, H. S. (1997: 272)

Black boys' resistance to schooling was pored over endlessly; black women (and black men who appeared too conformist) tended to be erased. However, a number of black women researchers broke with the masculinist assumptions of subcultural resistance theory and explored instead ways in which black girls' lived experiences of schooling differed from those of rebel boys. By the 1990s a distinctive body of black feminist research had accumulated, addressing gender, race and education from diverse standpoints. Since then black feminist scholarship in Britain has included the work of: Maud Blair (on schooling and identity); Cecile Wright and Debbie Weekes (on gender and school exclusions); Audrey Osler (on adolescence and citizenship), Iram Siraj-Blatchford (on teacher education); Avtar Brah and Nira Yuval-Davis (on diaspora); Amrit Wilson (on Asian women's experiences); Lola Young and Lisa Palmer (on gender, race and media representations); Valerie Amos, Ratna Lachman and Yasmin Alibhai-Brown (on equalities and social policy); Jasmine Rhamie and Uvanney Maylor (on black educational success); and Gargi Bhattacharyya (on academia and student experiences).

Ethnic gaps, gender gaps

This turn was not only driven by feminist theory; it was also informed by increasing awareness of the disparities between the educational experiences of different black communities and the ways in which these intersected with gender. In the 1970s and 80s a series of studies had revealed that Indian and Chinese children's educational outcomes, measured in terms of literacy levels and examination results, were significantly better than those of African-Caribbean and, in some cases, white British children (Black People's Progressive Alliance and Redbridge Community Relations Council, 1978; Runnymede Trust, 1980). These studies, being based on local and incomplete data were not conclusive. However, they engendered increased caution 'about the extent to which one can generalize about the success and failure of all black children' (Runnymede Trust, 1980: 102).

The disaggregation of black pupils' profile of educational achievement was influenced by the weakening of political blackness, insofar as individual community groups demanded more precise research into their children's schooling. It also, in cyclical fashion, influenced the shift away from political blackness, in that the disparities in the achievement of different black groups challenged, for some activists, the logic of unifying around issues that appeared to affect communities differentially (see Modood, 1994). In the literature on race and *gender* and education, fragmentation became even more pronounced because of the gap in achievement that opened up from around 1988 onwards between the achievement of boys and girls, across all major ethnic groups (Phoenix, 2002; Pilkington, 2003).

In 1988 the Education Reform Act introduced the National Curriculum and Key Stage Assessment; it was in 1988 also that the first GCSE (General Certificate of Secondary Education) exams were taken by sixteen-year-olds, following the abolition of the old two-tier O-Level/CSE exam qualification system. Prior to this, girls had outperformed boys by two or three percentage points but from the late 1980s the percentage point gap between boys and girls gaining five GCSEs at grades A–C rose markedly in favour of girls (Gillborn and Mirza, 2001). That gender gap has remained throughout the 1990s and 2000s, as recent English figures demonstrate. In 2006/07, 41.7 per cent of boys achieved five GCSEs at grades A*–C (including Maths and English), as against 49.9 per cent of girls. By 2010/11 the gender gap was 54.6 per cent (boys) to 61.9 per cent (girls). However, the gender disparity is greater among, for instance, African-Caribbean pupils. So, in 2006/07, 26.9 per cent of African-Caribbean boys gained five GCSEs at grades A*–C (including Maths and English), as against 39.1 per cent of African-Caribbean girls. The GCSE achievement figures for African-Caribbean pupils in 2010/11 were 42.3 per cent (boys) and 54.8 per cent (girls) (Department for Education, 2012). These achievement statistics are included here only as small examples, as context, and it should be noted that the gender and ethnic gaps have been subjected to contrasting readings by educational researchers (Gorard, 1999; Gillborn and Mirza, 2001; Pilkington, 2003; Gillborn, 2008). Here they serve only to illustrate why, in addition to their theoretical reservations about masculinist research on race and education, researchers have argued the need to nuance the particular experiences of black girls in British schools.

Education, resistance and inclusive acts

The work of Heidi Safia Mirza has contested the equation of black educational experiences with male resistance and underachievement (Mirza, H. S., 1992, 2009). Importantly, Mirza has argued the need to 'theorize the paradox of inclusive acts by excluded groups' (Mirza, H. S., 1997: 269). For Mirza, the paradox that had to be unpacked was this: if institutional racism persisted in the school system then how could the apparent commitment to 'getting on' in education among the African-Caribbean girls she encountered in her research be understood as more than just buying into myths of meritocracy? Her analysis was a response to the growing evidence of the 1990s that significant numbers of African-Caribbean and Asian girls were not rejecting schooling and were not failing in education. However, these girls were often rendered invisible by the dominance of the black underachievement paradigm. Moreover, where the recent educational successes of black girls had been observed, they had rarely been discussed critically or given meaning. Mirza's response was to 'reveal the subversive and transformative possibilities of their actions' (Mirza, H. S., 1997: 269). Taking issue with Mac an Ghaill's (1988) analysis of black girls' relative conformity as 'resistance through accommodation', Mirza argued that black girls had created their own distinctive educational ethos, networks and practices that actively refused the racist discourse of black failure. 'In certain circumstances,' argued Mirza, *'doing well can become a radical strategy.* An act of social transformation...' (Mirza, H. S., 1997: 274, italics in original).

As explained by Mirza, black Caribbean girls' strategies for doing well were not built upon denial of school and labour market inequalities but upon creative negotiation. For instance, in the classroom the girls Mirza studied were not deferential but they developed strategies for avoiding overt conflict with teachers. They were willing to stay in education longer (often using the 'back door' of further education and Access courses), in order to gain qualifications. They chose realistically attainable careers but ones that they felt would offer subsequent opportunities to gain promotion, continuing professional development and, in some cases, access to higher education. In developing 'positive educational orientation in the context of persistent labour-market inequality' (Mirza, H. S., 1992: 1–2) these second and third generation African-Caribbean girls were neither uncritically buying into the system nor resisting in defensive fashion but, through their own agency, were creating educational and labour market spaces of which they felt some ownership, on terms that were liveable and did not bow to systemic racism.

Sacred spaces

The creation of black spaces – spaces of self-definition – has been a salient theme in Mirza's subsequent research with white academic Diane Reay on black supplementary schools (Reay and Mirza, 1997, 2001). Their gendered analysis of the historical development, pedagogy and ethos of black (Caribbean) supplementary schools drew upon Patricia Hill Collins' and bell hooks' writing on the distinctive forms of opposition developed by black women educators. Reay and Mirza's claims also recalled other black British feminist writing on politicized black parenting, such as Julia Jarrett's:

> One of my responsibilities as a Black parent is to anchor my son in a cultural identity with its roots stretching back to Africa via the Caribbean. We, his parents, are the products of the intellectually demanding Black liberation movement of the 1960s and the 1970s. We emerged from that period with strong political views on Black achievement, past, present and future. Our generation's thirst for knowledge and information encouraged by our young aunts and uncles and parents gave rise to the concept of Black culture as cultural resistance.
>
> Jarrett (1996: 130)

In Reay and Mirza (1997, 2001) a form of political blackness still held sway. They explored how the cultural and educational politics of Black Power had translated into the pragmatic, credentialist supplementary schooling of the 1990s, while arguing also that the female educators who formed the larger part of their teaching staff were nurturing 'spaces of radical blackness', born out of acute consciousness of the racism black children continued to negotiate in mainstream schooling. These women teachers operated 'against the grain of the dominant discursive constructions of blackness as a negative reflection of whiteness which still prevail across British society' (Reay and Mirza, 2001: 96). From this starting position, the supplementary schools that Reay and Mirza studied offered a fertile counter-space:

> In creating a sanctuary in which the black child is re-centred black women decentre the popular pervasive public myth of black underachievement and educational alienation. As radical educators black women challenge the knowledge claims, pedagogy, and praxis of the mainstream schooling, and harness their own radical version of education as a means of transforming their lives ... However the very thing – spaces of blackness – which makes black supplementary schools so inviting for black pupils and the women who create and nurture them constitutes its threat for the white majority.
>
> Reay and Mirza (2001: 97)

While Reay and Mirza's (2001) depiction of supplementary schooling may have contained a degree of idealization, they pointed convincingly both to the continuing ambivalence of the school sector to black supplementary schools and again to another form of deceptive conformism to dominant definitions of educational success. Thus although supplementary schooling was designed to support mainstream achievement, it could simultaneously be read as an act of black self-definition: a rejection of low expectations and of the othering of black experiences in the 'white' world of mainstream schooling – but in ways that offered a positive re-centring of black identities, not merely a 'defence' against racism. These schools offered 'parallel spaces of contestation ... in which goals of enabling young black people to achieve academically are combined with a simultaneous opposition to the system ... encoded discursively rather than enacted antagonistically' (Reay and Mirza, 2001: 100).

From triple oppression to intersectionality

Analyses of black women's educational identities, like those developed by Mirza, have depicted black women in education as actual subjects of political practice. Where triple oppression was, in the 1970s and 80s, preferred shorthand for representing lived experiences of black women in fields such as education, a concept increasingly favoured in the twenty-first century is 'intersectionality'. Black British educators who have utilized the concept include Avtar Brah, Ann Phoenix, Nira Yuval-Davis, Kalwant Bhopal, Shirin Housee, Lorna Roberts and Uvanney Maylor.

The term 'intersectionality' entered the black feminist lexicon through African-American thinkers Kimberley Crenshaw and Patricia Hill Collins' critiques of the 'paralleling' of race and gender (Crenshaw, 1991; Collins, P. H., 1990). It offers a theoretical framework for understanding the political and experiential implications of regarding gender, race, class, faith, sexuality and so forth as co-constituted. Its impact on contemporary black British feminists' analyses of race, gender and education has been profound (Ali *et al.*, 2010; Bhopal and Preston, 2011; Bhopal and Maylor, 2013). Brah and Phoenix explain its conceptual value:

> We regard the concept of 'intersectionality' as signifying the complex, irreducible, varied, and variable effects which ensue when multiple axis of differentiation – economic, political, cultural, psychic, subjective and experiential – intersect in historically specific contexts.
>
> Brah and Phoenix (2004: 76)

The first implication of intersectionality is that because identities and oppressions intersect black women's lived experiences they cannot be partitioned out into parallel struggles. Secondly, the ways in which these oppressions intersect is historically specific, shaped by the particular forms of domination operated at legal, bureaucratic, cultural and interpersonal levels at any historical point (Collins, P. H., 1990). Consequently, there is no single homogenous or essential female experience or black experience or working-class experience – no innocent notion of identity. Moreover, because the oppressions of gender, race and class criss-cross, categories that are used as shorthand for particular experiences must be subject to multiple interrogations. So not only does the meaning and experience of being a 'black woman' shift historically, but what it means to be a 'mother', a 'professional', a 'teacher' or a 'pupil' is not static either. Gender stratification is not consistent across ethnic or class lines. In addition, drawing from one of the key lessons of feminism, intersectionality again calls into question the ostensible division between public and private in women's lives (Collins, P. H., 1990). So within home–school relationships, what it means to be a working-class Bangladeshi mother does not, in all senses, equate with what it means to be a white middle-class British mother. Yet these intersecting oppressions and the inequalities of experience and outcomes they produce are concealed by legislative and bureaucratic claims to guarantee neutrality, fairness and equal treatment. Contemporary black feminist researchers have drawn upon intersectionality to challenge the education system's claims to neutrality and meritocracy.

Contemporary black feminism and education

Since the late 1990s black British women intellectuals have opened up new areas of research on education, such as black cultural capital (Jasmine Rhamie, Carol Tomlin, Farzana Shain); the educational strategies of black middle-class families (Nicola Rollock, Uvanney Maylor); school exclusions (Maud Blair, Cecile Wright); black teachers' professional identities (Audrey Osler); pedagogy and identity among black academics (Gargi Bhattacharyya, Kalwant Bhopal, Cecily Jones, Yvette Summers); black students' experiences in HE (Shirin Housee, Vini Lander); and Critical Race Theory (Lorna Roberts, Namita Chakrabarty).

Among these, Audrey Osler's study of Asian and African-Caribbean teachers' career trajectories and identities located their lived experiences within the wider social antagonisms of migration, race relations, education and social policy in the post-war period (Osler, 1997). Often driven by their own experiences of racism and inequality as pupils, black teachers were committed to education as transformative, as a driver of social justice. Osler offered insights into many instances of black teachers' success in wielding influence and changing pupils' lives but did not shy away from the personal costs to individuals of operating 'in a context where black and minority ethnic people still experience widespread racism in employment, particularly when they move outside of those sectors which are recognized as traditional areas of black and minority ethnic employment' (Osler, 1997: 204).

Gargi Bhattacharyya, Cecily Jones, and Nicola Rollock have explored black educators' experiences in academia. Jones (2006) has addressed the unspoken racialization of academic life, examining the ramifications of shifts away from models of equalities from the 1980s and 90s to 'the adoption of diversity management as a strategy of organisational policy' (Jones, C., 2006: 145). Jones questions British universities' grasp of new equalities concepts, their relationship to wider issues of social justice and to failures to counter the continued marginalization of black academics. Nicola Rollock, meanwhile, has employed concepts drawn from American Critical Race Theory, in order to address the tacit 'micro-aggressions' that isolate and derogate black academics within their institutions (Rollock, 2012). Gargi Bhattacharyya, an alumna of CCCS, has continued to cross-pollinate cultural studies, black Marxism and feminism, examining the position of black women as both students and teachers in a world in which the 'powerful hog the privilege of the norm and the rest of us squeeze in behind, around, wherever there is room' (Bhattacharyya, 1997: 250).

Other recent black feminist research has focused on how black students, parents and educators have created their own powerful networks, akin to the kinds of black spaces described in Reay and Mirza (2001). Cecile Wright's critical ethnographies have destabilized the frameworks of black underachievement and school failure by focusing on relationships that emphasize forms of black social and cultural capital often overlooked in educational research (Wright *et al.*, 2010). Jasmine Rhamie's (2007) *Eagles Who Soar* places similar emphasis on the distinctive social and cultural capital generated in African-Caribbean communities, which informs students' conceptions of success within schooling and post-compulsory education. Like Rhamie, Jan McKenley's (2006) *Seven Black Men: An Ecological Study of Education and Parenting* stands as a major corrective, not only to the pathologization of black homes and educational values that have persisted but also to the understandable resistance, post-Coard, to studies of black home life, 'lest they be used against us as factors in the underattainment of our children' (McKenley, 2001: 310). In exploring the lives of black fathers in contemporary Britain, McKenley focuses powerfully on how black parents' lived experiences as black schoolchildren in the 1970s and 80s have informed the educational values they negotiate with their own children.

Conclusion

The work of black British feminists has reframed sociological understandings of the ways in which race, class, gender and sexuality are lived, and, in particular, the ways in which they are lived in institutional contexts. They have drawn attention to the diversity of gendered and racialized experiences, to multiple racisms and to the fact that black underachievement does not define the total experience of black people in education. In fact, it could be argued that it is black British feminists who have most trenchantly addressed the questions raised by Paul Gilroy (1987) about what black Britons stand for, as well as what they have organized against. In seeking to move beyond defensive anti-racism, black women intellectuals writing on race and education have arguably provided part of the answer. The final two chapters of this book explore how, in the context of the twenty-first century, black British scholars and activists have continued to develop understandings of race, education and social justice and how they have continued to trouble understandings of black British life.

8 New critical theories of race and education

> In order to transcend current race relations, which is a concrete possibility, we must first go *through* race in order to have any hopes of going *beyond* it.
>
> Leonardo (2009: 125)

Introduction

The first two decades of the twenty-first century have prompted new questions about race, education and social justice in Britain. These new questions have, in significant part, been prompted by black intellectuals, and they have also challenged black intellectuals to address anew the tropes of blackness, multiculturalism and anti-racism. What is certain is that education has remained a site of contest and a barometer of wider shifts in black British thought. For example, in recent years seductive claims have been made across the political spectrum to suggest that race no longer carries the salience that it once did in British society (Mirza, M., 2010; Sewell, 2011). It has been argued that the lived experience of the young, in particular, is no longer shaped by racism and that educators, sociologists and policy-makers should be cautious about equating black communities with social disadvantage and educational underachievement. Some commentators have spoken of society as post-racial and have urged a post-multicultural approach in education and social policy (Goodhart, 2004, 2013). Others have argued that post-racial claims are premature and have cautioned against over-eagerness to 'move on'. They point to the lessons of the Stephen Lawrence case, the rise of Islamophobia, hostility to new migrants and the continued educational underachievement of particular ethnic groups (Solomos, 2003; Kundnani, 2007; Gillborn, 2008; Chakrabortty, 2010), all of which are taken as signs of the mutability of racism, rather than its decline.

Few would deny that 'black' experiences of education and society have diversified as we become ever more distanced from the black explosion. Amidst these sociological changes, black thinkers themselves have had to ask which parts of racial analysis can be usefully retained and which parts should be jettisoned. Chapters 8 and 9 of this book explore three very different contemporary approaches to race, education and social justice. They are a 'post-black' multiculturalism that rejects black/white dualism, in favour of focusing on ethnicity, faith and language; Critical Race Theory, with its analysis of what it regards as continued, endemic 'taken-for-granted' racism; and what might be termed the new black social conservatism, which involves a rejection of traditional black left thought. These are significant new intellectual approaches: firstly, because they have defined themselves largely in relation to youth and education and, secondly, because they have become platforms for new, sometimes iconoclastic, black and anti-racist voices. Though in some ways analytically opposed, they all address questions of how, in putatively 'post-racial', 'post-multicultural' contexts, we might rethink race, education and social justice. This chapter begins, therefore, by examining the social and intellectual shifts that have destabilized understandings of race and identity in twenty-first-century Britain.

Are we 'post-racial' yet?

First of all, what form have 'post-racial' claims taken? What does the term 'post-racial' mean? The American critical theorist of race and education, Zeus Leonardo, has argued for a definition of the 'post-racial' that avoids the easy assumption that race has lost its salience, and that the fight against racism is done:

> The "post" in post-racial signals the possibility of a social formation without race but this would be its most obvious reading. A more nuanced reading suggests that the post-movement opens up new possibilities for critique, new questions to be posed about race in a way that was not possible heretofore.
>
> Leonardo (2009: 6)

Yet defining the term 'post-racial' remains highly problematic because it has been used to signify very different, some would say opposing, claims about the social salience of race. Some use it to suggest boldly that racism has declined as a feature of social life in many western societies. Witness, for instance, the heady optimism that accompanied Barack Obama's election as president of the United States; in some quarters Obama's success indicated that, in electing its first black president, the USA had finally transcended the original sins of slavery and racism. This definition of a 'post-racial' society implies that race, or *racism*, is no longer the social problem it once was and that social policy efforts should be re-directed towards class, poverty and social cohesion.

For other commentators, however, the 'post-racial' denotes a more complex social analysis. For instance, there have long been strains of Marxist thinking that regard race as an unreal social relation, placing the word in scare quotes and treating racism primarily as a technology of class. In Britain this position has been extensively argued by Robert Miles (1989). For these 'post-racial' thinkers, opposition to racism requires the complete jettisoning of race as an analytical concept on the grounds that sociologies of race, however well intentioned, serve to reproduce racialized views of the world. After all, if race is an incoherent, unscientific category, Miles and his followers have argued, how can it be employed to understand social relations? Critics of Miles, however, suggest that this kind of race-is-not-real fundamentalism fails to acknowledge the racialized assumptions of its own social theory and that, moreover, it remains unconvincing to those who continue to experience daily racism (Leonardo, 2009; Warmington, 2009, 2011).

A different 'post-racial' position is one that Zeus Leonardo (2005, 2011) terms 'race ambivalence'. This is a helpful term because it signifies that while race is indeed unreal in the sense that it is not a coherent scientific category, its effects, including the shaping of social relationships and the formation of our identities, are still real and salient. This position recognizes that race-is-unreal fundamentalism carries with it the risk of underestimating the continuing effects of racialized thinking and practice. In other words, as long as we continue to live *as if* race were real, and as long as racism forms part of our lived experience, sociology must retain a 'race-consciousness'. So, in conceptual terms, working within a terrain in which race is regarded as simultaneously 'real' *and* 'unreal' means 'being critical of race and being race critical of theory while still employing race categories, unlike a Marxist theorist of race who does not lend much credence to them' (Leonardo, 2009: 5). Those who hold this kind of race ambivalent position frequently point out it is not just an academic conceit. British writers such as Paul Gilroy, Miri Song and Yasmin Gunaratnam have all argued that black Britons, particularly the young, work with just this kind of paradox every day, learning quickly where racial identities are strategically useful and where they are not, where race has salience and where it has none (see, for instance, Song, 2003).

The de-racialization of education

There have also been critiques of education and social policy in both the USA and Britain that suggest not so much a post-racial field but a field in which education and social policy discourses have been deliberately de-racialized. At the end of the 1990s the late Manning Marable argued that there had been a profound de-racialization of public policy discourses in the USA, claiming that what used to be termed race issues had now been 'subsumed under a murky series of policy talking points, such as affirmative action, minority economic set-asides, crime, welfare reform and the urban "underclass"' (Marable, 1998: 1). In Britain an equivalent set of policy items for the 1990s and 2000s might be catalogued, including educational standards, academic underachievement and community cohesion.

It has been argued that, since the decline in municipal multiculturalism that came with the demise of ILEA in 1990, reductions in funding of ethnic minority community projects and the dispersal of many of the independent black networks active in the 1980s and early 90s, education policy in Britain has, in several respects, become a de-racialized field, wherein a new discourse of educational standards has switched attention away from racial inequalities in education (Tomlinson, 2005, 2008; Archer and Francis, 2007). Since the early 1990s, British education policy has been increasingly embedded within the discourse of standards and achievement. As numerous educators have observed, this was the outcome of the drift towards credentialism, wherein the success of the education sector, of individual schools and individual pupils was quantified through exam performance (Ball, 2008; Benn, 2011).

Thus the gaining of five GCSEs at A*–C grade became the benchmark for successful compulsory schooling up to the age of sixteen. The performance of each individual school could be measured and ranked according to the proportions of pupils gaining such benchmarks, and standards within the education sector as a whole could be judged by the proportions of successful or failing schools and by the overall proportions of pupils gaining particular credentials at age sixteen (GCSE) and age eighteen (A-Level), as well as through testing at earlier ages. In their study of the educational experiences of British-Chinese pupils, Louise Archer and Becky Francis argued that the dominance of the achievement paradigm, rooted in a narrow, credentialist conception of education experience and achievement, was:

> amply illustrated by the proliferation of testing regimes, academic league tables and the regular, high profile publication of achievement statistics from children's earliest years through to GCSEs and into post-compulsory education. Indeed we would assert that achievement is not just an educational issue – for the current government, it is *the* educational issue.
>
> Archer and Francis (2007: xiii)

The gold standard qualifications, A-Levels and GCSEs, and the vocational BTECs and NVQs themselves became a quantification or objectification of the exchange-value of education within the labour market and the higher education sector. At the level of national economic policy, the drive towards credentialism reflected a kind of faith in the potential of qualifications to generate jobs and opportunities; in terms of social policy, participation in education became a measure of social inclusion and cohesion (Tomlinson, 2005). Moreover, education policy was entrenched in an ideology that insisted there was no contradiction between the belief in education as a driver of economic performance and belief in education as a driver of social justice. Where did this leave questions of racial equality?

Colour-blind fairness?

Sally Tomlinson (2008) argued that structural analyses of racial inequality were a casualty of wider reconfigurations in national politics. 'The Conservative government,' she reasoned had, 'between 1990 and 1997, virtually removed issues concerning racial and ethnic inequalities in education from political consideration' (Tomlinson, 2008: 153) insisting instead on a colour-blind model of fairness. The New Labour government that succeeded the Conservatives in 1997 ensured continuity with many of the Conservative party's market reforms in education, while being keen to voice a greater commitment to social justice and diversity. The result, Tomlinson (2008) claimed, was a painfully atrophied framework for addressing racial inequality in education:

[A] continuation of Conservative market policies of choice and diversity in schooling and a targeting of 'failing' schools exacerbated school segregation and racial inequalities. Policies intended to improve the achievement of minority groups have had some success, but the higher achievements of Indian and Chinese groups have led to facile comparisons which further pathologise young people of African-Caribbean and Pakistani origin. Failure to develop a curriculum for a multiethnic society has contributed to an increase in xenophobia and racism, and there were no educational policies to deal with increased hostility towards young Muslims. Home Office policies targeting refugees and asylum seekers have encouraged racial hostility towards their children despite amended race relations legislation.

Tomlinson (2008: 153)

The underachievement paradigm

One of the effects of the concern with standards and achievement was that it drew attention to education as a site in which the outcomes of 'black and minority ethnic' (BME) groups were increasingly differentiated. By the 1990s there were credible sociological reasons for querying the usefulness of umbrella definitions of blackness and what Tariq Modood termed black/white racial dualism (Modood, 1992, 1994, 2007). However, ethnic monitoring of achievement and under-achievement was not merely a descriptor of a prior phenomenon; it also enabled policy-makers to *account for* racial inequality in education and to discount racism as a continued factor in the experiences of black or BME students. The atrophying of discourses around race, racism and education was summed up by Archer and Francis:

[I]ssues of race/ethnicity are really only acknowledged by or addressed by education policy within the context of 'underachievement' ... issues of race have been subject to a pernicious turn in policy discourse which removes the means for engaging with inequalities, naturalises differences in achievement between ethnic groups and places the responsibility for achievement differentials with minority ethnic individuals. This discourse denies racism as a potential cause of differences in achievement and hides inequalities within congratulatory public statements.

Archer and Francis (2007: 1)

In short, by shying away from the structural – the racialized dimensions of resourcing, curriculum, credentialization, teacher training, labelling of pupils, disciplinary systems – and tending to individualized explanations of underachievement – behaviour, aspiration, family backgrounds – the achievement discourse offered a means to normalize racial inequalities and to return to the pathologization of particular black communities, pupils and parents, albeit decked out in new social democratic language. This was apparent not least in what Tomlinson (2008) and Gillborn (2008) have identified as the construction of model minorities. If racism was a persistent factor in education, ran the implication, why did Chinese pupils succeed where African-Caribbeans failed? Why did Indian pupils succeed where Pakistani pupils failed? So it was that black parenting, educational aspirations, youth subcultures, faith and self-segregation again became the usual suspects in debates over black underachievement.

The ethnic turn

Where did this leave black intellectuals and the remnants of the black education movements? As Chapters 5 and 6 of this book have suggested, there were multiple reasons that political blackness lost purchase. By the early 1990s there was dissolution of many of the black radical groupings that had fired black intellectual activism between the 1960s and 80s. The 1990s saw an increasing shift in focus from 'race' to 'ethnicity'. Critics of political blackness were able to charge that referring to people of colour as black obscured their historical, cultural and social diversity. The adoption of ethnicity as the key category would, it was hoped, dispense once and for all with the ghost of racial pseudo-science and encourage us to think in terms of the interplay between open categories of culture, faith, language and nationality. This is simplificatory but it captures something of the dilemmas in which black British intellectuals were caught up in the 1990s and 2000s. Those who emphasized the progressive possibilities of addressing social inequalities via ethnic and cultural models often invoked Stuart Hall's pioneering conceptualization of 'new ethnicities' (Hall, 1988). Hall had, after all, reflected that:

> the plurality of antagonisms and differences that now seek to destroy the unity of black politics, given the complexities of the structures of subordination that have been formed by the way in which we were inserted into the black diaspora, is not at all surprising. These are the thoughts that drove me to speak, in an unguarded moment, of the end of the innocence of the black subject or the end of the innocent notion of an essential black subject.
>
> Hall (1996b: 474)

Those who have favoured ethnicity and culture as ways of understanding social antagonisms have argued that a 'non-essentialised approach to ethnicity allows us to understand ethnic identities as forever "in process", constructed through the social, cultural and discursive, and integrally tied to the construction of identity' (Archer and Francis, 2007: 28). No doubt – but the categories of culture and ethnicity were not new and were often liable to become as rigid and essentialist as the categories they sought to supplant, producing what Paul Gilroy (1993b: 65) describes as 'ethnic absolutism'.

Against black/white dualism

However, the ethnic turn was not just a policy effect; it was also favoured by thinkers who had become increasingly sceptical of the priorities implied by political blackness. In studies of youth and education the most strident theorist of ethnicity over political blackness has been Tariq Modood (1992, 1994, 2007). In the early 1990s Modood critiqued the 'racial dualism' (Modood, 1992: 27) that he regarded as the legacy of the African-Caribbean-dominated radical black politics of the 1960s and 70s. For Modood (1992: 28) 'long historical experience of white racism and the knowledge of its contemporary existence in Britain' had meant that black and anti-racist politics was 'over influenced by' three core assumptions. The first was that 'being white or not is the single most crucial factor in determining the sociological profile of any non-white group in contemporary Britain' (Modood, 1992: 28) and that race was assumed to dwarf and determine profiles of class, gender, employment, education, faith and ethnicity. The second, Modood argued, was that 'until racial prejudice and discrimination in all its forms is eliminated ... all non-white groups ... will form a racial underclass' (Modood, 1992: 28). Finally, in direct reference to the hothouse of British Black Power, Modood queried the belief that the 'only way "Black" people can improve their condition as a group is through political militancy and/or substantial state action; they are therefore, a natural ally and integral component of left-wing movements' (Modood, 1992: 28). While Modood recognized the socio-political value of these assumptions as a means of naming the pervasiveness of racism within the social formation, they were, he asserted, limited by a static model of identity that too rigidly linked race, colour and socio-economic disadvantage (see also Rattansi, 1992).

In particular, Modood argued that black/white racial dualism tended to relegate the experiences of South Asian communities. For Modood, the ostensibly inclusive definition of political blackness no longer matched either the objective experiences of educational and economic success evident among Indian and, to an extent, Bangladeshi communities or the public identities of communities for whom language, faith and ethnicity carried complex purchase, prior to any identification with political blackness. Modood remains influential among those who have distanced themselves from older forms of British political blackness. His work also reflects shifts in public policy around, for instance, ethnic monitoring, state resourcing and official terminology since the 1990s, wherein Asian communities have largely ceased to be seen merely as a 'black' sub-category. Kalwant Bhopal (2010) and Farzana Shain (2010) are among those who have built upon Modood's nuancing of Indian, Pakistani and Bangladeshi students' educational experiences.

However, Modood's approach has also been criticized for risking a retreat into a particular form of racialization, wherein South Asian communities are seen to possess 'culture', while African-Caribbeans possess only 'colour'. In her article 'Beyond black: re-thinking the colour/culture divide' Claire Alexander (2002) queried the growing sociological preference for disaggregating black Britishness. While acknowledging the potential reductionism of cleaving to simplistic notions of unified blackness, Alexander (2002) also argued that the theoretical splintering of Caribbean and Asian categories was premature, since in many communities African-Caribbean and Asian populations continued to experience similar disadvantages in education, housing and employment. Neither had the decentring of political blackness necessarily pluralized black histories or increased the visibility of Asian experiences. Alexander suggested that, in fact, Caribbean and Asian communities had become framed by two opposing models of difference. African-Caribbeans had come to symbolize vibrant cultural diversity in post-war Britain, embodied in Windrush histories and Black History Months, a difference that could be incorporated into a vision of a forward-looking, Cool Britannia. In contrast, Asians, and Muslims particularly, were used in news media and policy discourses to signify a problematic difference: supposedly closed cultures at odds with contemporary, liberal Britain (Alexander, 2002).

So by the late 1990s and early 2000s black British intellectuals were perhaps more than ever bound up in questions of representation. What did the word 'black' encompass? For whom did black intellectuals now speak? Was there a viable anti-racist movement? Without acknowledging these debates, the directions taken by new black voices in the field of education in the 2000s are not readily understood.

Lawrence and Macpherson

While post-racial and de-racialized discourses exerted powerful influence on educational debates, the first decades of the twenty-first century cannot be depicted wholly in these terms. In education, as in other areas of social policy, the case of Stephen Lawrence and the resultant Macpherson Inquiry renewed structural analyses of institutional racism, making race and racism explicit issues again. The Lawrence campaign became a cultural marker, shaping understandings of race, education and social justice, as Scarman and Swann did in the 1980s.

In April 1993 black teenager Stephen Lawrence was murdered in an unprovoked, racially motivated attack by white youths in south-east London. Failures in police surveillance of the suspects and the collapse of the initial Crown Prosecution case (it was not until January 2012 that two of the five murder suspects were convicted) led Stephen's parents, Doreen and Neville Lawrence, to mount a lengthy and difficult campaign for justice. In July 1997 the Home Office initiated a judicial inquiry headed by Sir William Macpherson into Stephen's killing and police handling of racially motivated crimes. During the inquiry the Metropolitan Police admitted to extensive failures in the handling of the murder case and, when published in February 1999, the Macpherson Report accused the Metropolitan Police of institutional racism.

The Macpherson Report's seventy recommendations addressed the police's organizational attitudes to racism but also proposed wider legal reforms and changes to the Race Relations Act that would touch all public bodies, including the education sector. The Race Relations (Amendment) Act 2000 that Macpherson prompted stipulated that public bodies in the UK now had a race equality duty. The implication of the new duty was that organizations should not only be alert to rectifying instances of racial discrimination that had occurred but should take proactive measures to ensure that their services met the needs of all communities. In schools, colleges and universities these measures included producing explicit race equality policies predicated upon monitoring the impacts of institutional practices upon minority ethnic communities. The cultural impact of the Macpherson Inquiry and the Lawrence campaign can be measured also by the fact that subsequently similar equalities duties were extended to cover areas such as disability and gender.

The Lawrence case and the Macpherson Inquiry informed black British intellectual work in the ensuing decade. Firstly, it brought to the fore the work of Doreen Lawrence, whose continued campaigning to raise awareness of and effect public action against racism has made her a commanding figure in British cultural politics. The Stephen Lawrence Charitable Trust, founded by Mrs Lawrence, and related bodies, such as the Stop Hate campaign, have worked extensively with young people, schools and policy-makers. Moreover, Doreen Lawrence's public presence has reasserted the primary role of black activism in achieving progress in anti-racist education and social policy. In 2013, the twentieth anniversary of her son's murder, Doreen Lawrence reflected on what she saw as the state's loss of focus on race equality issues in the years since the Macpherson Inquiry, alluding to residual institutional racism in the education system, and asserting the need for education policy to show commitment to greater equality of outcome: 'We want a society in which not just the opportunities but also the outcomes for education and career success are fairly balanced across all ethnic groups' (Doreen Lawrence, quote in Townsend, 2013).

Macpherson on institutional racism

Importantly, the Macpherson Report reasserted the concept of institutional racism in relationships between black communities and the state. Macpherson's root definition of institutional racism is now well known:

> The collective failure of an organisation to provide an appropriate and professional service to people because of their colour, culture, or ethnic origin. It can be seen or detected in processes, attitudes and behaviour which amount to discrimination through unwitting prejudice, ignorance, thoughtlessness and racist stereotyping which disadvantage minority ethnic people.
>
> Macpherson/Home Office (1999, para 6:34)

As Chapter 4 of this book has explained, the concept of institutional racism dates back at least as far as Carmichael and Hamilton (1967). It has long informed anti-racists' definitions of indirect racism, although the term was often treated nervously by legislators, policy-makers and public service managers. Bhikhu Parekh (2000) commented on the significance of Macpherson's employment of the concept:

> The report did not set out a detailed theoretical framework. Its acknowledgement of institutional racism, however, was a major step forward.

For 30 years British officialdom had consistently denied that it had any meaning when applied to Britain. Now, however, it has become part of the conceptual vocabulary of substantial numbers of people. It recognises that, to thrive, racism does not require overtly racist individuals, and conceives of it rather as arising through social and cultural processes. Culture regulates conduct.

Parekh (2000: 71)

For Sarah Neal, comparing news media and policy responses to Macpherson with the responses to Lord Scarman's report on the Brixton riots twenty years previously, '[t]he Macpherson recognition that systematic processes of racial exclusion existed and that these were reinscribed by racialized cultures within organisations officially put institutional racism on the social policy map, bringing the concept in from the political cold of 1980s town halls' (Neal, 2003: 66). Neal noted the willingness of British news media (even those who regarded Macpherson as going too far in his condemnation of police racism) to at least countenance the concept of institutional racism in ways that had not been evident in media coverage of the Scarman Report.

Community cohesion

Yet Neal (2003) also reflected upon the rapidity of the backlash against Macpherson among policy-makers, news media and the Metropolitan Police. Bloch and Solomos (2010: 96) have pointed out that 'Macpherson's conclusions and recommendations were still being digested by the police and government when serious rioting broke out in several northern towns between white and Asian youths' in spring and summer of 2001. If the Lawrence family's campaign and the Macpherson Report reintroduced anti-racism to social policy discourse, party political responses to the disturbances in Oldham, Burnley and Bradford, initiated its converse, the scraping out of the remnants of party support for state multiculturalism.

Yet for commentators with a historical awareness of post-war migration, intergenerational stresses and the collapse of educational and labour market compacts in the mill towns in which the textile sector was in terminal decline, the eruptions among young Asians in 2001 were best explained still in terms of structural racism and social exclusion. Arun Kundnani wrote in autumn of 2001:

Their violence was ad hoc, improvised and haphazard. It was no longer the organised community self-defence of 1981 ... the fires this time were lit by the youths of communities falling apart from within, as well as from without; youths whose violence was, therefore, all the more desperate ... Across the Pennine Hills, from Oldham, Burnley, Accrington, Blackburn and Preston to Bradford and Leeds, a string of Pakistani and Bangladeshi communities were among Britain's most impoverished...

Kundnani (2001: 105)

However, voices such as Kundnani's failed to resonate in the wider fields of media and social policy. Two reports that interrogated the outcomes of state multiculturalism were, however, influential. The first was Sir Herman Ouseley's (2001) report *Community Pride Not Prejudice: Making Diversity Work in Bradford*. Ouseley was one of Britain's most respected black public intellectuals. Between 1993 and 2000 he headed the Commission for Racial Equality and was well aware of the longstanding socio-economic fissures in the mill towns. In his report on Bradford, which had been commissioned prior to the 2001 riots, Ouseley was particularly careful to highlight the potential role of youth work and educational projects in addressing young people's disengagement. Yet it was Ouseley's use of the term 'self-segregation' to describe the outcome of years of socio-economic impoverishment that was picked up by news media after the riots in the north of England. Ouseley's report referred to the:

> very worrying drift towards self-segregation, the necessity of arresting and reversing this process through and the role of education in tackling ignorance and bigotry as well as identifying excellent exemplary projects and initiatives that point the way forward.
>
> Ouseley (2001: ii)

The use of the phrase 'self-segregation' has proved contentious, insofar as it suggested that Asian communities in Bradford might, in part, be the drivers of their own social exclusion. Commissioned by the government in the wake of the northern riots, the Cantle Report (2001) expanded on the idea of 'self-segregation', homing in particularly on areas in the north of England in which different communities lived out 'parallel lives' in education, housing, employment and leisure (Cantle, 2001: 9). The Cantle Report's primary concern was disintegration between white and South Asian Muslim communities and its motif was community cohesion. Bloch and Solomos' (2010) perceptive reading of the Cantle Report highlights some of its key messages and contradictions, not least the suggestion that municipal multiculturalism had proven counter-productive:

> According to Cantle, government initiatives had fostered 'enclavisation' and a perception of unfairness in the allocation of public resources in virtually every section of the localities. Without opportunities and spaces to cultivate commonalities, resentments, mythologies and racist attitudes had increased, allowing illiberal communities to close in on themselves ... The lack of cross-cultural contact at neighbourhood level was compounded by the absence of a shared notion of Britishness and little attachment to national identity. Of concern were the difficulties Muslims found in reconciling their strong sense of religious identity with the looser identity requirements of a multicultural secular society.
>
> Bloch and Solomos (2010: 96)

Bloch and Solomos (2010) note the highlighting of certain players in Cantle's depiction of social fragmentation: conservative Muslims, local authority funding mechanisms, lack of concern with shared 'British' values, but also the near absence of other actors. They comment, for instance, that Cantle's Report has 'remarkably little to say about policing philosophy and practice' (Bloch and Solomos, 2010: 97). As Chapter 9 of this book shows, during the 2000s the community cohesion discourse, with its critique of liberal multiculturalism and increased scrutiny of the cultural practices of ethnic minority communities, was to set the tone for the arguments of conservative black thinkers who sought to distance black communities from left politics, and for whom education became a particular site of contest.

Anti-racism in the twenty-first century

The remainder of this chapter explores the ways in which the tensions between the legacies of Macpherson and Cantle inflected black and anti-racist thought on race, education and social policy. The most radical critique of the retreat from Macpherson and the Race Relations (Amendment) Act 2000 was crafted by white British educator David Gillborn in his 2008 book, *Racism and Education: Coincidence or Conspiracy?* Since the 1990s Gillborn, along with Heidi Safia Mirza and Deborah Youdell, had produced a series of influential studies on racial inequalities in education, arguing that systemic racism remained endemic in UK schooling, with policies on selection, exam entry and school exclusions producing persistent, normalized inequalities (Gillborn and Youdell, 2000; Gillborn and Mirza, 2001; Gillborn, 2005). In *Racism and Education*, however, the conceptual tools that Gillborn applied, increasingly present in his work since the mid-2000s, were largely new to British education research. Gillborn spoke of Macpherson and the Race Relations (Amendment) Act 2000 in terms of institutional racism but also as examples of 'interest convergence', as 'contradiction-closing cases' and, most challengingly for a British readership, spoke of education and social policy as being embedded in 'White racial domination' (Gillborn, 2008: 133). The language was drawn from developments in American Critical Race Theory that had been carved out over the previous two decades by Bell (1992), Crenshaw *et al.* (1995) and Delgado and Stefancic (2000, 2001).

For Gillborn, the Stephen Lawrence case had produced several key shifts in race relations policy and ultimately some of the world's strongest legislation on race discrimination. He credited the Macpherson Report with 'putting the notion of institutional racism back into the public domain' (Gillborn, 2008: 134). Yet Gillborn cautioned that 'contradiction-closing cases' such as Lawrence/ Macpherson were always at risk of falling into a pattern that truncated long-term change. Initially hailed as landmark victories against racism, they could be taken as proof in public policy circles that racism had been dealt with, its contradictions 'closed'. They became, therefore, a signal that institutions could 'move on' from issues of race and racism, while subsequently being interpreted locally in so narrow a way as to impact only minimally on daily racial inequalities.

An example, warned Gillborn and the young black anti-racist thinkers who converged around Critical Race Theory (CRT), lay in the gradual retreat from the mandatory duties that the Race Relations (Amendment) Act 2000 placed upon institutions such as schools to produce written race equality policies, to monitor school practices and pupils' achievements and to develop active strategies against racial inequality. After 2007 the gradual modification of those duties through the principle of proportionality increasingly left definitions of appropriate and proportionate action on inequalities to the discretion of individual school bodies. 'Contradiction-closing cases' thus provided a lesson 'not that change is impossible but that change is always contested and every step forward must be valued and protected' (Gillborn, 2008: 134).

The origins of Critical Race Theory

The conceptual tools that Gillborn (2005, 2008) utilized to examine education policy were drawn from CRT. CRT emerged in the USA during the 1970s and 80s as a framework for understanding the endemic presence of race within the American social and political formation. Its origins lie in the breaks made by scholars of colour with the American Critical Legal Studies movement during the 1970s. Theorists such as Derrick Bell and Kimberlé Crenshaw insisted upon the need for a race-conscious analysis of race in US legislation, as opposed to slippage into regarding race as merely a technology of class (Crenshaw *et al.*, 1995). Some of CRT's key concepts, such as interest convergence, contradiction closure and storytelling, were crafted out of revisionist critiques of US civil rights law's liberal assumptions about the progress made in the fight against racism. CRT aimed to counter the ideological claims to neutrality and meritocracy customarily proffered in fields such as law, social policy, news media and education. Through CRT's analyses the 'taken for granted' racialized processes embedded in those fields were made visible; education and law were not neutral fields but instead reproduced and maintained racialized inequalities at manageable levels (Taylor, 2009).

CRT's analytic framework

CRT is now well established in the USA through the work of academics and activists such as Gloria Ladson-Billings, William Tate, Larry Parker, Richard Delgado and Jean Stefancic but it is a relatively new presence in the United Kingdom. Its emergence in the field of education has been detailed in the USA in Dixson and Rousseau (2006) and in Britain by Warmington (2012). Among its theoretical principles are:

- the definition of race as the product 'of social thought and relations ... not objective, inherent or fixed' (Delgado and Stefancic, 2001: 7);
- an understanding of racism as an endemic presence within the political and social formation (Dixson and Rousseau, 2006; Parker, 1998);

- the definition of racism as 'ordinary, not aberrational ... the usual way that society does business' (Delgado and Stefancic, 2001: 7); in other words, as comprising normalized, tacit assumptions and practices, not merely the overt racial hatred espoused by extremist groups;
- the notion of 'interest convergence': that apparently progressive legislative and policy moves against racial inequality are initiated when they converge with the self-interest of white elites and that such measures are often portrayed as having resolved problems of racism, rendering further action unnecessary and excessive (Bell, 1980);
- a commitment to intersectionality, in that CRT's focus on race and racism is also a focus on 'how racism works with, against and through additional axes of differentiation including class, gender, sexuality and disability' (Gillborn, 2008: 36);
- the suggestion that judgements about the credibility and objectivity of analyses of race and racism in fields such as education, law and social policy are regulated by 'rules of racial standing' that privilege (conservative) white discourses over black readings that take issue with the status quo (Bell, 1992).

CRT's adherents argue that these conceptual tools open up a potential space for understanding what Leonardo (2005: 405) terms 'the complete racialization of daily life'. By regarding whites, and not just blacks, as racialized subjects, CRT's social constructionism is apparent in its sometimes controversial usage of the concepts of whiteness and white supremacy: concepts that attempt to name specifically and historically the dominant mode of racism in western modernity but also attempt to distinguish white people from whiteness as ideology. CRT's insistence upon racism as non-aberrational and its way of unpacking whiteness as ideology and practice has met with resistance from UK critics such as Cole (2009).

Racial inequality equals business as usual

The CRT analyses that Gillborn, Shirin Housee, Lorna Roberts, John Preston and other British academics began to develop from the mid-2000s reasserted, with new inflections, the position that racial inequalities in education could only be diagnosed and addressed by placing understandings of schooling within a critical understanding of the wider social antagonisms of racialization and racism. This approach echoed Gilroy's (1987) insistence in *There Ain't No Black in the Union Jack* that racism must be understood not in terms of peripheral, extremist race-hate but as something central to the social formation, an everyday, 'normal' set of social relationships – what CRT often terms 'business as usual' racism (Delgado and Stefancic, 2000: xvi).

Gillborn has used CRT primarily to focus on UK education policy and its reproduction of racial inequalities, particularly among African-Caribbean pupils. These included concerns that had persisted among black communities and anti-racist educators since the 1960s: racialized patterns in setting, the causal relationship between setting and final achievement and the role of teachers' perceptions in ensuring that African-Caribbean pupils were less likely to be placed in upper sets early in their secondary schools careers. Gillborn (2008) also drew attention to GCSE tiering, a practice of which he claimed many parents were unaware, and which was structured so that children entered in lower tiers could not achieve the higher GCSE grades, no matter how well they performed.

In addition, Gillborn (2008) made a series of controversial claims based on data produced by LEAs that conducted ethnic monitoring of children's performance from age five. Their baseline assessment data indicated that at age five African-Caribbean children were among the highest achieving groups entering compulsory schooling, yet at age sixteen African-Caribbean pupils were the lowest performing of the main ethnic groupings. What Gillborn went on to examine were subsequent changes in the assessment of pupils on entry to school. In the five years after Gillborn and Mirza's (2001) study the old baseline assessments were replaced by a new Foundation Stage profile, initial data from which repositioned African-Caribbean pupils' on-entry attainment, claiming that their performance on-entry was lower than that of white and Indian children. Gillborn concluded that this new mode of early years assessment had the effect of diminishing concerns about African-Caribbean pupils' drop off and about the features of schooling that might shape black Caribbean pupils' underachievement.

CRT and tacit racism

For CRT's adherents, such examples of routine practice illustrated a 'tacit intentionality' (Gillborn, 2005: 499) that worked to disadvantage particular groups of BME pupils (particularly African-Caribbean, mixed race and Pakistani pupils) at key points in their school careers. The choice of the term tacit intentionality indicated a reproduction, over generations, of racial inequality in education that was neither deliberate *nor* accidental, in that the British education system appeared to be knowingly committed to achievement type policies and practices on setting, assessment, exam entry and exclusions that were proven to be detrimental to black pupils:

> [W]e know enough about education policy and practice to go a long way to eradicating race injustice in education (funding urban schools to a realistic level; securing testing regimes that do not unfairly discriminate on racial lines; abandoning selective teaching and grouping; broadening the curriculum; diversifying the teaching force; and genuinely acting on the results of ethnic monitoring would all be a good start). In practice, however, high stakes testing, school performance tables and selection by 'ability' are all being used increasingly – despite their known detrimental impact on Black students … racist measures are not only retained, but actually extended…
> Gillborn (2005: 499)

CRT in Britain

How then might CRT articulate with older black British intellectual currents? CRT's transfer to the UK warrants scrutiny. One reason for caution is that CRT has uttered its key conceptual claims in both global and local registers. Speaking globally, Taylor (2009: 4) draws on Charles Mills' dictum that '[r]acism is global White supremacy and is itself a political system, a particular power structure of formal and informal rule, privilege, socio-economic advantages'. However, CRT has 'local' origins that lie specifically in American Critical Legal Studies. The paper that signalled the transfer of CRT to the field of education, Gloria Ladson-Billings and William Tate's (1995) 'Toward a critical race theory of education', speaks CRT at the local US level, asserting that '[r]ace continues to be a significant factor in determining inequity in the United States' (Ladson-Billings and Tate, 1995: 48). There is nothing peculiar about this; all social theory originates somewhere along the line in local observations. However, it does mean that we should pay due attention to the local, historically grounded materials out of which CRT might evolve in the UK, not least the historical resources of black British thought and activism (Warmington, 2012).

For instance, one issue for CRT in the UK is how to define 'black', particularly in fields such as education. In the USA CRT's foundation texts prioritized the racialized experiences of African-Americans. That African-Americans have remained the dominant focus of the 'core' CRT movement is apparent from the fact that 'offshoots' such as LatCrit, Queer-Crit and Critical Race Feminism have developed in order to apply CRT's framework to the experiences of other minoritized groups. In the UK thus far CRT's focus has varied (see, for instance, the collection of writing in Hylton *et al.*, 2011). Gillborn has used the term black to refer solely to African and African-Caribbean people, and has applied CRT mainly to the experiences of African-Caribbean pupils in English schools. By contrast, Shirin Housee's (2008) research has examined the experiences of black university lecturers (in the umbrella sense); Housee (2010) has also focused on South Asian Muslim students. At present, it is unclear whether CRT in the UK will continue to house both definitions of black identity (signifying an adherence, albeit qualified, to 'traditional' UK notions of political blackness) or whether quasi-discrete strands of CRT will emerge to address, for instance, Islamophobia.

Over the past decade CRT has made significant impacts in British academia and educational research. One way in which UK CRT has adapted is that analysis of educational and social *policy* has tended to replace the focus on legislation that has historically driven the development of CRT in the USA. The work of Namita Chakrabarty and John Preston (Chakrabarty and Preston, 2008; Preston, 2010) has focused on the racialization of policy discourses around national security and David Skinner (2011) has drawn upon aspects of CRT to scrutinize racial categorizing in social policy and in sociological methodologies.

Elsewhere, educators such as Kevin Hylton (2009), Lorna Roberts (Parker and Roberts, 2011) and Shirin Housee (2008, 2012) have studied professional practices and learners' experiences, in schooling, higher education and informal settings, focusing on how unequal relations are maintained through classroom discourses and institutional practices. The racialization of professional practices and relationships in education have also been explored in Nicola Rollock's (2012) work on racialized relationships within academia. Rollock's examination of academics' interpersonal relationships, in part, returns to black British intellectuals' concerns about poor BME representation in academia (see also non-CRT analyses, such as Modood and Acland, 1998; ECU, 2011; Shepherd, 2011; Singh, 2011) but it also refers back to Derrick Bell's analyses of the ways in which equalities legislation and policy attend to crude and overt racism, whilst leaving untouched the everyday practices that reproduce white privilege. In this respect CRT also overlaps with emergent critical whiteness studies in the UK (see Garner, 2007; Preston, 2013).

Conclusion

It remains to be seen how far CRT's proponents are able to wield influence in policy and practice, and at the level of community activism. In contrast, Modood's 'post-black' form of multiculturalism both reflects and has been strongly influential upon shifts in theorization and policy developments around race, education and social justice. However, currently CRT's importance in the field of education is twofold. Firstly, it has become an intellectual space around which a new generation of black and anti-racist thinkers has coalesced. Secondly, CRT has reinserted a particular kind of political blackness into educational research and activism. CRT's approach reverts explicitly to anti-racism and has little use for discourses of ethnicity and diversity *per se*. This, of course, has led its critics to attack what they see as its dependence on black/white binaries (Cole, 2008).

Arguably, it is the 'white' component of that binary that has proven most challenging for CRT's critics. For what CRT, and related work in critical whiteness studies, insists upon is the need to match interrogations of black identities with equally rigorous interrogations of white identities and practices. One of the residual limitations of sociologies of race in Britain has, since the days of Rex and Banton, lain in the focusing of its gaze on black subjects – black masculinities, black cultural practices, black resistance – without subjecting white practices and identities to the same scrutiny. Too often even now blacks, but not whites, are implicitly seen as 'possessing' race. One of CRT's challenges is that, in refusing colour-blind analyses of institutional practices, it treats white people too as racialized subjects. CRT has offered one set of possibilities for addressing race and education, post-Macpherson and post-Cantle. However, other new black intellectuals have taken a very different approach: one that may represent a major break with the post-war black British politics. The final chapter of this book examines the emergence of a new black social conservatism and its claims about education.

9 'Post-multicultural' education?

> What is the special responsibility of black intellectuals as we enter a new century? ... Can we rethink what we mean by black and/or progressive politics, and craft a new, more effective paradigm for activism? Can we construct a theory and practice which challenges racism but also addresses the contradictions and inequalities of gender, class and community? Can we redefine the category of 'blackness' itself, away from its racial and biological concepts and identity-based politics, towards a progressive politics and common language that brings together oppressed people with very distinct ethnicities, cultures and traditions? ... The future of black liberation is inextricably linked to our ability successfully to answer these questions, speaking to the vast majority of humanity.
>
> Marable (1997: 12–13)

Introduction

This book began by discussing the ways in which Britain's black intelligentsia has historically grown up around sites of educational desire. The influence that black intellectual movements have had on British education since the 1960s forms a substantial but often hidden history. Yet with the decline of the black education movements, of multicultural education and of some of the traditional bases of independent black politics, has the flow of black intellectual activism in education stemmed? Leading black thinkers have, for instance, questioned whether a British anti-racist movement still exists in any meaningful sense (Kundnani, 2007; Younge, 2013). Black commentators from across the political spectrum have pointed also to the decline of independent black politics, eroded, in part, by the broader retreat of progressive left politics and, in part, by the fragmentation of British political blackness into its constituent parts (Phillips, M., 2001; Harker, 2011; Woolley, 2011). In academia, meanwhile, senior figures such as Harry Goulbourne and Heidi Safia Mirza have expressed concerns about the dearth of black academics in the UK (Shepherd, 2011; Williams, R., 2013). On the other hand, as Chapter 8 has shown, new currents, still recognizably within traditions of black radical thought, have emerged in the past decade.

This chapter reflects further on how new understandings of race, education and social justice are being shaped by wider black intellectual shifts, in a landscape that might be described as 'post-multicultural'. To use the term 'post-multicultural' is not to chime in unquestioningly with facile claims that multiculturalism is dead, still less that racial inequalities in education are no longer significant; it does, however, suggest spaces for new questions about equalities and cultural diversity. This chapter begins by considering debates that have emerged recently among black thinkers who have argued, almost heretically, the need for a break with the political traditions of the black left. They claim that black progressives have misrecognized and misrepresented the essentially conservative nature of black communities, particularly with regard to youth and education. Does this new black social conservatism offer a radical rethinking of education or has it gained its standing through downplaying the persistence of institutional racism? This last chapter traces the contours of black Britain at the start of the twenty-first century and asks how fertile the landscape that bred generations of black intellectual activity around race and education is today?

Black intellectual heresies

One respect in which black British thought differs from American models is that in Britain there is no real archetype of the black conservative public intellectual. Being a black British public thinker has, almost by definition, meant being located somewhere on the liberal-left spectrum, with all that implies in terms of analyses of race, class and education. However, in the past decade a number of black conservative intellectuals have explicitly positioned themselves in opposition to the anti-racist traditions of the left. Their iconoclastic rhetoric has, in large part, been developed around debates on youth and education. The new black conservative analyses share several discursive features: critiques of multiculturalism; suggestions that black pupils have been ill-served by liberal teaching methods; and a renewed 'behavioural' focus on black parenting, youth culture and educational values. They represent their position as speaking for a socially conservative Britain that they claim is authentic.

In relation to the politics that produced the post-war black education movements, these new social conservatives, such as Tony Sewell, Katharine Birbalsingh and Munira Mirza, comprise a heretical strain in black British thought. Whereas other contemporary black thinkers have pointed to the mutability of racism, identifying new manifestations of nativism and Islamophobia, the black social conservatives make the bold claim that racism has not shifted shape but has actually receded. Making an explicit break with the multiculturalism of the 1980s and 90s, Munira Mirza (Deputy Mayor for Education and Culture for London) has claimed that: 'Old prejudices have faded ... Race is no longer the significant disadvantage it is often portrayed to be' (Mirza, M., 2010: 31–2). Meanwhile, black educator Tony Sewell has argued that the continuation over forty years of disproportionate rates of exclusion among African-Caribbean boys is a symptom whose contemporary causes are quite distinct from those of the 1980s. For Sewell and others the premises of British multiculturalism have ceased to match the landscape of fact.

Post-multicultural claims

Of course, attempts to think beyond multiculturalism have not been solely the work of black conservatives. As discussed in Chapters 4 and 5 of this book, sections of the black left have been strident critics of what they regard as evasive, tokenistic state multiculturalism. More recently, cultural theorists such as Paul Gilroy and Kwame Anthony Appiah have argued that multiculturalism has proven to be an ambiguous tool in the struggle against racism. Gilroy instead has proposed 'conviviality' (Gilroy, 2004: xi) as a framework for reimagining the possibilities offered by cultural pluralism. Gilroy's conviviality signifies the 'processes of cohabitation and interaction that have made multiculture an ordinary feature of social life in Britain's urban areas' (Gilroy, 2004: xi). For Gilroy, it is these ordinary, daily practices that suggest ways of countering defensive models of British identity predicated on maintaining people of colour as immigrant outsiders:

> the briefest look around confirms that multicultural society has not actually expired. The noisy announcements of its demise is itself a political gesture, an act of wishful thinking ... aimed at abolishing any ambition toward plurality and at consolidating the growing sense that it is now illegitimate to believe that multiculture can and should be orchestrated by government in the public interest.
>
> Gilroy (2004: 1)

Gilroy has suggested that young, black intellectuals have the resources to develop understandings of Britain's social formation that might draw upon colonial histories, in order to critique not just racism but the entire concept of race: 'These insights are not ours alone but will belong to anyone who is prepared to use them' (Gilroy, 2004: 61). In short, Gilroy has argued for the weakening of cultural essentialism, while retaining a commitment to plurality. This is one form of 'post-multicultural' ambition.

The new black social conservatism

However, since the mid-2000s another, quite different 'post-multicultural' black intellectual discourse has emerged, one that has defined itself through public pronouncements on youth and education. Although far from cohesive, it might usefully be described as a new black social conservatism. The new black social conservative discourse offers an intriguing parallel with Critical Race Theory (CRT). Like CRT, its analysis of education and society looks to intellectual influences other than the sociology of Hall and Gilroy that has dominated since the 1980s. Like CRT, it suggests that those seeking to understand and better the experiences of black people in British society should heed black voices. And like CRT, its analysis of race and education is central. Unlike CRT, however, black social conservatism has a very problematic relationship to black radical traditions. This is perhaps why the new black conservative voices have rarely been remarked upon sociologically. Yet, while black conservative intellectuals are a minority within a minority, they have garnered significant media space and forged links with policy-makers.

The new black social conservatism encompasses figures with diverse political histories but its central claim is that state multiculturalism and alliances between black radicals and the British left produced misrecognition of the values of black British communities. The hothouse of anti-racist politics, runs the argument, denied the strong vein of social conservatism in African-Caribbean, African and Asian communities. The consequences have been an atrophied black politics, ossified in discourses of oppression and rebellion, and generations (particularly of African-Caribbean youth) locked into patterns of educational underachievement. In a 2011 radio broadcast Trevor Phillips historicized the black social conservative discourse:

> In a sense, what you saw in the first half of the 80s was the left outsourcing its anger and its outrage to ethnic minorities. And that is what really characterised "black" politics. Though it's fantastic for those who are politically active, those who are radical and particularly those who are on the left, it's not fantastic for the majority of the community. First of all, it put the African Caribbean community in a box, parts of which it doesn't feel comfortable with. African Caribbeans historically are socially conservative and there are some aspects of left politics that that community as a whole is not comfortable with...
>
> Phillips, T. (BBC, 2011: 6)

Phillips, former Head of the UK's Commission for Racial Equality (2003–06) and subsequently Chair (2007–12) of it successor, the Equality and Human Rights Commission, remains one of the most prominent black voices in the field of social policy. A veteran equalities activist, with a background in the National Union of Students and the Runnymede Trust, he has also been closely aligned with the upper echelons of the Labour Party. As a black public intellectual, Phillips has epitomized a particular double bind, sometimes being depicted by the black left as an establishment figure, and at other times being demonized by the right-wing press as a radical multiculturalist. In 2005, for instance, Phillips was decried in conservative news media when he suggested that separate classes might enable black boys to overcome poor school achievement (Lightfoot, 2005). Phillips' repositioning of himself in relation to historical alliances between black communities and left politics was, therefore, a notable shift.

A break with the past?

The major black British public intellectual currents of the post-war period have not, by any means, been homogenous but almost all have been positioned on the broad left. This has implied at an 'economic' level concern with, for instance, the redistribution of wealth, strong welfare provision, countering the social effects of neo-liberal economics; at a 'cultural' level, the politics of pluralism and recognition; and at an 'institutional' level the need to address the continued presence of structural racism and discrimination (Shukra, 1998). Black left discourses have been based on claims that:

- racism remains salient in the social and political formation, necessitating continued commitment to anti-racist struggle;
- the structures of education, the labour market and criminal justice tend to reproduce racial inequalities;
- black educational underperformance must be understood as the product of wider deprivation and social antagonisms;
- independent black thinkers should be critical of assimilationist politics, and advocate cultural pluralism as part of wider drives for social justice;
- black communities constitute, in alliance with other disadvantaged social groups, a potentially progressive political force.

Certainly, there have been black thinkers who have critiqued particular elements of these positions (for instance, Gilroy, 1987, 2000). However, such critiques have still been positioned in recognizably left-wing thought. Even Maureen Stone's (1985) rejection of multicultural education drew upon Gramsci, Bernstein and Bourdieu in its theorization of social reproduction.

In contrast, putative black social conservatism is characterized by deliberate breaks with the social analyses of the black and anti-racist left, and is predicated on the claim that black social conservatism is an authentic voice historically marginalized by black activists' alliances with the broader, socially liberal left. Alongside this claim to cultural and historical authenticity, the black social conservative discourse also makes a claim to innovation, arguing the need to 'move on' politically, to cease replaying the battles of post-war black politics, embedded as they were in discourses of conflict and oppression. This variant of post-multiculturalism has converged closely with the renewed critiques of multiculturalism that emerged in British politics in the early 2000s, following the events of 9/11 and 7/7, the disturbances in the north of England, concerns about 'self-segregation' and anxieties over the radicalization of Muslim communities (see Modood, 2005; Kundnani, 2007; Bunting, 2011). What distinguished these critiques of multiculturalism was that they were advanced not just from traditional heartlands of anti-multiculturalism, located in what Gilroy (2004) describes as the melancholia of post-imperial Britain, but also from commentators on the centre-left and 'modernizing' centre-right.

Too diverse?

The community cohesion agenda of the early 2000s raised questions, explicit and implicit, about the role of municipal policies in fostering ethnic divisions in urban centres (Cantle, 2001). In February 2004, a wider set of questions about tensions between cultural diversity and social solidarity were posed in a widely noted think piece by the editor of the left-leaning *Prospect* magazine, David Goodhart. It was titled: 'Too diverse? Is Britain becoming too diverse to sustain the mutual obligations behind a good society and the welfare state?' Goodhart's comment focused on questions about the degree to which a sustainable welfare state was dependent on its members feeling social solidarity – a sense of common culture and reciprocity – with those fellow citizens with whom national wealth is to be shared. For Goodhart, the increasing social diversity of Britain presented:

> one of the central dilemmas of political life in developed societies: sharing and solidarity can conflict with diversity. This is an especially acute dilemma for progressives who want plenty of both ... the left's recent love affair with diversity may come at the expense of the values and even the people that it once championed.
>
> Goodhart (2004: 1)

While Goodhart's initial depiction of a 'too diverse' Britain ranged beyond race and ethnicity, he acknowledged, perhaps disingenuously, that the 'visibility of ethnic difference means that it often overshadows other forms of diversity' (Goodhart, 2004: 3). Certainly, in the subsequent reporting and debates over Goodhart's article, ethnic diversity and state multiculturalism became the hinges of anxiety. The year after the *Prospect* article Trevor Phillips, then Head of the Commission for Racial Equality, delivered a widely reported speech in Manchester speculating that the political focus on cultural diversity had undermined community cohesion, leaving Britain 'sleepwalking into segregation'. In the changing mood Tariq Modood (2005), Sivanandan (2006) and the IRR's Jenny Bourne (2007), in the past by no means uncritical of state multiculturalism, all penned pieces in defence of the principles of multiculturalism.

The discourse of black conservatism

The years 2008–11 saw these new black conservative voices solidify as a public presence. This was a period that saw the demise of the New Labour government that had held office from 1997 to 2010. Within a few months of coming to office the new Conservative Prime Minister David Cameron declared that multiculturalism had 'failed' (Doward, 2011). Summer 2011 saw the most widespread rioting in England's major cities since the mid-1980s. Political responses to the riots invoked the image of a broken society, a discourse in which the youth of multi-ethnic urban centres figured strongly. Moreover, anxieties over multiculturalism produced a moral panic over the educational inequalities experienced by fractions of the white working class (see Gillborn's, 2010, analysis of this turn). White victim narratives emerged in media commentaries on multiculturalism, education and political representation. In the field of education, these dovetailed with concerns about gender gaps in educational achievement, creating particular concern over the school performance of disadvantaged white working-class boys.

It was in this context that black thinkers such as Tony Sewell, Trevor Phillips and Katharine Birbalsingh were accorded levels of media attention rarely given to black commentators. Some of these black critics of multiculturalism were established public intellectuals, who had roots in anti-racism but who now appeared to reposition themselves. Educator Tony Sewell had, in the 1990s, developed analyses of race and schooling that explored complex dynamics of cultural racism, hyper-masculinity, school conflict and survival (Sewell, 1997). A decade later, Sewell's writing shifted in emphasis towards behavioural explanations of black boys' underachievement and criticism of the impact of liberal teaching methods on their school experiences.

Others invoking black social conservatism included voices from both the Conservative Party, such as Shaun Bailey, Samuel Kasumu and Kwasi Kwarteng MP, and from the Labour Party. David Lammy, Labour MP for the racially mixed ward of Tottenham, north London, offered thoughtful reflections on the riots of summer 2011 in his book *Out of the Ashes: Britain After the Riots* (Lammy, 2011). However, subsequent media coverage chose to home in on Lammy's criticisms of liberal middle-class culture's opposition to corporal punishment. Among the newer voices was teacher and writer Katharine Birbalsingh, who became prominent following a controversial speech to the Conservative Party Conference in 2010, in which she attacked what she saw as cultures of low expectations and failure in Britain's state schools (Birbalsingh, 2010b). In the aftermath Birbalsingh lost her job as a deputy head, was widely defended within the Conservative Party and the centre-right press, and protested in her online account of events that she would not be 'silenced while our children are betrayed by schools' (Birbalsingh, 2010a).

While its origins were diverse, therefore, the black conservative discourse contained some recurrent features. These entered territory long considered out of bounds by black educators and activists, who had opposed explanations of educational failure that they regarded as pathologizing black pupils and their communities. Overlapping themes included:

- suggestions that race and racism have declined in salience in the UK;
- arguments that black (African-Caribbean) underachievement is due, at least in part, to anti-school cultures and poor parental support for schools and children;
- arguments that multicultural education and other liberal learning and teaching approaches have failed black children and are culturally at odds with the 'social conservatism' of black communities;
- claims that multiculturalism and anti-racism have promoted cultures of victimhood, particularly among black male pupils;
- claims that the educational success of high achieving minority ethnic groups casts doubt on arguments that structural/institutional racism is a significant factor in schooling.

Black boys: anti-school behaviours?

Threaded through black conservative analyses of education was the claim that liberal multiculturalists were too ready to blame institutional racism for black pupils' continued underachievement (particularly that of African-Caribbean boys), while shying away from black pupils' own part in creating damaging school relationships. In the 1990s Tony Sewell's influential *Black Masculinities and Schooling: How Black Boys Survive Modern Schooling* (Sewell, 1997) exemplified perennial tensions between structural and behavioural analyses of race and education. In *Black Masculinities* Sewell began by offering a structural reading of how African-Caribbean boys were located in a school system that reproduced racial inequalities. However, Sewell's real preference was for subcultural analysis and in the latter part of the book Sewell's constructions of pupils as 'rebels', 'innovators', 'retreatists' and 'conformists' largely superseded structural analysis of the school system.

Sewell's early work, therefore, was pitched in the midst of a dialogue – or non-dialogue – akin to the one that Cornel West described in the US context, wherein:

> [o]n the one hand, there are those who highlight the *structural* constraints on the life chances of black people. This point of view involves a subtle historical and sociological analysis of ... job and residential discrimination, skewed unemployment rates, inadequate healthcare, and poor education. On the other hand, there are those who stress the behavioral impediments to black upward mobility ... the waning of the Protestant ethic – hard work, deferred gratification ... Those in the first camp – the liberal structuralists – call for full employment, health, education and child-care programs, and broad affirmative action ... the second camp – conservative behaviorists – promote self-help programs, black business expansion, and non-preferential job treatment.
>
> West (1992: 37)

In Britain liberal structuralists have tended to dominate black educational debates. In contrast, Sewell's study of black masculinities marked a tentative return to behavioural analyses of black youth, albeit decked out in subcultural theory. His reliance on subcultural analysis also raised perennial issues about subcultural approaches to studying disadvantaged pupils' experiences: namely, whether the emphasis on pupils' social practices exaggerated the power of black or working-class children to shape their educational outcomes and whether subcultural analyses were limited by their attraction to the most visible, supposedly authentic, anti-school rebels.

A decade on, when Sewell published *Generating Genius: Black Boys in Search of Love, Ritual and Schooling* in 2009, his position was less agnostic. *Generating Genius* comprised Sewell's own evaluation of his intervention projects that were based around intensive summer schools for African-Caribbean boys. In his account of how rebel boys might, like Heidi Safia Mirza's black girls, resist racism by placing value on educational desire, Sewell explicitly rejected what he saw as an overly structural approach: '[t]he idea that students are powerless victims in a wider "game" of institutional racism is nothing less than patronising. Even when faced with white racism, these black students are their own worst enemies' (Sewell, 2009: 55). For Sewell the error of many structural analyses of black boys' underachievement lay in seeing only top-down institutional power. Sewell now explored the under-acknowledged power of peer pressure: the deriding of educational success by some black boys as 'acting white', cults of anti-intellectualism and dependence on defensive hyper-masculinity. However, in his subsequent analysis, Sewell did not entirely abandon the notion of black boys as structural victims; he spoke of the Generating Genius project as a process of shielding black boys 'from those who want them to wallow in self-pity' (Sewell, 2010: 34). For Sewell, it seemed, generations of black boys had become victims of liberal approaches to multiculturalism and education that 'excused' black failure on the grounds that it was the inevitable product of wider social disadvantage.

'Has multiculturalism had its day?'

During 2010–11 *Prospect* magazine began to provide a platform for black British intellectuals who were publicly critical of multiculturalism and whose analyses of youth and education were embedded in the discourse of black social conservatism. In autumn 2010 Sewell was among four black thinkers featured in *Prospect* magazine's cover story, titled 'Rethinking race: has multiculturalism had its day?' Encompassing views on education, mental health, the arts and social policy, the thematic thrust was against the ghettoization, low educational expectations and weak analyses of social justice that the authors claimed derived from Britain's attachment to outdated liberal models of multiculturalism. Tony Sewell's contribution, 'Master class in victimhood', was typically outspoken: 'I believe black underachievement is due to the low expectations of school leaders, who do not want to be seen as racist and who position black boys as victims' (Sewell, 2010: 33). Years of lip-service to anti-racism in education had, Sewell suggested, developed young blacks' sense of being victims within the school system:

> The bad boys in that class had a default reaction – all their experience was seen through the lens of racism. They had no measure to understand their lives other than that of the victim ... We have a generation who have all the language and discourse of the race relations industry but no devil to fight ... Much of the supposed evidence of institutional racism is flimsy.
>
> Sewell (2010: 34)

In a kind of double-victimology, therefore, Sewell argued that black boys must abandon the false consciousness of victimhood, while also insisting that black boys *really were* victims – but victims of a kind of liberal racism. This became a motif among black conservative commentators. Katharine Birbalsingh's controversial blogs on schooling became the basis of her book, *To Miss with Love*

(Birbalsingh, 2011b). In the book Birbalsingh positioned herself as both heretical and authentic: a comprehensive pupil who had progressed to Oxford, an Oxford graduate who taught for many years in inner-city schools, a teacher unafraid of critiquing the assumptions that she insisted enabled teachers and pupils to co-exist in failure:

> Black kids all have that winning ace up their sleeve, which they can play when the going gets really tough – the race card: 'It's cause I is black, innit ... She hates us 'cause we is black' ... if the black kid has got himself a slightly scared new white teacher, he is in serious business. He has got them running scared.
>
> Birbalsingh (2011b: 55)

Here the echoes of Sewell, even of Maureen Stone, were coarsened into caricature: black victim of failed liberal schooling bests white teacher; white liberal teacher abandons black child.

The framing of commentators such as Sewell and Birbalsingh as authentic voices with long experience of inner-city schooling was itself strangely contradictory. These critics of multiculturalism's identity politics were themselves apparently validated by their authentic identities. For example, *Prospect*'s 'Rethinking Race' edition was introduced by Munira Mirza with the assertion that:

> [t]he following articles are by people who want to change the way in which racism and diversity are discussed in Britain and question the assumptions of some "official anti-racism". None of them is white and therefore cannot easily be dismissed as ignorant, naïve or unwittingly prejudiced.
>
> Mirza, M. (2010: 31)

Moreover, the classroom accounts of Sewell and Birbalsingh often had the ring of allegory, rather than ethnography. For instance, Sewell recounted winning over a table of (black) bad boys, encouraging them to excel in a classroom task, by the lure of a prize of a box of chocolates:

> There we have it: the trauma of 400 years of racism, slavery and oppression overcome by the desire for a soft-centre ... At the end of the lesson ... [t]he winner was Table 5. They had worked with their meagre resources and come up with something magnificent.
>
> Sewell (2010: 33)

The allegory was clear. Here structures, institutions and history were downplayed. Black pupils could pull themselves up by marshalling their meagre resources into success. Like Maureen Stone, Sewell's analysis of race and schooling is embedded in what Fisher (2009) has termed 'capitalist realism', wherein contemporary neo-liberalism is represented as permanent, the only realistically attainable mode of social organization. Writing at opposite ends of the neo-liberal era both Stone and Sewell take education in capitalism as a given, with all that implies about the permanence of inequalities produced by credentialism, higher education and differential cultural capital.

In autumn 2011 BBC Radio Four devoted an edition of its current affairs programme *Analysis* to the emergence of what it termed 'A New Black Politics'. Presented by *Prospect*'s David Goodhart, it featured contributions both from veteran black 'left' commentators, including Trevor Phillips, Linda Bellos, Stafford Scott and David Lammy MP, and from newer 'conservative' voices, including Kwasi Kwarteng MP and Shaun Bailey. The programme focused on whether the responses of black thinkers and activists to that summer's riots signalled a rift between older black British left traditions and newer figures who questioned the discourses of anti-racism. Did activists who had grown up with the racial politics of the 1970s and 80s speak for black Britain in 2011 or were they, as Goodhart (BBC, 2011: 13) put it, old generals still 'fighting the last war'? The programme offered reflections on the disparities between underachievement in African-Caribbean communities and the greater successes in education and employment of East African Asians, the legacies of the schooling of black children in the 1960s and 70s, and the ways in which black politics was shaped by the politics of anti-racist protest in the 1980s. Once again, social conservatism was proposed as an authentic representation of silent black values. In the broadcast Conservative parliamentary candidate Shaun Bailey (described as an 'authentically "street" black west Londoner', BBC, 2011: 3) crafted an antithesis between multiculturalism and 'authentic' cultural diversity: 'I think now black communities are reaching a point where they think well hold on a second, at our heart, at least socially, we're very conservative and we are now beginning to compromise some of our core beliefs' (Bailey, BBC, 2011: 3).

Pointedly, the programme repeatedly asked whether the priorities of the black and anti-racist left had truncated the aspirations of young black people in education and employment, particularly young African-Caribbean men. Here Goodhart's editorial comments echoed the rhetoric of Sewell and Birbalsingh:

> Is British society still to blame for some of the real problems facing some young black, urban men, or are they the authors of their own misfortune or at least victims of an ideology that says they can only fail in British society, thus ensuring that they do?
>
> Goodhart (BBC, 2011: 11)

Thus the building blocks of the new black conservatism include the creation of antitheses between 'liberal' teachers and 'conservative' black parents, and between underachieving black (African-Caribbean) children and other, better achieving 'model' ethnic minorities, such as Chinese and Indian pupils. Black 'conservative' discourses also create equivalences, so that black pupils' underachievement is equated (and held to be the product of) anti-school subcultures. Multiculturalism is equated with a culture of victimhood – and, insofar as they subscribe to discourses of victimhood, young black people become actual victims of anti-racist ideology. Because the rationale of the new black conservatism is dependent on depictions of underachieving African-Caribbean young men, it remains largely silent on the experiences of black women and of Asian communities, except those that serve as model minorities in the discourse. The 'conservatism' of Muslim communities, of course, remains too problematic to be absorbed into the black conservative discourse.

Where are we now?

After decades embedded in what Trevor Phillips termed the 'politics of protest' (BBC, 2011: 12), might these new black conservative analyses provide a standpoint from which to re-open behavioural analyses of black parenting, community values and student cultures? Or are such claims premature? Are the advocates of black social conservatism, in fact, the beneficiaries of what CRT terms enhanced racial standing, the exceptional status accorded to 'the black person who publicly disparages ... other blacks who are speaking or acting in ways that upset whites' (Bell, 1992: 114)?

It is not only adherents of CRT or traditional anti-racism who have queried the claims of black social conservatives. Aditya Chakrabortty, whose journalism focuses on economic and social policy, has argued that assertions about the decline of racism are more a rhetorical claim to 'newness' and political vitality than a factual description of current social relationships:

> Read enough of these pieces, or pay attention to what senior politicians from all parties tell you, and you might think that Britain is now in the middle of a national re-enactment of the Cosby Show. Colour is just an incidental feature and certainly no bar to pulling one's self up by the bootstraps. Talk such as this gives austerity minded coalition politicians all the excuse they need to cut funding to all those old fashioned community groups.
>
> Yet race remains a massive factor in determining our opportunities and life chances. Two in three British Bangladeshi children grow up in poverty in the UK (compared with two in ten of their white counterparts). Even those at the top of the career ladder, who have been dealt all the right cards and played them correctly, are still subject to what ... Tariq Modood calls an "ethnic penalty" ... Since time immemorial ethnic-minority children have been told they need to work two, three times as hard as their white friends: that rule hasn't expired yet.
>
> Chakrabortty (2010: 5)

So what is the current state of black Britain's intellectual life, its thoughts on education and social justice? How central will education remain to the leading edge of black intellectual activity in Britain, given the disparity of educational experiences among minority ethnic communities and the decline of the traditional black education movements?

By the beginning of the twenty-first century successive shifts had redrawn the ethnic profile of Britain's state schools. By 2003 three in four primary pupils in

England and Wales, and four in five secondary pupils, fitted the description 'white British'. South Asian pupils formed the second largest ethnic group in schools: around 7 per cent in primary schools and 6 per cent at secondary level. Of these, children of Pakistani origin were the biggest Asian group in primary schools and Indian pupils the largest in secondary schools. Moreover, primary schools now had more black African pupils than black Caribbean children. Immigration patterns meant that despite Britain's quarter-century membership of the EU, only 2 per cent of pupils were from white backgrounds other than British and Irish (Bhattacharyya *et al.*, 2003; DfES, 2004). In 2011, 24.3 per cent of pupils in state schools in England and Wales were from ethnic minority backgrounds. In primary schools 26.5 per cent of pupils were from ethnic minority backgrounds. In secondary schools 22.2 per cent of pupils were from an ethnic minority (compared with 17.7 per cent in 2006) (DfE, 2011).

Census data from 2011 also indicated wider changes in the country's population. In England and Wales the proportion of people identifying themselves as 'white British' declined from 87 per cent to just over 80 per cent between 2001 and 2011, with Indians comprising the largest 'black and minority ethnic' (BME) group (2.5 per cent of the population of England and Wales). Black African people (1.76 of the population) and 'mixed race' people (2.19 per cent) both now outnumbered black Caribbeans (1.06 per cent). In the decade between the censuses of 2001 and 2011 the Muslim population of England and Wales had risen from 4.1 per cent to 6.7 per cent (BRAP, 2011). Notable too was the growth in minority ethnic populations other than the traditional communities established in the 1950s, 60s and 70s. Race and racism might not have disappeared but ideas about race, ethnicity, nationality and identity – as Stuart Hall had predicted long before – were being substantially redefined.

Between the censuses of 2001 and 2011 the education landscape had also, in true British style, continued to shift, albeit still within the embedded frameworks of standards, achievement and parental choice. Tony Blair's New Labour government had come to power in 1997 professing education to be its priority. New Labour's flagship academies programme further weakened local authorities' control of state schools. Initially designed to serve disadvantaged districts, the academy schools were funded under contracts between individual schools and central government. Their grand claim was to offer schools greater managerial autonomy, allowing scope for greater curriculum flexibility, the provision of particular subject specialisms, and partnerships between schools and sponsors from industry (BBC, 2010). First applied to secondary schools under special measures as a panacea for low achievement, the academies programme was expanded and by 2010, when New Labour left office, there were around two hundred in England and Wales.

The succeeding Conservative government took up and further promoted the academies programme 'extending it far beyond the impoverished inner-city areas that it was originally intended to serve' (Benn, 2011: 4). The Conservatives also developed the free schools initiative (DfE, 2013a, 2013b). Like the academies, the free schools were publicly funded but outside of local authority management.

Where they differed from academies was in the emphasis they placed on the potential for parents, teachers and community groups to create new free schools, giving them the 'added ideological appeal of appearing to emanate from the combined dynamism and desperation of parents and teachers up and down the country' (Benn, 2011: 4). Dynamism and desperation had historically characterized the black education movements. Both among education ministers keen to sell the concept of the free schools project and black educators seeking to build new educational routes, the free schools were depicted as an opportunity to build on the legacies of supplementary schools. In 2011 Katharine Birbalsingh launched her own attempt to create a free school.

With many applications for free school status still under consideration, whether free schools will advantage black communities, particularly the socially excluded, is a contentious issue. Optimists see opportunities to renew independent black educational initiatives (Birbalsingh, 2011a); others doubt that black parents, teachers and pupils will be among those to benefit from a schools revolution they suspect will entrench, rather than challenge inequalities of race and class in education (BBC, 2013). As yet black communities have featured largely as respondents to the free schools agenda, rather than drivers.

Conclusion: black renewal or decline?

There is no shortage of black intellectual activity in Britain today. Nowhere is this more apparent than in the arts where Zadie Smith, Caryl Phillips, Roy Williams, Andrea Levy, Dreda Say Mitchell, Kwame Kwei-Armah, Julian Joseph, Lemn Sissay and Benjamin Zephaniah remain vital presences. Print, blog and broadcast journalism too have produced significant black public voices, including Gary Younge, Aditya Chakrabortty, Ratna Lachman, Joseph Harker, Yasmin Alibhai-Brown, Hugh Muir and Sarfraz Manzoor. Popular historians Colin Grant and Kwasi Kwarteng have also garnered attention in media circles.

Yet the interplay between black intellectual work and the worlds of education and social policy is, some would argue, less than robust. At the beginning of the twenty-first century Owusu (2000: 12) still regarded Stuart Hall and Sivanandan as 'the two most formidable veterans of Black intellectual debate'. Anyone who has attended British conferences on race, sociology and education will attest to the influence that the generation of black thinkers that emerged in the 1970s and 80s still wields. One explanation for lack of high-profile successors to Hall, Gilroy and Sivanandan may be the withering of independent black politics in Britain. Sivanandan's Institute of Race Relations maintains its presence but, as discussed in Chapters 5 and 8 of this book, the independent networks that produced the black education movements, Race Today and the Asian Youth Movements, have dissipated (Phillips, M., 2001; Alleyne, 2002; White et al., 2005). Many supplementary schools arguably now operate as adjuncts to a marketized and credentialized education system (John, G., 2005). Non-governmental organizations such as Runnymede (under the auspices of Director Rob Berkeley) and the Joseph Rowntree Trust exert valuable influence on debates around race and education but both occupy established third sector roles.

When considering how future grassroots black activism might emerge and how it might impact upon policy and politics another area of debate has been traditional relationships between black activists and the broader left. In the 1970s and 80s black public intellectual spaces grew out of the new social movements of the left and local and national left-wing politics. The question of how far the fortunes of independent black politics have waned with the fortunes of the organized left in Britain is a larger one than can be addressed fully here (see Chakrabortty, 2011; Williams, S., 2012; Goodhart, 2013) but it would be disingenuous to seek like-for-like comparison between the political field that produced New Beacon, Gus John and even the Labour Party's Black Sections and the political landscape in which today's young black activists seek space. The left of the 1970s and 80s also produced white interlocutors who were concerned with dialogues with black activists. Gargi Bhattacharyya is among those who have asked whether the white, policy-making interlocutor still exists; that question returns us to claims about the de-racialization of British politics and consequent constraints on the emergence of new black public intellectual voices.

There is currently also widespread disenchantment over British academia's support for new black voices (see Jones, C., 2006; Wright *et al.*, 2007; Equality Challenge Unit, 2011; Singh, 2011). In recent years headlines such as 'Black intellectual seems an oxymoron in England' (Phillips, S., 2004), 'How Britain treats its black academics' (Boateng, 2013) and '14,000 British professors – but only 50 are black' (Shepherd, 2011) have periodically appeared in the British press, highlighting the continued marginalization of black academics in British higher education, in both numbers and seniority. The brain drain of black British social scientists to the USA (Phillips, S., 2004) may be cited as further evidence of the marginal status of race-conscious scholarship in British academia. It should be noted that currently an online forum exists specifically for black academics who are considering relocating outside Britain. It is hard to calculate the educational losses that result from this conceptual and bodily attrition.

However, before decrying the weakening of links between black academia, grassroots black politics and educational activism, we should again acknowledge the demographic shifts in 'black' Britain. There is no reason why the grassroots educational movements of the twenty-first century should resemble the post-Windrush, first and second generation Caribbean dominated activism that shaped protest and debate among earlier generations. Thinkers whose identifications are shaped by faith, language and ethnicity may produce new forms of educational activism, as the new migrant communities surely will (see Pillai *et al.*, 2007; Harris, 2009; Howson and Sallah, 2009).

Moreover, perhaps we should not over-inflate anxieties about the extent to which black public intellectuals remain marginalized or, conversely, about the extent to which some black public voices might become co-opted into popular anti-multicultural discourses. For as this book suggested at its outset, black British intellectual life has always been the product of a kind of double consciousness, moving between margins and centre, alienation and belonging, alignment and critique. Current anxieties about the readiness with which black educational voices are heard should not be allowed to obscure the very real impacts of the post-war black presence on our understandings of education and social justice.

When I began documentary research in archives such as London's George Padmore Institute and the Black Cultural Archives, consulted growing on-line resources and returned also to major published works, I was simultaneously daunted and gladdened by the scale of the research task, by the range and complexity of black voices speaking on education and by the hidden histories out of which spaces had emerged for conversation, critique, activism and dissent. I was struck by how so much of what black intellectuals and educators struggled for in decades past has become integral to British education, its absence now unimaginable. Their hopes and ambitions remained embedded in realistic appraisals of the current educational conditions without succumbing to pessimism; their activism was produced by local conditions but was also informed by universal ideals of transformative education. The myriad examples of black intellectual work confirmed my belief that the agency of black thinkers and communities had produced a history far richer than the problem–victim paradigm of black underachievement reveals. In examining landmarks in the work of black British academics, educators and activists, this book is but one attempt to illuminate how and why competing understandings of education in and for cultural diversity have developed in Britain, and how educational struggles helped to produce a sense of being black and British. For, although we did not come alive here, Britain's black communities were, in both senses of the word, schooled here.

References

Adi, H. (1995) *The History of African and Caribbean Communities in Britain*, Hove: Wayland.

Adi, H. (2000) 'Pan-Africanism and West African nationalism in Britain', *African Studies Review*, 43(1): 69–82.

Adi, H. and Sherwood, M. (1995) *The 1945 Manchester Pan-African Congress Revisited*, London: New Beacon.

Ajegbo, K., Kiwan, D. and Sharma, S. (2007) *Diversity and Citizenship: Curriculum Review*, London: Department for Education and Skills.

Alexander, C. (1996) *The Art of Being Black: The Creation of Black British Youth Identities*, Oxford: Clarendon.

Alexander, C. (2002) 'Beyond black: re-thinking the colour/culture divide', *Ethnic and Racial Studies*, 25(4): 552–71.

Ali, S., Mirza, H. S., Phoenix, A. and Ringrose, J. (2010) 'Intersectionality, Black British feminism and resistance in education: a roundtable discussion', *Gender and Education*, 22(6): 647–61.

Alibhai-Brown, Y. (1999) 'To be or not to be Black', in C. Prescod and H. Waters (eds) *A World to Win: Essays in Honour of A. Sivanandan*, London: Institute of Race Relations, pp. 163–70.

All Faiths for One Race (AFFOR) (1982) *Talking Chalk: Black Pupils, Parents and Teachers Speak About Education*, Birmingham: AFFOR.

Alleyne, B. (2002) *Radicals Against Race: Black Activism and Cultural Politics*, Oxford: Berg.

Alleyne, B. (2007) 'Anti-racist cultural politics in post-imperial Britain: the New Beacon Circle', in R. Day, G. De Peuter and M. Coté (eds) *Utopian Pedagogy: Radical Experiments against Neoliberal Globalization*, Toronto: University of Toronto Press, pp. 207–26.

Amos, V. and Parmar, P. (1981) 'Resistances and responses: the experiences of black girls in Britain', in A. McRobbie and T. McCabe (eds) *Feminism for Girls: An Adventure Story*, London: Routledge and Kegan Paul, pp. 129–48.

Andrews, K. (2013) *Resisting Racism: Race, Inequality and the Black Supplementary School Movement*, Stoke: Trentham.

Appiah, K. A. (2007) *Cosmopolitanism: Ethics in a World of Strangers*, New York: Norton.

Archer, L. and Francis, B. (2007) *Understanding Minority Ethnic Achievement: Race, Gender, Class and 'Success'*, Abingdon: Routledge.

Arnott, C. (2008) 'David Dabydeen; the loose-tongued ambassador', *Guardian*, 1 April, Online: http://www.guardian.co.uk/education/2008/apr/01/higher educationprofile.highereducation (last accessed 8 July 2013).

Asian Youth Movement (AYM) Bradford (1984) *Policy Statement on Religious Separate Schools*.

Avis, J. (1993) 'Post-Fordism, curriculum modernisers and radical practice: the case of vocational education and training in England', *Vocational Aspect of Education*, 45(1): 3–14.

Ball, S. (2008) *The Education Debate: Policy and Politics in the Twenty-first Century*, Bristol: Policy Press.

Banner-Haley, C. (2010) *From Dubois to Obama: African American Intellectuals in the Public Forum*, Carbondale, IL: Southern Illinois University Press.

Banton, M. (1977) *The Idea of Race*, London: Tavistock.

BBC (2010) *Q&A: Academies and Free Schools*. Online: http://www.bbc.co.uk/news/ 10161371 (last accessed 15 September 2012).

BBC (2011) *Analysis: A New Black Politics*, broadcast BBC Radio 4, 31 October.

BBC (2013) 'London mother challenges free school refusal decision', 4 March 2013. Online: http://www.bbc.co.uk/news/uk-england-london-21658926 (last accessed 30 June 2013).

Bell, D. (1980) 'Brown v. Board of Education and the interest convergence dilemma', *Harvard Law Review*, 93: 518–33. Reprinted in K. Crenshaw, N. Gotanda, G. Peller and K. Thomas (eds) (1995) *Critical Race Theory: The Key Writings that Formed the Movement*, New York: New Press.

Bell, D. (1992) *Faces at the Bottom of the Well: The Permanence of Racism*, New York: Basic.

Benn, M. (2011) *School Wars: The Battle for Britain's Education*, London: Verso.

Benyon, J. (ed.) (1984) *Scarman and After: Essays Reflecting on Lord Scarman's Report, the Riots, and their Aftermath*, Oxford: Pergamon.

Bergman, C. (1971) 'Making children subnormal', *Times Educational Supplement*, 7 May, p. 4.

Best, W. (1991) 'John La Rose: the man and the idealist and the shrewd political operator', in John La Rose Tribute Committee (eds) *Foundations of a Movement: A Tribute to John La Rose on the Occasion of the 10th International Book Fair of Radical Black and Third World Books*, London: John La Rose Tribute Committee, pp. 12–19.

Bhattacharyya, G. (1997) 'The fabulous adventures of the mahogany princesses', in H. Mirza (ed.) *Black British Feminism: A Reader*, London: Routledge, pp. 240–52.

Bhattacharyya, G., Ison, L. and Blair, M. (2003) *Minority Ethnic Attainment and Participation in Education and Training: The Evidence*, London: DfES.

Bhopal, K. (2010) *Asian Women in Higher Education: Shared Communities*, Stoke: Trentham.

Bhopal, K. and Maylor, U. (eds) (2014) *Educational Inequalities: Difference and Diversity in Schools and Higher Education*, London: Routledge.

Bhopal, K. and Preston, J. (eds) (2011) *Intersectionality and 'Race' in Education*, London: Routledge.

Birbalsingh, K. (2010a) 'I won't be silenced while our children are betrayed by schools', *Daily Mail*. Online: http://www.dailymail.co.uk/debate/article-1319025/ KATHARINE-BIRBALSINGH-I-wont-silenced-children-betrayed-schools. html (last accessed 1 December 2012).

Birbalsingh, K. (2010b) Speech to Conservative Party Conference, October 2010.

Birbalsingh, K. (2011a) 'My new school will free parents from the tyranny of the bossy middle classes', *The Telegraph* blog, 19 April. Online: http://blogs.telegraph. co.uk/news/katharinebirbalsingh/100084370/my-free-school-will-free-parents-from-the-tyranny-of-the-bossy-middle-classes/ (last accessed 5 June 2013).

Birbalsingh, K. (2011b) *To Miss with Love*, London: Viking.

Black Cultural Archives (2010) *The Papers of Jan McKenley*, Archives Hub. Online: http://archiveshub.ac.uk/contributors/blackculturalarchives.html (last accessed 15 November 2012).

Black Parents Movement and Black Students Movement (1976) *What are the Black Parents Movement and the Black Students Movement?* Statement of the Black Parents Movement and the Black Students Movement Committee, 20 August 1976.

Black People's Progressive Alliance and Redbridge Community Relations Council (1978) *Cause for Concern: West Indian Pupils in Redbridge*, Redbridge: Redbridge Council.

Black Vision (undated) 'Editorial', *Black Vision*, 1, p. 1.

Blair, M. (2001) *Why Pick on Me? School Exclusion and Black Youth*, Stoke: Trentham.

Bloch, A. and Solomos, J. (2010) *Race and Ethnicity in the 21st Century*, London: Palgrave Macmillan.

Boateng, O. (2013) 'How Britain treats its black academics', *New African*, 8 January 2013. Online: http://www.newafricanmagazine.com/features/diaspora/how-britain-treats-its-black-academics (last accessed 20 June 2013).

Bonilla-Silva, E. (2006) *Racism Without Racists: Color-blind Racism and the Persistence of Racial Inequality in the United States*, Lanham: Rowman and Littlefield.

Bourne, J. (2007) *In Defence of Multiculturalism*. IRR Briefing Paper No. 2, London: Institute of Race Relations.

Bourne, J. and Sivanandan, A. (1980) 'Cheerleaders and ombudsmen: the sociology of race relations in Britain', *Race Class*, 21(4): 331–52.

Bourne, J., Bridges, L. and Searle, C. (1994) *Outcast England: How Schools Exclude Black Children*, London: Institute of Race Relations.

Bowles, S. and Gintis, H. (1976) *Schooling in Capitalist America: Educational Reform and the Contradictions of Economic Life*, New York: Basic Books.

Brah, A. (1996) *Cartographies of Diaspora, Contesting Identities*, London and New York: Routledge.

Brah, A. and Phoenix, A. (2004) 'Ain't I a woman? Revisiting intersectionality', *Journal of International Women's Studies*, 5(3): 75–86.

BRAP (2011) *Census 2011: Religion and Ethnicity Data Overview*, www.brap.org.uk/ index.php/component/.../doc.../96-brapcensus2011 (last accessed October 2012).

Bridges, L. (1983) 'Book review of *The Empire Strikes Back*: race and racism in 70s Britain', *Race and Class*, 25(1): 99–100.

Bryan, B., Dadzie, S. and Scafe, S. (1985a) 'Chain reactions: Black women organising', *Race and Class*, 27(1): 1–28.

Bryan, B., Dadzie, S. and Scafe, S. (1985b) *The Heart of the Race: Black Women's Lives in Britain*, London: Virago.

Buhle, P. (1988) *CLR James: The Artist as Revolutionary*, London: Verso.

Bullock Report (1975) *A Language for Life: Report of the Committee of Inquiry into Reading and the Use of English*, London: HMSO.

Bunting, M. (2011) 'Cameron is wrong. Multicapitalism is to blame, and not multiculturalism', *Guardian*, 7 February, p. 25.

Bygott, D. (1992) *Black and British*, Oxford: Oxford University Press.

Cantle, T. (2001) *Community Cohesion: A Report of the Independent Review Team*, London: Home Office.

Carby, H. (1982a) 'Schooling in Babylon', in Centre for Contemporary Cultural Studies (eds) *The Empire Strikes Back: Race and Racism in 70s Britain*, London: Hutchinson, pp. 183–211.

Carby, H. (1982b) 'White woman listen! Black feminism and the boundaries of sisterhood', in Centre for Contemporary Cultural Studies (eds) *The Empire Strikes Back: Race and Racism in 70s Britain*, London: Hutchinson, pp. 212–35.

Carby, H. (1999) *Cultures in Babylon: Black Britain and African America*, London: Verso.

Carmichael, S. and Hamilton, C. (1967) *Black Power: The Politics of Liberation in America*, New York: Vintage.

Carretta, V. (1996) *Unchained Voices: An Anthology of Black Authors in the English-speaking World of the Eighteenth Century*, Lexington: University Press of Kentucky.

Carrington, B. (2010) 'Improbable grounds: the emergence of the black British intellectual', *South Atlantic Quarterly*, 109(2): 369–89.

Carter, B., Harris, C. and Joshi, S. (1993) 'The Conservative government 1951–1955 and the racialisation of black immigration', in W. James and C. Harris (eds) *Inside Babylon: The Caribbean Diaspora in Britain*, London: Verso, pp. 55–71.

Cashmore, E. and Troyna, B. (2005) *Introduction to Race Relations*, 2nd edition, Basingstoke: Falmer.

Centre for Contemporary Cultural Studies (CCCS) (eds) (1982) *The Empire Strikes Back: Race and Racism in 70s Britain*, London: Hutchinson.

Chakrabarty, N. and Preston, J. (2008) 'Posturing fear in a world of performed evil: terrorists, teachers and evil neo-liberals', in R. Fisher (ed.) *Perspectives on Evil and Human Wickedness*, Oxford: Oxford Inter-Disciplinary Press, pp. 227–38.

Chakrabortty, A. (2010) 'When it comes to race, the move-on brigade can't get away with merely saying the problems are old hat', *Guardian G2*, 28 September, p. 5.

Chakrabortty, A. (2011) 'UK riots: political classes see what they want to see', *Guardian*, 10 August. Online: http://www.guardian.co.uk/uk/2011/aug/10/uk-riots-political-classes (last accessed 24 June 2013).

Chen, A. (2013) 'Working class history's been ethnically cleansed', *Guardian*, 17 July, p. 28.

Chessum, L. (2000) *From Immigrants to Ethnic Minority: Making Black Community in Britain*, Farnham: Ashgate.

Chitty, C. (2007) *Eugenics, Race and Intelligence in Education*, London: Continuum.

Christian, M. (2005) 'The politics of the Black presence in Britain and Black male exclusion in the British education system', *Journal of Black Studies*, 35(3): 327–46

Coard, B. (1971a) 'Black and white marks', *Guardian*, 4 May, page number unknown.

Coard, B. (1971b) *How the West Indian Child is Made Educationally Subnormal in the British School System*, London: New Beacon, reprinted in B. Richardson (ed.) (2005) *Tell It Like It Is: How Our Schools Fail Black Children*, London: Bookmarks/Trentham, pp. 29–61.

Cole, M. (2008) *Marxism and Educational Theory: Origins and Issues*, London: Routledge.

Cole, M. (2009) *Critical Race Theory and Education: A Marxist Response*, London: Palgrave Macmillan.

Collins, P. H. (1990) *Black Feminist Thought: Knowledge, Consciousness and the Politics of Empowerment*, New York: Routledge.

Collins, R. (1971) 'Functional and conflict theories of educational stratification', *American Sociological Review*, 36(6): 1002–19.

Craig-James, S. (2006) 'Tribute to John La Rose', *The Trinidad Memorial Tribute to John La Rose Organised by the Oilfield Workers Trade Union*, 8 April. Online: http://www.georgepadmoreinstitute.org/node/108 (last accessed 1 May 2011).

Crenshaw, K. (1991) 'Mapping the margins: intersectionality, identity politics, and violence against women of color', *Stanford Law Review*, 43(6): 1241–99.

Crenshaw, K., Gotanda, N., Peller, G. and Thomas, K. (eds) (1995) *Critical Race Theory: The Key Writings that Formed the Movement*, New York: New Press.

Cruse, H. (1967) *The Crisis of the Negro Intellectual*, New York: William Morrow.

Cudjoe, S. and Cain, W. (eds) (1995) *CLR James: His Intellectual Legacies*, Amherst: University of Massachusetts Press.

Curtis, L. (1984) *Nothing But the Same Old Story: The Roots of Anti-Irish Racism*, London: Information on Ireland.

Dabydeen, D. (ed.) (1985a) *The Black Presence in English Literature*, Manchester: Manchester University Press.

Dabydeen, D. (1985b) *Hogarth's Blacks: Images of Blacks in Eighteenth-century English Arts*, Kingston-upon-Thames: Dangaroo.

Dabydeen, D. (1988) *Handbook for Teaching Caribbean Literature*, Oxford: Heinemann.

Dabydeen, D. and Wilson-Tagoe, N. (1988) *A Reader's Guide to West Indian and Black British Literature*, London: Hansib.

Dabydeen, D., Gilmore, J. and Jones, C. (eds) (2007) *The Oxford Companion to Black British History*, Oxford: Oxford University Press.

Delgado, R. and Stefancic, J. (eds) (2000) *Critical Race Theory: The Cutting Edge*, 2nd edition, Philadelphia: University Press.

Delgado, R. and Stefancic, J. (2001) *Critical Race Theory: An Introduction*, London: New York University Press.

Dennis, F. (1988) *Behind the Frontlines: Journey into Afro-Britain*, London: Victor Gollancz.

Department for Education (DfE) (2011) *Schools, Pupils and their Characteristics: January 2011*. Online: https://www.gov.uk/government/publications/schools-pupils-and-their-characteristics-january-2011 (last accessed 15 April 2013).

Department for Education (DfE) (2012) *GCSE and Equivalent Attainment by Pupil Characteristics in England: 2011 to 2012*. Online: https://www.gov.uk/government/publications/gcse-and-equivalent-attainment-by-pupil-characteristics-in-england (last accessed 15 July 2013).

Department for Education (DfE) (2013a) *Free Schools*. Online: http://www.education.gov.uk/schools/leadership/typesofschools/freeschools (last accessed 1 July 2013).

Department for Education (DfE) (2013b) *Increasing the Number of Academies and Free Schools to Create a Better and More Diverse School System*. Online: https://www.gov.uk/government/policies/ (last accessed 1 July 2013).

Department for Education and Skills (DfES) (2004) *Ethnicity and Education: The Evidence on Minority Ethnic Pupils*, Nottingham: DfES. Online: http://webarchive.nationalarchives.gov.uk/20130401151715/https://www.education.gov.uk/publications/eOrderingDownload/RTP01-05.pdf (last accessed 15 March 2013).

Department of Education and Science (DES) (1971) *The Education of Immigrants*, London: HMSO.

Department of Education and Science (DES) (1974) *Educational Disadvantage and the Needs of Immigrants*, London: HMSO.

Department of Education and Science (DES) (1977) *Education in Schools: A Consultative Document*, London: HMSO.

Dhondy, F. (2001) *C.L.R. James: Cricket, the Caribbean and World Revolution*, London: Weidenfeld and Nicolson.

Dhondy, F., Beese, B. and Hassan, L. (1985) *The Black Explosion in British Schools*, London: Race Today.

Dixson, A. and Rousseau, C. (2006) *Critical Race Theory in Education: All God's Children Got a Song*, Abingdon: Routledge.

Donnell, A. (2003) 'Una Marson: feminism, anti-colonialism and a forgotten fight for freedom', in B. Schwarz (ed.) *West Indian Intellectuals in Britain*, Manchester: Manchester University Press, pp. 114–31.

Doward, J. (2011) 'David Cameron's attack on multiculturalism divides the coalition', *Guardian*, 6 February. Online: http://www.guardian.co.uk/politics/2011/feb/05/david-cameron-attack-multiculturalism-coalition (last accessed 1 July 2013).

Du Bois, W. E. B. (1965) *The World and Africa*, New York: International.

Duffield, I. (1992) 'Dusé Mohamed Ali, Afro-Asian solidarity and Pan-Africanism in early twentieth-century London', in J. Gundara and I. Duffield (eds) *Essays on the History of Blacks in Britain*, Aldershot: Avebury, pp. 124–49.

Edwards, P. (1967) 'Introduction', in O. Equiano, *Equiano's Travels*, London: Heinemann, pp. vii–xix.

Equality Challenge Unit (ECU) (2011) *Experience of Black and Minority Ethnic Staff in H.E. in England*, London: ECU.

Equality and Human Rights Commission (EHRC) (2009) *All Together Now: A Portrait of Race in Britain*, London: EHRC. Online: http://www.equalityhuman rights.com/uploaded_files/raceinbritain/alltogethernow.pdf (last accessed 16 May 2013).

Equiano, O. (1987) 'The interesting narrative of the life of Olaudah Equiano or Gustavus Vassa, the African, written by himself', in H. L. Gates (ed.) *The Classic Slave Narratives*, New York: Mentor, pp. 1–182.

Fanon, F. (1963) *The Wretched of the Earth*, New York: Grove.

Farrar, M. (1992) 'Racism, education and black self-organisation', *Critical Social Policy*, 35: 1–24.

Farrar, M. (2004) 'Social movements and the struggle over "race"', in M. Todd and G. Taylor (eds) *Democracy and Participation: Protest and New Social Movements*, London: Merlin Press. Online: www.maxfarrar.org.uk/docs/StruggleOverRace Merlin1.pdf (last accessed 10 April 2012).

Farrar, M. (2011) Phone discussion with Paul Warmington, 18 June.

Farred, G. (1994) 'Victorian with the rebel seed: C. L. R. James, postcolonial intellectual', *Social Text*, 38: 21–38.

Farred, G. (ed.) (1996) *Rethinking CLR James*. Oxford: Blackwell.

File, N. and Power, C. (1981) *Black Settlers in Britain 1555–1958*, London: Heinemann.

Fisher, M. (2009) *Capitalist Realism. Is There No Alternative?* Winchester: Zero.

Fryer, P. (1984) *Staying Power: The History of Black People in Britain*, London: Pluto.

Garner, S. (2007) *Whiteness: An Introduction*, London: Routledge.

Gates, H. L. (1987) 'Introduction', in H. L. Gates (ed.) *The Classic Slave Narratives*, New York: Mentor, pp. ix–xviii.

Gates, H. L. (1992) 'The black man's burden', in M. Wallace and G. Dent (eds) *Black Popular Culture*, Seattle: Bay Press, pp. 75–83.

Gates, H. L. (2000) 'A reporter at large: black London', in K. Owusu (ed.) *Black British Culture and Society: A Text Reader*, London: Routledge, pp. 169–80.

Geiss, I. (1974) *The Pan-African Movement*, London: Methuen.

Gerrard, J. (2013) 'Self-help and protest: the emergence of black supplementary schooling in England', *Race Ethnicity and Education*, 16(1): 32–58.

Gerzina, G. (1995) *Black London: Life Before Emancipation*, New Brunswick, NJ: Rutgers University Press.

Gibson, A. and Barrow, J. (1986) *The Unequal Struggle*, London: Centre For Caribbean Studies.

Gifford, Z. (1992) *Dadabhai Naoroji: Britain's First Asian MP*, London: Mantra.

Gillborn, D. (1990) *'Race' Ethnicity and Education: Teaching and Learning in Multiethnic Schools*, London: Unwin Hyman.

Gillborn, D. (2005) 'Education policy as an act of white supremacy: whiteness, critical race theory and education reform', *Journal of Education Policy*, 20(4): 485–505.

Gillborn, D. (2008) *Racism and Education: Coincidence or Conspiracy?* Abingdon: Routledge.

Gillborn, D. (2010) 'The white working class, racism and respectability: victims, degenerates and interest-convergence', *British Journal of Educational Studies*, 58(1): 2–25.

Gillborn, D. and Mirza, H. S. (2001) *Educational Inequality: Mapping Race, Class and Gender*, London: Ofsted.

Gillborn, D. and Youdell, D. (2000) *Rationing Education: Policy, Practice, Reform and Equity*, Buckingham: Open University Press.

Gilroy, P. (1980) 'Managing the "underclass": a further note on the sociology of race relations in Britain', *Race and Class*, 22(1): 47–62.

Gilroy, P. (1982a) 'Police and thieves', in Centre for Contemporary Cultural Studies (eds) *The Empire Strikes Back: Race and Racism in 70s Britain*, London: Hutchinson, pp. 143–82.

Gilroy, P. (1982b) 'Preface', in Centre for Contemporary Cultural Studies (eds), *The Empire Strikes Back: Race and Racism in 70s Britain*, London: Hutchinson, pp. 7–8.

Gilroy, P. (1987) *There Ain't No Black in the Union Jack*, London: Routledge.

Gilroy, P. (1993a) *The Black Atlantic: Modernity and Double Consciousness*, London: Verso.

Gilroy, P. (1993b) *Small Acts: Thoughts on the Politics of Black Cultures*, London: Serpent's Tail.

Gilroy, P. (2000) *Against Race: Imagining Political Culture Beyond the Color Line*, Cambridge, MA: Harvard University Press.

Gilroy, P. (2004) *After Empire: Melancholia or Convivial Culture?* Abingdon: Routledge.

Gilroy, P., Grossberg, L. and McRobbie, A. (eds) (2000) *Without Guarantees: In Honour of Stuart Hall*, London: Verso.

Goodhart, D. (2004) 'Too diverse? Is Britain becoming too diverse to sustain the mutual obligations behind a good society and the welfare state?', *Prospect*, 20 February. Online: http://www.prospectmagazine.co.uk/magazine/too-diverse-david-goodhart-multiculturalism-britain-immigration-globalisation/#.Uds3dft wbIU (last accessed 8 July 2013).

Goodhart, D. (2013) *The British Dream: Successes and Failures of Post-war Immigration*, London: Atlantic.

Goodman, M. (1964) *Race Awareness in Young Children*, New York: Collier.

Gorard, S. (1999) 'Keeping a sense of proportion: the "politician's error" in analysing school outcomes', *British Journal of Educational Studies*, 47(3): 235–46.

Gosai, N. (2011) *Perspectives on the Educational Experiences of African-Caribbean Boys*, Newcastle: Cambridge Scholars.

Goulbourne, H. (ed.) (1990) *Black Politics in Britain*, Aldershot: Avebury.

Graham, M. (2001) 'The "miseducation" of Black children in the British education system – towards an African-centred orientation to knowledge', in R. Majors (ed.) *Educating Our Black Children: New Directions and Radical Approaches*, London: Routledge Falmer, pp. 61–78.

Grant, C. (2008) *Negro With a Hat: The Rise and Fall of Marcus Garvey and His Dream of Mother Africa*, London: Jonathan Cape.

Griffith, J., Henderson, J., Usborne, M. and Wood, D. (1960) *Coloured Immigrants in Britain*, London: IRR.

Grimshaw, A. (ed.) (1992) *The CLR James Reader*, Oxford: Blackwell.

Grosvenor, I. (1997) *Assimilating Identities: Racism and Educational Policy in Post 1945 Britain*, London: Lawrence and Wishart.

Gunaratnam, Y. (2003) *Researching 'Race' and Ethnicity: Methods, Knowledge and Power*, London: Sage.

Gundara, J. and Duffield, I. (eds) (1992) *Essays on the History of Blacks in Britain*, Aldershot: Avebury.

Guptara, P. (1986) *Black British Literature: An Annotated Bibliography*, Oxford: Dangaroo.

Gutzmore, C. (1983) 'Capital, "black youth" and crime', *Race and Class*, 25(2): 13–30.

Hall, S. (1984) 'Reconstruction work: images of post-war black settlement', *Ten 8*, 16. Reprinted in J. Procter (ed.) *Writing Black Britain 1948–1998*, Manchester: Manchester University Press, pp. 82–93.

Hall, S. (1988) 'New ethnicities', in K. Mercer (ed.) *Black Film/British Cinema: ICA Document 7*, London: Institute of Contemporary Arts.

Hall, S. (1989) 'Ethnicity: identity and difference', Speech to Hampshire College, Amherst, Massachusetts, Spring 1989. Online: http://www.csus.edu/indiv/l/leekellerh/Hall,%20Ethnicity_Identity_and_Difference.pdf (last accessed March 2010).

Hall, S. (1990) 'Cultural identity and diaspora', in J. Rutherford (ed.) *Identity: Community, Culture, Difference*, London: Lawrence and Wishart, pp. 222–37.

Hall, S. (1996a) 'Cultural Studies and its theoretical legacies', in D. Morley and K. Chen (eds) *Stuart Hall: Critical Dialogues in Cultural Studies*, Abingdon: Routledge, pp. 262–75.

Hall, S. (1996b) 'What is this "black" in black popular culture?', in D. Morley and K. Chen (eds) *Stuart Hall: Critical Dialogues in Cultural Studies*, Abingdon: Routledge, pp. 465–75.

Hall, S. (1997) *Representation: Cultural Representations and Signifying Practices*, London: Sage.

Hall, S. (2000) 'Conclusion: the multi-cultural question', in B. Hesse (ed.) *Un/settled Multiculturalisms: Diasporas, Entanglements, Disruptions*, London: Zed, pp. 209–41.

Hall, S. and Chen, K. (1996) 'The formation of a diasporic intellectual: an interview with Stuart Hall by Kuan-Hsing Chen', in D. Morley and K. Chen (eds) *Stuart Hall: Critical Dialogues in Cultural Studies*, Abingdon: Routledge, pp. 484–503.

Hall, S. and du Gay, P. (eds) (1996) *Questions of Cultural Identity*, London: Sage.

Hall, S. and Gieben, B. (eds) (1992) *Formations of Modernity*, Cambridge: Polity Press.

Hall, S. and Jefferson, T. (eds) (1993) *Resistance through Rituals*, London: Hutchinson.

Hall, S. and Walmsley, A. (1987) Stuart Hall interviewed by Anne Walmsley, research on Caribbean Artists Movement, October 1987, George Padmore Institute Archives, CAM 6/23.

Hall, S., Critcher, C., Jefferson, T., Clarke, J. and Roberts, B. (1978) *Policing the Crisis: Mugging, the State, and Law and Order*, Basingstoke: Macmillan.

Hall, S., Held, D. and McGrew, T. (eds) (1992) *Modernity and its Futures*, Cambridge: Polity.

Haringey Communist Party (1969) Letter to Haringey Borough Council re: banding proposals.

Harker, J. (2011) 'For black Britons, this is not the 80s revisited. It's worse', *Guardian*, 11 August. Online: http://www.guardian.co.uk/commentisfree/2011/aug/11/black-britons-80s-mps-media (last accessed 9 July 2013).

Harris, R. (2000) 'Openings, absences and omissions: aspects of the treatment of "race", culture and ethnicity in British cultural studies', in K. Owusu (ed.) *Black British Culture and Society: A Text Reader*, London: Routledge, pp. 395–404.

Harris, R. (2009) *New Ethnicities and Language Use*, London: Palgrave Macmillan.

Harris, R. and White, S. (eds) (1999) *Changing Britannia: Life Experience with Britain*, London: New Beacon, pp. 193–225.

Haydon, G., White, J., Jones, M., White, P., McLaughlin, T. and Devall, S. (1987) *Education for a Pluralist Society: Philosophical Perspectives on the Swann Report*, London: University of London.

Hebdige, D. (1979) *Subculture: The Meaning of Style*, London: Routledge.

Heineman, B. (1972) *The Politics of the Powerless: A Study of the Campaign Against Racial Discrimination*, London: Oxford University Press.

Henry, D. with Ruddock, R. (1991) *Thirty Blacks in British Education: Hopes, Frustrations, Achievements*, Crawley: Rabbit Press.

Henry, P. and Buhle, P. (eds) (1992) *C.L.R. James's Caribbean*, Durham, NC: Duke University Press.

Hinds, D. (2008) 'The West Indian Gazette: Claudia Jones and the black press in Britain', *Race and Class*, 50(1): 88–97.

Hiro, D. (1973) *Black British, White British: A History of Race Relations in Britain*, London: Grafton.

Homan, R. (1986) 'The all black school: development and implications', in S. Modgil, G. K. Verma, K. Mallick and C. Modgil (eds) *Multicultural Education: The Interminable Debate*, Lewes: Falmer, pp. 167–80.

Home Office (1964) *Immigration from the Commonwealth*, London: HMSO.

Hooker, J. R. (1967) *Black Revolutionary: George Padmore's Path from Communism to Pan-Africanism*, London: Pall Mall.

hooks, b. (1994) *Outlaw Culture: Resisting Representations*, New York: Routledge.

hooks, b. and West, C. (1991) *Breaking Bread: Insurgent Black Intellectual Life*, Boston: Southend Press.

Housee, S. (2008) 'Should ethnicity *matter* when teaching about "race" and racism in the classroom?', *Race Ethnicity and Education*, 11(4): 415–28.

Housee, S. (2010) 'When silences are broken: an out of class discussion with Asian female students', *Educational Review*, 62(4): 421–34.

Housee, S. (2012) 'What's the point? Antiracism and students' voices against Islamophobia', *Race Ethnicity and Education*, 15(1): 101–20.

Howe, D. (1988) *From Bobby to Babylon: Blacks and the British Police*, London: Race Today.

Howe, D. (2011) 'New Cross: the blaze we cannot forget', *Guardian*, 17 January. Online: http://www.guardian.co.uk/commentisfree/2011/jan/17/new-cross-fire-we-cant-forget (last accessed 9 July 2013).

Howson, C. and Sallah, M. (2009) *Europe's Established and Emerging Immigrant Communities: Assimilation, Multiculturalism or Integration*, Stoke: Trentham.

Hoyles, M. (2013) *William Cuffay: The Life and Times of a Chartist Leader*, Hertford: Hansib.

Humphry, D. and John, G. (1972) *Because They're Black*, Harmondsworth: Pelican.

Hunte, J. (1966) *Nigger Hunting in England?* London: West Indian Standing Conference.

Hylton, K. (2009) *'Race' and Sport: Critical Race Theory*, Abingdon: Routledge.

Hylton, K., Pilkington, A., Warmington, P. and Housee, S. (eds) (2011) *Atlantic Crossings: International Dialogues on Critical Race Theory*, Birmingham: CSAP/ Higher Education Academy.

Inner London Education Authority (ILEA) (1977) *Multi-Ethnic Education*, London: ILEA.

Inner London Education Authority (ILEA) (1982) *Anti-Racist School Policies*, London: ILEA.

Institute of Race Relations (IRR) (1982) *Roots of Racism*, London: IRR.

James, C. L. R. (1980) *The Black Jacobins*, London: Allison and Busby.

James, C. L. R. (1983) *Beyond a Boundary*, London: Serpent's Tail.

James, C. L. R. (1984) *At the Rendezvous of Victory*, London: Allison and Busby.

James, W. and Harris, C. (eds) (1993) *Inside Babylon*, London: Verso.

Jarrett, J. (1996) 'Creative space? The experience of Black women in British art schools', in D. Jarrett-Macauley (ed.) *Reconstructing Womanhood, Reconstructing Feminism: Writings on Black Women*, London: Routledge, pp. 121–35.

Jarrett-Macauley, D. (1998) *The Life of Una Marson, 1905–1965*, Manchester: Manchester University Press.

John, D. W. (1969) *Indian Workers Associations in Britain*, Oxford: Oxford University Press.

John, G. (2005) 'Parental and community involvement in education: time to get the balance right', in B. Richardson (ed.) *Tell It Like It Is: How Our Schools Fail Black Children*, London: Bookmarks/Trentham, pp. 97–107.

John, G. (2006a) 'John La Rose in the cause of social liberation across the continents', in *The Trinidad Memorial Tribute to John La Rose organised by the Oilfield Workers Trade Union on 8 April 2006*, http://www.georgepadmoreinstitute.org/john-la-rose-tributes/trinidad-memorial-at-owtu-2006 (last accessed July 2011).

John, G. (2006b) *Taking a Stand: Gus John Speaks on Education, Race, Social Action and Civil Unrest 1980–2005*, Manchester: Gus John Partnership.

John, G. and Walmsley, A. (1988) Gus John interviewed by Anne Walmsley, research on Caribbean Artists Movement, February 1988, George Padmore Institute Archives, CAM 6/35.

Johnson, B. (1985) *'I Think of My Mother': Notes on the Life and Times of Claudia Jones*, London: Karia.

Johnson, L. K. (2012) 'Trust between the police and the black community is still broken', *Guardian*, 28 March. Online: http://www.guardian.co.uk/commentisfree/2012/mar/28/trust-police-black-community-riots (last accessed 10 July 2013).

Jones, C. (2006) 'Falling between the cracks: what diversity means for black women in higher education', *Policy Futures in Education*, 4(2): 145–59.

Jones, V. (1986) *We Are Our Own Educators! Josina Machel: From Supplementary to Black Complementary School*, London: Karia.

Josephides, S. (1991) *Towards a History of the Indian Workers' Association*, Research Paper in Ethnic Relations No. 18, Coventry: Centre for Research in Ethnic Relations, University of Warwick.

Keith, M. (1993) *Race, Riots and Policing: Lore and Disorder in Multi-racist Society*, London: UCL Press.

Kirp, D. (1979a) *Doing Good by Doing Little: Race and Schooling in Britain*, Berkeley: University of California Press.

Kirp, D. (1979b) 'The vagaries of discrimination: busing, policy, and law in Britain', *The School Review*, 87(3): 269–94.

Kundnani, A. (2001) 'From Oldham to Bradford: the violence of the violated', *Race and Class*, 43(2): 105–31.

Kundnani, A. (2007) *The End of Tolerance: Racism in 21st century Britain*, London: Pluto.

La Rose, J. (1984) *The New Cross Massacre Story: Interviews with John la Rose*, London: Alliance of the Black Parents Movement.

Ladson-Billings, G. and Tate, W. (1995) 'Towards a critical race theory of education', *Teachers College Record*, 97(1): 47–68.

Lammy, D. (2011) *Out of the Ashes: Britain After the Riots*, London: Guardian Books.

Larsen, N. (1996) 'Negativities of the popular: C.L.R. James and the limits of "cultural studies"', in G. Farred (ed.) (1996) *Rethinking CLR James*, Oxford: Blackwell, pp. 85–102.

Lawrence, E. (1982) 'In the abundance of water the fool is thirsty: sociology and the black "pathology"', in Centre for Contemporary Cultural Studies (eds) *The Empire Strikes Back: Race and Racism in 70s Britain*, London: Hutchinson, pp. 47–94.

Leonardo, Z. (2005) 'Through the multicultural glass: Althusser, ideology and race relations in post-civil rights America', *Policy Futures in Education*, 3(4): 400–12.

Leonardo, Z. (2009) *Race, Whiteness and Education*, Abingdon: Routledge.

Leonardo, Z. (2011) 'After the glow: race ambivalence and other educational prognoses', *Educational Philosophy and Theory*, 43(6): 675–98.

Lewis, D. L. (1993) *W.E.B. Du Bois, 1868–1919: Biography of a Race*, New York: Henry Holt.

Lewis, R. (1988) *Marcus Garvey: Anti-colonial Champion*, Trenton, NJ: Africa World Press.

Lightfoot, L. (2005) 'We cannot accept this school apartheid', *Telegraph*, 8 March. Online: http://www.telegraph.co.uk/news/uknews/1485158/We-cannot-accept-this-school-apartheid.html (last accessed 15 June 2013).

Little, K. (1948) *Negroes in Britain: A Study of Racial Relations in English Society*, London: Kegan Paul.

Mac an Ghaill, M. (1988) *Young, Gifted and Black: Student–Teacher Relations in the Schooling of Black Youth*, Milton Keynes: Open University.

Macdonald, I., Bhavani, R., Khan, L. and John, G. (1989) *Murder in the Playground: The Report of the Macdonald Inquiry into Racism and Racial Violence in Manchester Schools*, London: Longsight.

MacDonald, R. (1973) 'Dr Harold Arundel Moody and the League of Coloured Peoples, 1931–47: a retrospective view', *Race*, 14(3): 291–310.

MacDonald, R. (ed.) (1976) *The Keys: The Official Organ of the League of Coloured Peoples 1933–1939*, New York: Kraus-Thomson.

MacDonald, R. (1992) '"The wisers who are far away": the role of London's Black press in the 1930s and the 1940s', in J. Gundara and I. Duffield (eds) *Essays on the History of Blacks in Britain*, Aldershot: Avebury, pp. 150–72.

McKenley, J. (c. 1978) *Black Women and Education*, working paper.

McKenley, J. (2001) 'The way we were: conspiracies of silence in the wake of the Empire Windrush', *Race Ethnicity and Education*, 4(4): 309–28.

McKenley, J. (2006) *Seven Black Men: An Ecological Study of Education and Parenting*, London: Aduma.

McKenley, J. (undated) *Black Women in Britain*, working paper.

Macpherson, W./Home Office (1999) *The Stephen Lawrence Inquiry: Report of an Inquiry by Sir William Macpherson*, London: HMSO.

McRobbie, A. (2000) 'Stuart Hall: the universities and the "hurly burly"', in P. Gilroy, L. Grossberg and A. McRobbie *Without Guarantees: In Honour of Stuart Hall*, London: Verso, pp. 212–24.

Male, G. (1980) 'Multicultural education and education policy: the British experience', *Comparative Education Review*, 24(3): 291–301.

Malik, K. (2009) *From Fatwa to Jihad: The Rushdie Affair and its Legacy*, London: Atlantic.

Malik, Z. (2012) *The Asian Youth Movements*, BBC Radio 4 broadcast, 26 March.

Marable, M. (1997) 'Rethinking black liberation: towards a new protest paradigm', *Race and Class*, 38(4): 1–13.

Marable, M. (1998) 'Beyond color-blindness', *The Nation*, 14 December. Online: http://www.hartford-hwp.com/archives/45a/561.html (last accessed 10 July 2013).

Marable, M. (2000) 'Introduction: black studies and the racial mountain', in M. Marable (ed.) *Dispatches from the Ebony Tower: Intellectuals Confront the African American Experience*, New York: Columbia University Press, pp. 1–28.

Martin, T. (1976) *Race First: The Ideological and Organizational Struggles of Marcus Garvey and the Universal Negro Improvement Association*, Dover, MA: Majority.

May, T. (2001) *Social Research: Issues, Methods and Process*, 2nd edition, Buckingham: Open University Press.

Miles, R. (1989) *Racism*, London: Routledge.

Milner, D. (1973) 'Racial identification and preference in black British children', *European Journal of Social Psychology*, 3(3): 287–95.

Mirza, H. S. (1992) *Young, Female and Black*, London: Routledge.

Mirza, H. S. (ed.) (1997) *Black British Feminism: A Reader*, London: Routledge.

Mirza, H. S. (1999) 'Black masculinities and schooling: a black feminist response', *British Journal of Sociology of Education*, 20(1): 137–47.

Mirza, H. S. (2007) 'The more things change, the more they stay the same', in B. Richardson (ed.) *Tell It Like It Is: How Our Schools Fail Black Children*, Second Edition, London: Bookmarks/Trentham, pp. 111–19.

Mirza, H. S. (2009) *Race, Gender and Educational Desire: Why Black Women Succeed and Fail*, Abingdon, Routledge.

Mirza, M. (2010) 'Rethinking race', *Prospect*, 175, pp. 31–2.

Modgil, S., Verma, G., Mallick, K. and Modgil, C. (eds) (1986) *Multicultural Education: The Interminable Debate*, London: Palmer.

Modood, T. (1992) *Not Easy Being British: Colour, Culture and Citizenship*, London: Runnymede/Trentham.

Modood, T. (1994) 'Political blackness and British Asians', *Sociology*, 28(4): 859–76.

Modood, T. (2005) 'A defence of multiculturalism', *Soundings*, 29. Online: http://www.leeds.ac.uk/educol/documents/153854.pdf (last accessed October 2011).

Modood, T. (2007) *Multiculturalism: A Civic Idea*, Cambridge: Polity.

Modood, T. and Acland, T. (eds) (1998) *Race and Higher Education: Experiences, Challenges and Policy Implications*, London: Policy Studies Institute.

Morley, D. and Chen, K. (1996) *Stuart Hall: Critical Dialogues in Cultural Studies*, Abingdon: Routledge.

Morris, G., Hussain, A. and Aura, T. G. (1984) 'Schooling crisis in Bradford', *Race Today*, July, pp. 8–11.

Mullard, C. (1973) *Black Britain (with an account of recent events at the Institute of Race Relations by Alexander Kirby)*, London: Allen and Unwin.

Mullard, C. (1982) 'Multiracial education in Britain: from assimilation to cultural pluralism', in J. Tierney (ed.) *Race, Migration and Schooling*, London: Holt, pp. 120–33.

Myers, K. and Grosvenor, I. (2009) 'Exploring supplementary education: margins, theories and methods', paper presented at International Standing Conference for the History of Education, Utrecht University, August 2009.

Neal, S. (2003) 'The Scarman Report, the Macpherson Report and the media: how newspapers respond to race-centred social policy interventions', *Journal of Social Policy*, 32(1): 55–74.

North London West Indian Association (1969a) *All West Indian Parents Beware*, NLWIA Flyer, April 1969.

North London West Indian Association (1969b) *Proposals of the North London West Indian Association Concerning Education in Haringey Schools*, letter to the Chairman of the Haringey Education Committee, December 1969.

Ogude, S. (1982) 'Facts into fiction: Equiano's Narrative reconsidered', *Research in African Literatures*, 13: 31–43.

Okokon, S. (1998) *Black Londoners 1880 to 1990*, Stroud: Sutton.

Oldfield, J. R. (1998) *Popular Politics and British Anti-Slavery: The Mobilisation of Public Opinion Against the Slave Trade 1787–1807*, Abingdon: Routledge.

Omi, M. and Winant, H. (1986) *Racial Formation in the United States: From the 1960s to the 1980s*, New York: Routledge.

Osler, A. (1989) *Speaking Out: Black Girls in Britain*, London: Virago.

Osler, A. (1997) *The Education and Careers of Black Teachers: Changing Identities, Changing Lives*, Buckingham: Open University Press.

Osler, A. (2008) 'Citizenship education and the Ajegbo Report: reimagining a cosmopolitan nation', *London Review of Education*, 6(1): 11–25.

Ouseley, H. (2001) *Community Pride Not Prejudice: Making Diversity Work in Bradford – The Ouseley Report*, Bradford: Bradford District Race Review Panel.

Owusu, K. (ed.) (2000) *Black British Culture and Society: A Text Reader*, London: Routledge.

Padmore, G. (1971) *Pan-Africanism or Communism*, foreword by Richard Wright, Garden City, NY: Doubleday.

Parekh, B. (1992) 'The hermeneutics of the Swann Report', in D. Gill, B. Mayor and M. Blair (eds) *Racism and Education: Structures and Strategies*, London: Sage.

Parekh, B. (2000) *The Future of Multi-Ethnic Britain: Report of the Commission on the Future of Multi-Ethnic Britain*, London: Profile.

Parekh, B. (2006) *Rethinking Multiculturalism: Cultural Diversity and Political Theory*, 2nd edition, Basingstoke: Palgrave Macmillan.

Parker, L. (1998) '"Race is … race ain't": an exploration of the utility of Critical Race Theory in qualitative research in education', *International Journal of Qualitative Studies in Education*, 11(1): 43–55.

Parker, L. and Roberts, L. (2011) 'Critical Race Theory and its use in social science research', in B. Somekh and C. Lewin (eds) *Theory and Methods in Social Research*, 2nd edition, London: Sage, pp. 78–85.

Parmar, P. (1982) 'Gender, race and class: Asian women in resistance', in Centre for Contemporary Cultural Studies (eds) *The Empire Strikes Back: Race and Racism in 70s Britain*, London: Hutchinson, pp. 236–75.

Phillips, C. (ed.) (1997) 'Preface', in C. Phillips (ed.) *Extravagant Strangers*, London: Faber and Faber, pp. xiii–xvi.

Phillips, M. (2001) *London Crossings: A Biography of Black Britain*, London: Continuum.

Phillips, M. and Phillips, T. (1999) *Windrush: The Irresistible Rise of Multi-racial Britain*, London: HarperCollins.

Phillips, S. (2004) 'Black intellectual seems an oxymoron in England', *Times Higher Education*, 29 October. Online: http://www.timeshighereducation.co.uk/story.asp ?storyCode=192064&sectioncode=26 (last accessed June 2010).

Phillips, T. (2005) 'Sleepwalking into segregation', Speech to Manchester Council for Community Relations, Manchester, September.

Phoenix, A. (1987) 'Theories of gender and black families', in G. Weiner and M. Arnot (eds) *Gender Under Scrutiny*, London: Hutchinson, reprinted in H. S. Mirza (ed.) *Black British Feminism: A Reader*, London: Routledge, pp. 63–6.

Phoenix, A. (2002) 'Mapping present inequalities to navigate future success: racialisation and education', *British Journal of Sociology of Education*, 23(3): 505–15.

Pilkington, A. (1999) 'Racism in schools and ethnic differentials in educational achievement: a brief comment on a recent debate', *British Journal of Sociology of Education*, 20(3): 411–17.

Pilkington, A. (2003) *Racial Disadvantage and Ethnic Diversity in Britain*, Basingstoke: Palgrave Macmillan.

Pillai, R. with Kyambi, S., Nowacka, K. and Sriskandarajah, D. (2007) *The Reception and Integration of New Migrant Communities*, London: IPPR/CRE.

Posnock, R. (1997) 'How it feels to be a problem: Du Bois, Fanon, and the "impossible life" of the black intellectual', *Critical Inquiry*, 23: 323–49.

Posnock, R. (1998) *Color and Culture: Black Writers and the Making of the Modern Intellectual*, Cambridge, MA: Harvard University Press.

Powell, E. (1968) 'Rivers of Blood', Speech to Conservative Party Association, Birmingham, 20 April, reprinted in *Telegraph*, 6 November 2007. Online: http://www.telegraph.co.uk/comment/3643823/Enoch-Powells-Rivers-of-Blood-speech.html (last accessed 10 July 2013).

Prescod, C. (1999a) 'Colin Prescod with John La Rose in the chair', in R. Harris and S. White (eds) *Changing Britannia: Life Experience with Britain*, London: New Beacon, pp. 193–225.

Prescod, C. (1999b) 'The Black intellectual liberated', in C. Prescod and H. Waters (eds) *A World to Win: Essays in Honour of A. Sivanandan*, London: Institute of Race Relations, pp. 171–4.

Prescod-Roberts, M. and Steele, N. (1980) *Black Women: Bringing It All Back Home*, Bristol: Falling Wall.

Preston, J. (2010) 'Concrete and abstract racial domination', *Power and Education*, 2(2): 115–25.

Preston, J. (2013) *Whiteness in Academia: Counter-stories of Betrayal and Resistance*, Newcastle: Cambridge Scholars Publishing.

Prince, M. (1987) 'The History of Mary Prince: a West Indian slave', in H. L. Gates (ed.) *The Classic Slave Narratives*, New York: Mentor, pp. 183–242.

Procter, J. (ed.) (2000) *Writing Black Britain 1948–1998*, Manchester: Manchester University Press.

Procter, J. (2003) *Dwelling Places: Postwar Black British Writing*, Manchester: Manchester University Press.

Pryce, K. (1979) *Endless Pressure: A Study of West Indian Life-styles in Bristol*, Harmondsworth: Penguin.

Pumfrey, P. and Verma, G. (eds) (1990) *Race Relations and Urban Education: Contexts and Promising Practices*, Basingstoke: Falmer.

Race, R. (2011) *Multiculturalism and Education*, London: Continuum.

Race Today (1988) 'Editorial: black cultural expression', *Race Today*, 18(2): 3.

Radke, M. and Trager, H. (1950) 'Children's perceptions of the social roles of Negroes and Whites', *Journal of Psychology*, 29: 3–33.

Ramamurthy, A. (2005) 'Secular identities and the Asian Youth Movements', Paper presented to 10th International Conference on Alternative Futures and Popular Protest, Manchester Metropolitan University, 30 March.

Ramamurthy, A. (2006) 'The politics of Britain's Asian Youth Movements', *Race and Class*, 48(2): 38–60.

Ramamurthy, A. (2007) *Kala Tara: A History of the Asian Youth Movements in Britain – Education Pack*, Preston: Tandana.

Ramdin, R. (1987) *The Making of the Black Working Class in Britain*, Aldershot: Wildwood House.

Ramdin, R. (1999) *Reimaging Britain: 500 Years of Black and Asian History*, London: Pluto.

Rampton Report (1981) *West Indian Children in Our Schools: Interim Report of the Committee of Inquiry into the Education of Children from Ethnic Minority Groups*, London: HMSO.

Ranson, S. (1988) 'From 1944 to 1988: education, citizenship and democracy', *Local Government Studies*, 14(1): 1–19.

Ratcliffe, P. (1981) *Racism and Reaction: A Profile of Handsworth*, London: Routledge and Kegan Paul.

Rattansi, A. (1992) 'Changing the subject? Racism, culture and education', in J. Donald and A. Rattansi (eds) *'Race', Culture and Difference*, London: Sage, pp. 11–48.

Reay, D. (2006) 'The zombie stalking English schools: social class and educational inequality', *British Journal of Educational Studies*, 54(3): 288–307.

Reay, D. and Mirza, H. S. (1997) 'Uncovering genealogies of the margins: black supplementary schooling', *British Journal of Sociology of Education*, 18(4): 477–99.

Reay, D. and Mirza, H. S. (2001) 'Black supplementary schools: spaces of radical blackness', in R. Majors (ed.) *Educating Our Black Children: New Directions and Radical Approaches*, London: Routledge Falmer, pp. 90–101.

Rex, J. (1970) *Race Relations in Sociological Theory*, London: Weidenfeld and Nicolson.

Rex, J. and Tomlinson, S. (1979) *Colonial Immigrants in a British City: A Class Analysis*, London: Routledge.

Rhamie, J. (2007) *Eagles Who Soar: How Black Learners Find the Path to Success*, Stoke: Trentham.

Robinson, C. (1983) *Black Marxism: The Making of the Black Radical Tradition*, London: Zed.

Rodney, W. (1972) *How Europe Underdeveloped Africa*, London: Bogle L'Ouverture.

Rollock, N. (2012) 'Unspoken rules of engagement: navigating racial microaggressions in the academic terrain', *International Journal of Qualitative Studies in Education*, 25(5): 517–32.

Rose, E., Deakin, N. *et al.* (1969) *Colour and Citizenship: A Report on British Race Relations*, Oxford: Oxford University Press.

Runnymede Trust (1980) *Britain's Black Population*, London: Heinemann.

Runnymede Trust (1985) *'Education for All': A Summary of the Swann Report*, London: Runnymede.

Rush, A. S. (2002) 'Imperial identity in colonial minds: Harold Moody and the League of Coloured Peoples 1931–50', *Twentieth Century British History*, 13(4): 356–83.

Rushdie, S., Hall, S. and Howe, D. (2000) 'The "Handsworth Songs" Letters', in J. Procter (ed.) *Writing Black Britain 1948–1998*, Manchester: Manchester University Press, pp. 261–5.

Saakana, A. S. and Pearse, A. (1986) *Towards the Decolonization of the British Educational System*, London: Karnak House.

Sahgal, G. and Yuval-Davis, N. (eds) (1992) *Refusing Holy Orders*, London: Virago.

Said, E. (1996) *Representations of the Intellectual*, New York: Vintage.

Sandhu, S. (2003) *London Calling: How Black and Asian Writers Imagined a City*, London: HarperCollins.

Sandiford, K. (1988) *Measuring the Moment: Strategies of Protest in Eighteenth-century Afro-English Writing*, London: Associated University Press.

Scafe, S. (1989) *Teaching Black Literature*, London: Virago.

Scarman, Lord L. G. (1982) *The Scarman Report: The Brixton Disorders 10–12 April 1981*, Harmondsworth: Pelican.

Schwarz, B. (2003a) 'Claudia Jones and the West Indian Gazette: reflections on the emergence of post-colonial Britain', *Twentieth Century British History*, 14(3): 264–85.

Schwarz, B. (2003b) *West Indian Intellectuals in Britain*, Manchester: Manchester University Press.

Searle, C. (1973) *The Forsaken Lover: White Words and Black People*, Harmondsworth: Penguin.

Select Committee on Race Relations and Immigration (SCRRI) (1969) *The Problem of Coloured School-Leavers*, London: HMSO.

Select Committee on Race Relations and Immigration (SCRRI) (1977) *The West Indian Community*, London: HMSO.

Sewell, T. (1990) *Garvey's Children: The Legacy of Marcus Garvey*, Oxford: Macmillan.

Sewell, T. (1997) *Black Masculinities and Schooling: How Black Boys Survive Modern Schooling*, Stoke: Trentham.

Sewell, T. (2009) *Generating Genius: Black Boys in Search of Love, Ritual and Schooling*, Stoke: Trentham.

Sewell, T. (2010) 'Master class in victimhood', *Prospect*, 175, pp. 33–4.

Sewell, T. (2011) 'Black students and the class ceiling', *Telegraph*. Online: http://www.telegraph.co.uk/education/8446571/Black-students-and-the-class-ceiling.html (last accessed 1 December 2012).

Shain, F. (2010) *The New Folk Devils? Muslim Boys and Education in England*, Stoke: Trentham.

Shepherd, J. (2011) '14,000 British professors – but only 50 are black', *Guardian*, 27 May. Online: http://www.guardian.co.uk/education/2011/may/27/only-50-black-british-professors (last accessed 10 July 2013).

Shepperson, G. (1960) 'Notes on Negro American influences on the emergence of African nationalism', *Journal of African History*, 1(2): 299–312.

Sherwood, M. (1995) *Manchester and the 1945 Pan-African Congress*, London: Savannah.

Sherwood, M., Hinds, D. and Prescod, C. (1999) *Claudia Jones: A Life in Exile*, London: Lawrence and Wishart.

Shukra, K. (1998) *The Changing Pattern of Black Politics in Britain*, London: Pluto.

Simon, D. (2005) 'Education of the Blacks: the supplementary school movement', in B. Richardson (ed.) *Tell It Like It Is: How Our Schools Fail Black Children*, London: Bookmarks/Trentham, pp. 64–71.

Singh, G. (1988) *Language, Race and Education*, Birmingham: Jaysons.

Singh, G. (2011) *Black and Minority Ethnic (BME) Students' Participation and Success in Higher Education: Improving Retention and Success – A Synthesis of Research Evidence*, York: Higher Education Academy. Online: http://bit.ly/zj31rI (last accessed 10 July 2013).

Sivanandan, A. (1974) *Race and Resistance: The IRR Story*, London: Race Today.

Sivanandan, A. (1982) *A Different Hunger: Writings on Black Resistance*, London: Pluto.

Sivanandan, A. (1983) 'Challenging racism: strategies for the 80s', *Race and Class*, 25(2): 1–11.

Sivanandan, A. (1989) 'Racism, education and the black child', in M. Reeves and J. Hammond (eds) *Looking Beyond the Frame: Racism, Representation and Resistance*, Oxford: Third World First, pp. 19–24.

Sivanandan, A. (2006) 'Attacks on multicultural Britain pave the way for enforced assimilation', *Guardian*, 13 September, p. 32.

Sivanandan, T. (2001) 'Black British writing: a review article', *Race and Class*, 43(2): 132–40.

Skinner, D. (2011) 'How might Critical Race Theory allow us to rethink racial categorisation?', in K. Hylton, A. Pilkington, P. Warmington and S. Housee (eds) *Atlantic Crossings: International Dialogues on Critical Race Theory*, Birmingham, CSAP/Higher Education Academy, pp. 115–31.

Smith, B. (1983) 'Introduction', in B. Smith (ed.) *Home Girls: A Black Feminist Anthology*, New York: Kitchen Table/Women of Color Press, pp. xix–lvi.

Solomos, J. (2003) *Race and Racism in Britain*, 3rd edition, Basingstoke: Macmillan.

Song, M. (2003) *Choosing Ethnic Identity*, Cambridge: Polity.

St. Louis, B. (2007) *Rethinking Race, Politics, and Poetics: C.L.R. James' Critique of Modernity*, London: Routledge.

Stephen, D. (1970) 'Improving understanding: a realistic education programme', *Race Today*, July, pp. 218–20.

Stone, M. (1985) *The Education of the Black Child: The Myth of Multiracial Education*, 2nd edition, London: Fontana.

Taylor, E. (2009) 'The foundations of Critical Race Theory in education: an introduction', in E. Taylor, D. Gillborn and G. Ladson-Billings (eds) *Foundations of Critical Race Theory in Education*, Abingdon: Routledge, pp. 1–16.

Tomlinson, S. (2005) 'Race, ethnicity and education under New Labour', *Oxford Review of Education*, 31(1): 153–71.

Tomlinson, S. (2008) *Race and Education: Policy and Politics in Britain*, Maidenhead: Open University Press.

Townsend, M. (2013) 'Doreen Lawrence launches centre to boost minority students' prospects', *Observer*, 16 February. Online: http://www.guardian.co.uk/uk/2013/feb/16/doreen-lawrence-minority-students-prospects (last accessed 11 July 2013).

Troyna, B. (1992) 'Can you see the join? An historical analysis of multicultural and antiracist education policies', in D. Gill, B. Mayor and M. Blair (eds) *Racism and Education: Structures and Strategies*, London: Sage, pp. 63–91.

Troyna, B. and Williams, J. (1986) *Racism, Education and the State: The Racialisation of Education Policy*, London: Croom Helm.

Visram, R. (2002) *Asians in Britain: 400 Years of History*, London: Pluto.

Wallace, M. (1990) *Invisibility Blues: From Pop to Theory*, New York: Verso.

Walmsley, A. (1992) *The Caribbean Artists Movement 1966–1972: A Literary and Cultural History*, London: New Beacon Books.

Walters, W. (2013) *Archives of the Black Atlantic: Reading Between Literature and History*, New York: Routledge.

Walvin, J. (1998) *An African's Life: The Life and Times of Olaudah Equiano 1745–1797*, Washington: Cassell.

Wambu, O. (ed.) (1998) *Empire Windrush: Fifty Years of Writing About Black Britain*, London: Victor Gollancz.

Warmington, P. (2009) 'Taking race out of scare quotes: race conscious social analysis in an ostensibly post-racial world', *Race Ethnicity and Education*, 12(3): 281–96.

Warmington, P. (2011) 'Some of my best friends are Marxists: CRT, sociocultural theory and the "figured worlds" of race', in K. Hylton, A. Pilkington, P. Warmington and S. Housee (eds) (2011) *Atlantic Crossings: International Dialogues on Critical Race Theory*, Birmingham, CSAP/Higher Education Academy, pp. 262–83.

Warmington, P. (2012) '"A tradition in ceaseless motion": Critical Race Theory and black British intellectual spaces', *Race Ethnicity and Education*, 15(11): 5–21.

Warmington, P. (2013) 'Agents of critical hope: black British narratives', in V. Bozalek, B. Leibowitz, R. Carolissen and M. Boler (eds) *Discerning Critical Hope in Educational Practices*, London: Routledge.

Weekes-Bernard, D. (2010) *Did They Get It Right? A Re-examination of School Exclusions and Race Equality*, London: Runnymede Trust.

Weinreich, P. (1979) 'Cross-ethnic identification and self-rejection in a black adolescent', in G. Verma and C. Bagley (eds) *Race, Education and Identity*, London: Macmillan, pp. 157–75.

West, C. (1992) 'Nihilism in Black America', in M. Wallace and G. Dent (eds) *Black Popular Culture*, Seattle: Bay Press, pp. 37–47.

West African Students Union (WASU) Project (2012) *Key Figures: Ladipo Solanke*. Online: http://wasuproject.org.uk/2012/01/29/key-figures-ladipo-solanke/ (last accessed 20 June 2013).

West Indian Standing Conference (WISC) (1970) *The Last Three Years, 1967–70: Executive Committee Working Party Report*, London: WISC.

White, S., Harris, R. and Beezmohun, S. (eds) (2005) *A Meeting of the Continents: The International Book Fair of Radical Black and Third World Books – Revisited*, London: New Beacon.

Williams, R. (2013) 'The university professor is always white', *Guardian*, 28 January, p. 30.

Williams, S. (2012) 'The Saturday interview: Stuart Hall', *Guardian*, 11 February. Online: http://www.guardian.co.uk/theguardian/2012/feb/11/saturday-interview-stuart-hall (last accessed 11 July 2013).

Willis, P. (1978) *Learning to Labour: How Working Class Kids Get Working Class Jobs*, Farnborough: Saxon House.

Wilson, A. (1978) *Finding a Voice: Asian Women in Britain*, London: Virago.

Winant, H. (2000) 'The theoretical status of the concept of race', in L. Back and J. Solomos (eds) *Theories of Race and Racism*, London: Routledge, pp. 181–90.

Woolley, S. (2011) 'We can't indulge in this nostalgia. Racism today is subtle and complex', *Guardian*, 15 August. Online: http://www.guardian.co.uk/commentisfree/2011/aug/15/modern-racism-complex-sophisticated-approach (last accessed 11 July 2013).

Worrell, K. (1972) 'All-black schools: an answer to under-performance', *Race Today*, 4(1): 7–9.

Wright, C., Standen, P., John, G., German, G. and Patel, T. (2005) *School Exclusion and Transition into Adulthood in African-Caribbean Communities*, York: Joseph Rowntree Foundation.

Wright, C., Thompson, S. and Channer, Y. (2007) 'Out of place: black women academics in British universities', *Women's History Review*, 16(2): 145–62.

Wright, C., Standen, P. and Patel, T. (2010) *Black Youth Matters: Transitions from School to Success*, Abingdon: Routledge.

Yekwai, D. (1988) *British Racism, Miseducation and the Afrikan Child*, London: Karnak House.

Young, L. (2000) 'What is black British feminism?', *Women: A Cultural Review*, 11(1/2): 45–60.

Younge, G. (2012) 'Growing up black: Dennis Morris's portrait of the 70s', *Guardian*, 26 March. Online: http://www.guardian.co.uk/artanddesign/2012/mar/26/growing-up-black-dennis-morris (last accessed 11 July 2013).

Younge, G. (2013) '"Race", nation and culture in a globalised world', Paper presented to Centre for Education for Racial Equality in Scotland (CERES) Conference, 26 June, University of Edinburgh.

Youth Development Trust (1967) *Young and Coloured in Manchester*, Manchester: Youth Development Trust.

Yuval-Davis, N. and Anthis, F. (eds) (1989) *Woman-Nation-State*, London: Macmillan.

Index

Islamophobia 125, 140, 143

James, C. L. R. i, ix, 1, 11, 21–30, 38, 54, 64, 83–4, 93–94, 106
John, Gus 4, 30, 42, 53, 57, 65, 70, 80, 87–8
Johnson, Linton Kwesi 21, 41, 85–6
Jones, Claudia i, 1, 12, 15, 36–7, 53, 84–5, 110–11

Klein, Gillian 82, 84
Kwarteng, Kwasi 148, 152, 155

La Rose, John ix, 2, 14, 23, 27, 37, 39, 46–7, 54, 58, 83, 92
Lachman, Ratna 118, 155
Ladson-Billings, Gloria 137, 140
Lammy, David 148, 152
Lawrence, Doreen 5, 133
Lawrence, Errol 94, 100, 101
Lawrence, Stephen: campaign 132–3; murder of 63, 132; impacts of Lawrence case 13, 125, 136; and Macpherson Inquiry 13, 63, 132–4, 136, 141
League of Coloured Peoples (LCP) 4, 25–7, 31, 36, 111
Leonardo, Zeus 9, 125–7, 138

Mac an Ghaill, Máirtín 103–4, 119
Makonnen, Ras 21, 24–5
Manchester Pan-African Congress (1945) 15, 21–4, 31, 51
Mangrove Nine 39, 64
Marable, Manning 1, 3, 127, 142
Marson, Una 9, 12, 15, 21, 27, 110–111
Marxism: black Marxism 9, 11, 15, 38, 46, 70, 88, 123; conflict theory 67–71, 115; Marxist educational theory 65, 67
Maylor, Uvanney 118, 121
McKenley, Jan 59–60, 116–17, 123
Miles, Robert 126
Mirza, Heidi Safia 4, 60, 103–5, 109, 117–25, 142, 149
Mirza, Munira 143, 151
Modood, Tariq 4, 6, 118, 129–31, 141, 147, 153
Moody, Harold 2, 4, 25–6, 31,
Morris, Olive 110, 111
Mullard, Chris 57, 63–4, 70, 76
multicultural education 4, 49, 72–81, 90; critiques of 12, 67–70, 81, 86–9; origins of 49, 73–9, 80–1
multiculturalism 73–81, 86, 90, 103, 135, 144, 156; and assimilation 34, 52, 60–4, 69, 76, 87; and community cohesion 26, 62, 91, 127, 134–6; cultural diversity 3–4, 13, 34, 62, 68, 72–5, 79, 88–90; 103, 132, 146–7, 152, 157; and disability

rights 73, 133, 138; and gay rights 73–4; post-multiculturalism' i, 1, 12–3, 103, 143–7; state multiculturalism 12, 71–5, 79–80, 90, 101, 103, 132–5, 144–7, 152, 157

Naoroji, Dadabhai 19, 21
New Beacon: bookshop 23, 47, 83–4; publishing 5, 58, 83; political grouping 2, 17, 27, 54, 65, 84–6, 98, 156
New Cross Fire 85–6
news media viii, 8, 145, 148, 155: reporting on race 116, 132, 134–5, 147
Nichols, Grace 90
Nkrumah, Kwame 20, 24, 31
North London West Indian Association (NLWIA) 37, 46–9, 53, 58, 59, 65, 68, 79, 98; and banding 15, 42, 45–9, 66, 70

Organisation of Women of Asian and African Descent (OWAAD) 5, 38, 111–16
Osler, Audrey 110, 118, 122–3
Ové, Horace 85–6
Owusu, Kwesi 95, 155

Padmore, George 4, 15, 21–5, 54, 67, 84
pan-Africanism 4, 11, 15, 20–7, 30–1, 37–8, 106, 110
Parekh, Bhikhu 74, 80, 133–4
Parmar, Pratibha 94, 100–1, 110
Phillips, Caryl 15, 85, 115
Phillips, Trevor 5, 31, 145–8, 152–3
Phoenix, Ann 106, 109, 110, 112–13, 121–2
Pilkington, Andrew 82, 104
policing 37, 39, 63, 69–71, 78, 93, 96–100, 111, 136; and black youth 39, 45, 68, 71, 78, 88, 96–8, 101, 117; and racism 39, 63, 68, 78, 96, 100, 117, 132–4
political blackness 4–5, 10, 12, 40, 90–1, 109–11, 118, 120, 130–2, 140–2; decline of 90–91
Posnock, Ross 8
post-colonial theory 1, 94–5, 106–7
Powell, Enoch 33, 38, 106
Prescod, Colin 38, 60
Preston, John 138, 140
Prince, Mary 17, 110
Prospect Magazine 146–7, 150–2

Race Relations (Amendment) Act (2000) 132, 136–7
race relations 13, 30, 40, 48, 123, 129, 136; early race relations policy 12, 26, 57, 76; sociology of 60–1, 96, 99; black critiques of race relations policy 62–4, 69, 86, 93, 100, 101, 150